Pledged A

STRATEGIC AND TACTICAL FAILURES OF THE 1916 EASTER REBELLION

Matthew Hoff

Pledged as a Rebel: The Founding Myth of the 1916 Easter Rebellion for Irish Independence
Cover from National Archives
This edition published in 2021

Winged Hussar Publishing is an imprint of

Winged Hussar Publishing, LLC
1525 Hulse Rd, Unit 1
Point Pleasant, NJ 08742

ISBN 978-1-950423-63-7 PB
ISBN 978-1-950423-78-1 EBK
LCN 2021946579

Bibliographical References and Index
1. History. 2. Ireland. 3. Irish Rebellion

For more information
visit us at www.wingedhussarpublishing.com and www.whpsupplyroom.com

Twitter: WingHusPubLLC
Facebook: Winged Hussar Publishing LLC

Pledged As A Rebel: The Founding Myth of The 1916 Easter Rebellion For Irish Independence

But while Ireland is not free I remain a rebel, unconverted and unconvertible. There is no word strong enough for it. I am pledged as a rebel, an unconvertible rebel, to the one thing - a free and independent Republic.[1] - Countess Markievicz Debating the Peace Treaty in the Dail Eireann, January 3rd, 1922

[1]Constance Markievicz, "Dail Eireann debate – Debate on Treaty", January 2021 [*Tithe an Orieachtais House of the Oireachtas*]< Available from < https://www.oireachtas.ie/en/debates/debate/dail/1922-01-03/2/>.

Dublin, 1900 (Irish Times)

Section 1: The Origins of a Revolution

Chapter 1: Introduction

The foundation for this book was my senior history thesis while I was a First-Class Cadet (Firstie) at West Point. Back then, the History Department granted selected Cadets the ability to travel internationally to conduct research for their thesis during our short summer breaks. Speaking no foreign languages and wanting to take advantage of this program severely limited my topics – especially considering that I would have rather taken an extra math class than done anything on the English Civil Wars. I came to the topic out of purely selfish reasons.

The Easter Uprising did not originally call to me in any way, and I thought that a brief and unsuccessful uprising would be easier to condense into a thesis than the later Irish Civil Wars. Like many Irish Americans, I knew some of *The Troubles* and had grown up with vague stories of a Bishop that was a relative's cousin who was very involved in the Rebellion. The names Pearce and Connelly were completely foreign to me. While the wider known de Valera and Michael Collins were very obscure.

With my ulterior motives fully in mind, I found a thesis advisor, wrote my proposal, completed my prerequisites and managed to get one of the few spots for the program. Between a summer training assignment, training raising Yearlings and the start of the start of my final academic year I spent a week in Dublin going through the archives at Trinity College Dublin, touring the different sites and meeting with local authorities on the Rebellion. I no plans or motivations to turn this into anything more and would have probably been a little disappointed to know that a decade later, I'd still be working on this same train of thought.

Although little more than a footnote to the Great War and an ignominious start to the Irish War of Independence, the characters and tragedies of 1916 deserve more than just a footnote's worth of attention. The intricacies of the doomed rebellion and the counterproductive effect of the British response contains lessons and parallels whose relevance extends beyond modern counterinsurgencies. Looking at the causes of the Rebellion, specifically the proximate cause of the repeated failures of the Home Rule Bill and the opportunity presented by the First World War, reveals how the failure to deliver on a long-sought promise can undermine and destroy a government's sovereignty over a people and land.

The British response and its failure mirror the failure of General Maxwell's peers to grasp the realities of modern war on the Western Front and predict the failure of subsequent generations of generals to adapt to the challenges of counterinsurgency. These same men who learned the lessons of the Somme, Passendale and Gallipoli so well were, for the most part, failures in learning how to win public opinion and treat it as a decisive point in the wars of post-colonial, Cold War and counterterrorism.

The lens through which modern historians and military professionals see counterinsurgency operations has changed greatly from the commonly held views of early 20th century military leaders. While writing my thesis in 2007, I not only had the knowledge and conclusions of hindsight and academic scholarship on the specific topic, but I also had dozens of similar conflicts as examples - the most recent lessons and practices from Iraq and Afghanistan to base my conclusions on.

While the US military was rewriting and refining what came to be known as counterinsurgency operations in the Middle East (coincidentally, in other former British dominions) I was finishing my Cadet studies in both the war I was soon to fight and in the academic courses that would earn my degree. That is not to say that the answers or the best practices are established or even apparent. The realization that these problems are more complex than the ancient linear battle or the early modern age of gentlemanly warfare is apparent. These problems are more complicated than three-dimensional warfare of World War II or the strategies of Armageddon of the theories third world war.

The men on both sides of the conflict in 1916 did not have this benefit; hindsight and serious study of revolutions and counterrevolutions did not exist at the time. Their decisions were either based off lore and enthusiasm from Ireland's history, Marxist theory or the barricades of Paris. At best, those who took the lessons of recent military history, like Irish Commandant Edward (Ned) Daly and some of the British officers, would have studied or been aware of the Boer War or other colonial conflicts. Others, like General Sir John Maxwell, would have had personal experience to base his decisions. There was no such thing as a doctrinal approach to anti-guerrilla operations, no serious concern given to the second order effects of suppressing a rebellion, no thought given to winning the hearts and minds. To a student who would be engaged in a similar conflict within a year and a half of submitting their thesis, the opportunity to learn from their successes and failures was enticing.

The men who fought on Dublin's streets viewed the world through the purview of the Victorian Englishmen and the nearly lost Irish Hibernianism. The leaders of the British forces, to included General Maxwell, were not ignorant of small-scale wars or local uprisings. Prior to the Great War, Britain's fighting men learned the lessons of combat in small, colonial wars scattered throughout the Empire. Unfortunately, the lessons they learned were drastically different than the lessons that 20th Century counterinsurgents would learn.

Victorian ideals of Anglo superiority resulted in not only an underestimation of opponents and ignorance to the local political climate, but also to draconian strategy and tactics. In previous generations, the British were able to win these wars and confirm these beliefs mainly due to the disparity of martial prowess that industrial societies had over their dominions. While the weapons available to the Mau Mau, Vietcong or Al-Qaida fighter give them more parity to lethality than the assegai of the Zulus or the bolos of the Moros, the tactics learned from The Long March, the Second World War and in Ireland in the decades following the Easter Rebellion amongst others dramatically change the dynamic between guerrilla and counter guerrilla.

Prior to the Rebellion, General Maxwell was an officer in good standing who was held in high esteem by his peers and the British government. He was experienced and competent. As with many of his fellow officers, he had served in the Boer Wars and was familiar with suppressing rebellious subjects to the crown.

While his immediate suppression of the Uprising was even seen by the Irish as fair and in line with the expectations of the day, his punitive measures were seen as an overreaction to the rebellion in its aftermath – especially the numerous executions, imprisonments, and restrictions. This draconian response and the centuries of heavy-handed rule seems to have snatched defeat from the jaws of victory for the Crown's forces.

These actions set the conditions that created a larger movement among the Irish people and the subsequent Irish Civil War eventually led to the creation of the Irish Free State. However, to the Fenians, all of this was an unexpected outcome for what many of them saw as nothing more than their generations' obligation to take a stand against the British crown and continue the narrative of the Irish rising up in arms against the oppression of their English overlords. Win or lose, the men and women who rebelled on Easter Week believed that: "For in Ireland we have an unbroken tradition of struggle for our freedom. Every generation has seen blood spilled and sacrificed cheerfully made that the tradition might live."[1]

Why this iteration of generational Fenian succession succeeded where all others has failed is fairly well established. However, there are more intriguing questions that we may never know the answer to that hold far more consequence for the advancement of the understanding of rebellions and guerrilla war.

The less consequential question is, "did the leaders of the Uprising believe they would succeed?" It is doubtful that there was a uniform consensus amongst the leaders and the ranks. When writing my thesis years ago, I pictured Pearse and Connolly in meeting halls discussing the people rising to their barricades to overthrow the English yoke. The amount of attention paid to the Easter Proclamation and iconography of the self-proclaimed republic had echoes of the Red and Black from the musical adaptation of *Les Miserable*s ringing in my ears.

While the men of this real-life rebellion may have been dourer and more Victorian in disposition than those who participated in the numerous continental rebellions a generation before, it is hard to believe that they would be any less enthusiastic about their cause or their chances. Most of the leaders were men late in their lives. They could not blame youthful exuberance or ignorance for their idealism. Their tone and their plan seemed far more fatalistic than the liberal rebellions based around Enlightenment ideals that occurred in the preceding century.

More likely than not, there was many men in the Fenian formation who believed in the potential for success. While common sense and the popular political rhetoric coming from the Irish Parliamentary Party believed that supporting Britain in her time of need during the Great War would solidify the passage of the *Home Rule Bill* upon the war's conclusion. With each proposal and passing year, the *Home Rule Bill* was getting closer and closer to passage. The leadership of the British government was well aware of the contributions that Irish men and goods were making towards the war aims. In some respects, the cracks in absolute British domination over its possessions were beginning to show. Growing nationalist movements manifesting in both political and insurgent pushes for independence or self-governance heralded an era in which England could no longer totally dominate their colonies and terri-

[1]Constance Markievicz, "Dail Eireann debate – Debate on Treaty", January 2021 [*Tithe an Orieachtais House of the Oireachtas*]< Available from < https://www.oireachtas.ie/en/debates/debate/dail/1922-01-03/2/>.p.xvii

tories. An increase in the Ireland's ability to govern itself was inevitable.

Why then, with the achievement of the goal of Home Rule so close by peaceful means and the chances of traditional military victory so unlikely would these men and women with so much to lose risk a rebellion?

Throughout this book, I will attempt to clarify several arguments that are often neglected by the Irish centric historians of the Rebellion. While there is a plethora of excellent scholarship, few fully acknowledge how poorly position the Fenian forces were. Their training, resources and planning were all wholly inadequate for the enemy they faced and to do anything other than offer a blood sacrifice. Second, Eoin MacNeill was not a villain whose actions doomed the Rebellion. There is no viable circumstance in which the overwhelming force of the British Army would not have defeated the Fenian forces. Third, while General Maxwell's actions turned the successful defeat of an insurrection into a civil war, he was not a bumbling or incompetent commander, and his appointment was well-reasoned and logically sound. He succeeded in his operational mission and failed in his strategic mission, but he could and should be categorized as a competent officer who failed in his task like McClellan, Westmoreland, Haig, Ludendorff or any number of other examples. Finally, that a Rebellion during the First World War was practically inevitable. Even if had one one-hundredth the participation and scope, there were factions in Ireland so committed to the idea that they would have acted alone if need be. While these assertions are not wholly original, they are important refutations of the common myths that surround a little known or understood event in centuries long history of Anglo-Irish violence.

Chapter 2: Historiography of the Rebellion

"One of the most terrible things about the English education System in Ireland is its ruthlessness...it is cold and mechanical, like the ruthlessness of an immensely powerful engine. A machine vast, complicated... It grinds night and day; it obeys immutable and predetermined laws; it is as devoid of understanding, of sympathy, of imagination, as is any other piece of machinery that performs an appointed task. Into it is fed all raw human material in Ireland; it seizes upon it inexorably and rends and compresses and remoulds..."[1] - Padraig Pease

At the turn of the 20th Century, history books tended to be written in what today is derisively called the "guns and trumpet" style. The focus was on the grand action, the great men behind those actions and had overt agendas to further specific causes. Following the Irish Civil War, the new Irish government went to great lengths to record the individual experiences of the participants. The trend in histories at the turn of the 21st Century is to tell the story of the common man, of voices heretofore unheard – like those of women and minorities – and to deemphasize the role of the great man theory. While ideology and agendas have not disappeared, bias is more freely acknowledged. This book is not the story of an epic battle or the tale of the common soldier or member of the *Cumann na mBan*. There is little assumption of prior knowledge of the events of that week or the history that lead to it. It does attempts to understand and critique the decisions and the history that lead the leaders on both sides of the barricades to make those decisions.

Understanding how the 1916 Easter Uprising has been written about in both the immediate aftermath and in the decades since the surrender of the Fenian forces is vital to understanding how a military action that failed to achieve any of its tactical or operational objectives managed to eventually achieve its goal. Current events and recent history rarely have a completely objective or analytical take. Those who are interested enough to write on a topic, especially the primary sources, generally have a motive or agenda when telling their stories. The writings of the Fenian leaders, the first-hand accounts of those whose loved

---

[1] Liz Curtis, *The Cause Of Ireland*, (Beyond the Pale Publications, Belfast 1994), pg. 190.This quote was taken from the original, in Padraig Pearse's book, *The Murder Machine*

ones were held and executed by the British and even the official staff reports from General Maxwell's office and staff all have their own agenda.

Further complicating the biases of the writings on Easter Uprising is the fact that most of the secondary work took place during a time of continuing violence in Ireland. Either during the *Irish Civil War*, the *Troubles of the 1980s* or the still volatile period in between. One hundred years removed; it is still difficult to truly perform objective work on *The Rebellion*. This is due in large part to the fact that the Easter Uprising has become the de facto founding story for the Irish Free State. The climax of a century's long story of the Irish clash against the English yoke. To the Fenian and many modern scholars on the subject, there is truth to the story arch that led from the Black Prince to the bombardment of the GPO and beyond. Especially taking the contemporary effects of the Irish Diaspora and the post-Colonial world, it is impossible to accurately recount and analyze the events of Easter Week in a vacuum. However, de-mythologizing this story is critical to understanding the juxtaposition inherent in the thesis that the Rebellion was a tactical failure and yet a strategic success.

The chronicles of the Easter Uprising are generally either fact driven news reports, romanticized lore, or footnotes to the larger history of the post-Victorian British Empire. While the firsthand accounts and primary source documents are readily available in Ireland, many Irish students learn of the Rebellion only through biased oral history.[2] The main reason for the lack of scholarly interpretation into the events of Easter Week is that primary accounts are so well preserved.[3] In fact, most works on the Easter Rebellion are mere records of the events and the people rather than analysis. The vast primary sources include: articles in the *Irish Times*, numerous journals, the official British records, the saved the correspondences of August Birrell - the Chief Secretary of Ireland - at Trinity College, and the Army of the Irish Free State complied an account from many of the witnesses and participants of the Uprising. There is such a large quantity of primary sources that illustrate the ineptitude of the founders of what would be become the Irish Free State that it prevents much of the romantic mythology that surrounds the founding stories of most nations. This also makes it harder for historians of the Rebellion to succumb to the same romanticizing of this insurrection that Victorian Irish historians are guilty of. Scholars of modern

[2]Eamon Collins, *Killing Rage* (London: Granta Books, 1997), p. 30.

[3]Lorcan Collins, "1916: The Easter Rising Walking Tour," Personal Interview, 13 July 2006.

Irish history seem to prefer to write on events that lack this wealth of primary sources either for the challenge or to appease their audience's biases.

The vast majority of scholarly works on the Easter Uprising contain a particularly Irish bias. Which seems obvious; of course, a nation will write more about their founding narrative than a defeated hegemon will. The great contrast between the British and Irish interpretations of the Easter Rebellion does not come from the record of events or from analysis of their implication into the later war. Both sides rely on the official record of the action and the papers of August Birrell. The difference is the relative importance of the Rebellion. While Easter Week was the founding event of an independent Irish state, in Britain the losses of the Western Front and the internal politics that ushered David Lloyd George into the post of prime minister eclipsed a quickly suppressed revolution. Even in many sources with an Irish bias, the events of Easter week and the decisions of the British command serve only an introductory purpose to the larger Fenian movement as manifested in the military action of well-known groups and figures such as the Irish Republican Army, Michael Collins, and Eamon de Valera. While almost all modern Irish histories mention the events of 1916 as the genesis of a larger movement, the battles and conflicts that followed tend to receive more attention.

The biases of the Irish scholarship into the Easter Uprising are typically transparent, especially in the primary sources. The traditional Gaelic names of many of the authors tend to betray the point of view in the way cover art never can. Many of the romanticizing historians feel that the Rebellion was a necessary event for change. The most recent accounts of *The Uprising*, many inspired by the relative peace of the past decade, have tried to move away from this romanticizing trend. However, interpretations from as recent as this century continue to lionize the Fenians. *The Troubles* served as a changing point for interpretations of Irish history.[4] The secondary sources written before and during the violent period of *The Troubles* - considered by some as revisionist - depicts *The Uprising* as unnecessary and bloody.[5] Many of the

---

[4]The Troubles were a violent period of Irish history that lasted from 1968 until the ceasefire of the Belfast Agreement of 1998. Popularly known as the Second Long War, the war was a contest between the Catholic Irish Republican Army who wished to reunify with the Southern states and the Protestant British.

[5]Conor Kostick and Lorcan Collins, *The Easter Rising: A Guide to Dublin in 1916* (Dublin: The O'Brien Press, 2000), p. 131.

personal accounts written after the Anglo-Irish Treaty of 1921, which granted independence for the twenty-six southern counties, focus solely on the achievements of the Rebellion while marginalizing the initially disapproving public response.

Published in 1963, Max Caufield's, *The Easter Rebellion,* was the first popular, comprehensive account of *The Uprising* outside of the primary sources. His book focused primarily on the mistakes and weaknesses of the insurgents in their fruitless attempt to create an Irish republic by force.[6] This book was the herald of decades of scholarship on the 1916 Rebellion written with the backdrop of *The Troubles* in Northern Ireland during the 1970s. There is comparatively little focus on the events that followed the rebellion. Although not meaning to mislead, Caufield minimized the effects of the executions of the leaders at Kilmainham Gaol and the declaration of martial law on public opinion. It is understandable that during a time of heightened nationalist tensions preceding a time of great violence that an author would want to minimize the link between the historic heroes of Ireland and later revolutions. This apparently antiquated interpretation of the primary sources is not enough to justify the revisionist label because there is no clear distinction between what is and is not revisionary.

Almost immediately after Caufield's work, several historians published accounts that focused on precisely the areas that Caufield avoided. Works such as R. Dudley Edwards', *The Achievement of 1916*, Ruth Edward's, *Patrick Pearse: The Triumph of Failure*, and Margaret Ward's, *Unmanageable Revolutionaries: Women and Irish Nationalism* all came within twenty years of Caufield's work and focused on what the revolutionaries achieved rather than what they failed to do. These revisions of the generally accepted history of 1916 tended not to lionize the men who died by firing squad nor did it aggrandize the fighting of Easter Week to something of lore. However, these works did acknowledge that the Easter Rebellion was an important turning point in the history of Irish nationalism. The revisions written during *The Troubles* ranged from ushering in of the modern romanticism or were the biographies that either demonized or exonerated the main characters of Easter Week.

Tim Pat Coogan is widely regarded as the preeminent scholar of modern Irish history both in Ireland and abroad. His works, *Ireland Since the Rising* and, *The IRA,* are the definitive works on the history of

---

[6]Max Caufield, *The Easter Rebellion* (New York: Holt, Rinehart, and Winston, 1963), p. 17.

the Irish Republican Army and the establishment of the Irish Free State stretching from its predecessors to the actions of Gerry Adams in recent history. His 2001 work, *1916: The Easter Rising*, epitomizes an era of reinterpretation of the events of Easter Week and the beginnings of the Irish Civil War. What separates Coogan's work from the multitude of works on the Rebellion is that it focuses on the parallels between the turn of the century Fenians and the Catholics of Ulster.[7] This modern relevance helped to usher in a new era of revision.

These new interpretations blur the distinction between history and historical fiction, creating representations of the events that focus more on virtues than on events. Combining history with storytelling, Peter De Rosa's 1990 *Rebels: The Irish Rising of 1916* is historical interpretation at its least academic. Despite De Rosa's extensive research, the book is a historical novel. Written by a former Catholic Priest, the work is full of overt religious references and impassioned rhetoric, and dramatically tells the tale in ways typically reserved for motion pictures.[8] While a great contribution to the mythology of 1916, the lionizing and demonizing of the leaders and events of Easter Week means that this book is hardly history.[9] Unfortunately, this historical fiction reflects the growing trend of romantic nationalism in many modern works on *The Easter Rebellion.*

The British interpretations of the importance of Easter Week differ greatly from the Irish views. From the British perspective, the Easter Rebellion was a minor incident. In 1916, the events and population,

---

[7]Robert Moore, "1916: the Easter Rising", Winter 2002 [EBSCO Publishing] Available from < http://bir1.epnet.com/BIRApp/BIR/results.aspx?sid=6B059F12-EE45 4FDFA5A698679EA9ECE7@sessionmgr2&control=brd&booleantex-t=%28%28XX%20%221916%3A%20The%20Easter%20Rising%22%29%29&-fuzzytext=&key=BJBG.THE.EASTER.RISING.COOGAN.TIM.PAT.Adult.NonFiction&ui=BK0006148769&sort=Standout&starthit=18&prevEndHit=28&dis-playText=1916%3A%20The%20Easter%20Rising&pagenumber=2&display-starthit=11&prox=255>; accessed 3 December 2006.

[8] Peter De Rosa, *Rebels: The Irish Rising of 1916* (New York: Fawcett Books, 1990), p. 171.

[9]"Rebels: The Irish Rising of 1916", February 1991 [Proquest Online]; Availale from <http://bir1.epnet.com/BIRApp/BIR/results.aspx?sid=F-8C9F042-961D-4DE7-A105-6FBD8B47AB58@sessionmgr7&control=brd&-booleantext=%28%28TX%20%22peter%20de%20rosa%22%29%29&-fuzzytext=&key=REBELS.THE.IRISH.RISING.OF.BJBG.DE.ROSA.PETER.Adult.Fiction&ui=BK0001833741&sort=Standout&starthit=27&pre-vEndHit=36&displayText=peter%20de%20rosa&pagenumber=3&display-starthit=21&prox=255>; accessed 3 December 2006.

shattering losses of the Western Front and the inabilities of Prime Minister Henry Asquith to create a Liberal government capable of running wartime Britain all overshadow the events and aftermath of the Rebellion. Britain had lost colonies before and since, but never during a time when the preservation of the Metropole was a legitimate concern. Most British accounts concerning the Uprising group it with the other events of 1916. Works such as David Boyce's article, "British Opinion, Ireland, and the War, 1916-1918" show that British historians tend to see the events of Easter Week as merely another casualty in the calamity of the First World War.[10] Regardless of whether the author lionizes the Rebellion or decries its failings, almost all sources agree with the reasons that the primary sources give for the causes for the Rebellion and for the quick British suppression of it.

The events of Easter Week reveal that the combination of an effective nationalist propaganda movement and tyrannical British reprisals led to the mobilization of a nation for revolutionary warfare. The Anglo-Irish War would not have occurred without the conversion of the people from supporters of Home Rule to supporters of an open and violent revolution. The populace provided more than moral support; in many cases they provided logistical, propaganda, intelligence, and auxiliaries for major operations. The Fenians in Ireland did not have the support and will of the people in early April 1916, but by launching a major offensive and by exploiting the British reaction, those who survived were able to create this base of support.

[10]David Boyce, "British Opinion, Ireland, and the War, 1916-1918," *The Historical Journal* 17 (Sept., 1974): 593.

Chapter 3: Success from Failure

"The fools, the fools, the fools! – they have left us our Fenian dead, and, while Ireland holds these graves, Ireland unfree shall never be at peace." [1] *- Padraig Pearse*

The Easter Rebellion in Dublin during the week of 24 to 30 April 1916 succeeded where previous rebellions had failed. It revived the dream of Irish independence which manifested itself in the Anglo-Irish War of 1918-1921 which created a separate Irish state with the signing of the Anglo-Irish Treaty. Easter Week was the moment that Irish nationalism began its phoenix-like rebirth from its decline during the last decade of the nineteenth century.[2] The great achievement of the Uprising was that it served as a catalyst for a change in Irish public opinion.[3] The 1916 Easter Rebellion differed from earlier Irish uprisings because it indirectly led to a separate state by serving as the cause that created an excessively harsh British response. This draconian response inspired the people to fight for self-determination. To say that Easter Week alone altered popular opinion is inaccurate; the British government's response and Irish nationalists' propaganda created and mobilized a base of popular support that the Fenians, the group of militant nationalists that fought in the Rebellion needed for a successful war with Britain. The term Fenian is the broadest umbrella term that covers the plethora of semi-connected groups that fought for and advocated Irish independence in the 18th and 19th centuries. Some of the most notable groups that fall under this umbrella are: The Irish Republican Brotherhood, the Fenian Brotherhood, The Irish Volunteers, Clan na Gael, Sinn Fein, and the Citizen Army.

The century prior to the Easter Rebellion had been disastrous for Ireland. In addition to the Potato Famine that caused a mass emigration, loss of life and poverty the politics of the Ireland became far more draconian as rule shifted from Dublin to London under the Act of

---

[1]Patrick Pearse, "O'Donovan Ross's Funeral Address at Graveside." Speech. Glasnevin Cemetery, Dublin, 1 August 1915.

[2]The Phoenix was an old symbol of Irish nationalism. A symbol of rebirth from the ashes of defeat, the Phoenix was a popular symbol among nationalist and lent its name to the expansive Phoenix Park - the site of the Fenian inspired murders of Thomas Henry Burke and Lord Frederick Cavendish in 1882 - outside of the city.

[3]R. Dudley Edwards, "The Achievement of 1916," in 1916: The Easter Rising. Ed. O. Dudley Edwards and Fergus Pyle (London: MacGibbon and Kee Ltd., 1968), p. 210.

Union that was passed in large part due to consequences and realities of England's wars against Napoleon from 1793 to 1815. The major catalyst for this legislation and the inspiration for the Easter Uprising was the rebellion of 1798. Subsequent rebellions occurred in 1803, 1848 and Fenian Rebellion of 1867.[4]

The vast majority of Irishmen - even among nationalists - before, during, and in the weeks immediately after the Uprising opposed the use of violence to win independence. From the countryside pulpits to the United Irish League, the Rebellion was wholly condemned as not reflecting the true sentiment of the island.[5] The harsh British reaction, especially that of General Sir John Maxwell, the officer commanding all forces in Ireland, changed Irish perceptions on the acceptability of force for freedom. The wide net cast by General Maxwell's response caught many innocent men, affected many families and coupled with a high number of executions to turn the Rebels from villains into heroes.

The British response to the Uprising was swift and decisive and initially had the support of the majority of Ireland. Although British artillery leveled Sackville Street at the heart of Dublin, many in Ireland blamed the rebels for the damage and castigated them as "ill-advised persons…[who have] chosen to shock and outrage public opinion."[6] Standing in such staunch opposition to the Rebellion were the lionized Irishmen in uniform who served the British effort during the First World War. In the public opinion, these men were rallying to a worthy cause: fighting for the Empire or in hopes of winning Home Rule for their nation. In private, they fought for their comrades and for the relatively generous benefits that service brought them and their families. For the most part, the Irish nation greatly supported the British war effort.

The reasons for support typically came from a sense of duty to the state, from a feeling that support of the war effort would lead to the passage of Home Rule legislation that Redmond promised, or from the benefits the British government gave to soldiers and their families. In fact, 10,235 Irishmen had joined the Royal Irish Constabulary at the

---

[4]R. Dudley Edwards, "The Achievement of 1916," in 1916: The Easter Rising. Ed. O. Dudley Edwards and Fergus Pyle (London: MacGibbon and Kee Ltd., 1968), p. 210.

[5]Pauline Codd, "Recruiting and the Responses to the War in Wexford," in Ireland and the First World War, ed. David Fitzpatrick (Dublin: Trinity History Workshop, 1986), p. 24.

[6]Irish Political Documents 1916-1949. "A Public Meeting in Galway Reacts to the Rising, 29 April 1916." Ed. Arthur Mitchell and Padraig O Snodaigh. Dublin: Irish Academic Press, Ltd., 1985, p. 21.

outbreak of the war.[7] Some of these soldiers publicly renounced the motives of the Fenians stating, "the real Irishmen out here [received news of the Rebellion] with profound regret and shame."[8] Letters and editorials such as these were very common and demonstrated that most in Ireland supported the British cause.

With the rebellion quickly quashed and a native population desperate to prove their loyalty to the Empire, the post-revolt decisions of the British authorities lead by General Maxwell turned the decisive defeat of the nationalists into their most important and most romanticized victory. The British were experienced colonial masters and had fought rebellions in Ireland and other colonies for centuries. It seems improbable that with this great wealth of experience in fighting rebellions and their intimate knowledge of this island and their tremendous advantages in manpower, firepower, and supply that defeat could come from an almost certain victory. While the Crown's track record was not flawless with missteps in India, the Sudan, the America and almost every other corner of the globe as well as in Ireland, the British should have made some effort over the centuries to learn and teach the lessons of their defeats and missteps. Had these lessons been inculcated into the British officer class, the decisions made immediately following the Uprising could have solidified a victory instead of setting the basis for a mobilization of the Irish people.

That the organizers of the Easter Rebellion had a grand strategic vision or a long-term strategy for a dramatic change in popular opinion is highly improbable. It is nearly impossible to determine how the leaders, riflemen and supporters of the Easter Rebellion viewed their chances. Every firsthand account, whether written before or after the events of Easter Week, is couched in either knowledge of the later Civil War or changing public opinion or was written as a rallying cry to Fenian supporters. There are no widely acknowledged primary source that stated: 'The Rebellion will fail during Easter Week. The people will fail to raise to the barricades and the insurmountable might of the British Army will defeat Irish Free State Forces at all locations. However, this is a necessary sacrifice. The loss, plus the subsequent retributions, imprisonments, penalties, and executions will cause a dramatic change in public opinion. This change will sway a nation on the cusp of Home

[7]CSO, Regd. Papers, 7319/1916.

[8]W. O'Brien, "An Irish Soldier and the Rebellion," The Irish Times, 9 May 1916, p. 25.

Rule, whose populace is heavily involved in a foreign war in support on Britain and heavily dependent upon its pensions and welfare to violently reject any form of British rule and rise in arms against the Crown. Further, these events will be so polarizing that the nascent nation will be able to sustain a bloody conflict for almost a year as well as a lower level, but violent nonetheless fight for the six years prior and six decades following the Civil War. The ultimate result being the establishment and recognition of an Irish Free State. Whether that means that the Fenians survivors did a thorough job of whitewashing their history or those who lacked faith in their chances for success chose not to record their feelings.

It took several missteps by the British, decades of careful cultural work and a vigorous and proactive control of the narratives surrounding the events of the Easter Uprising to cause the metamorphosis that changed the short-lived revolution from an operational and tactical failure into a strategic success. It is doubtful that the Fenian leaders had the language or even the vision to foresee this ultimately successful strategy. At a time when military theorists were just beginning to formalize and understand concepts such as the decisive point, it is unlikely that anyone in 1916 Dublin foresaw and understood the importance of – not to mention how to capture – the hearts and minds of the people. While these men grew up in a world where contemporaries both on mainland Europe and in the colonies participated in both failed and semi-failed revolutions. The most logical assumption is that their rebellion would proceed in a linear fashion from the Easter Proclamation, through a successful conflict on Dublin's streets into Ireland's green hills, to inflicting enough losses on a British Army already strained by the Great War to the establishment of a fully independent country in a peace declaration. Regardless of if they overestimated their chances for success or marched stoically into a mortal sacrifice; the indirect success of the rebellion would most have likely surprised the Rebels. The violence of the next ten years of Irish history and beyond transpired largely due to the lack of vision on the Rebel side for what the next steps in the rebellion would be more than from the counteractions of the British forces.

There was a strong Fenian tradition of a generational sacrifice. Nearly all of the leaders of the Easter Uprising wrote and spoke to the great Irish tradition and centuries of struggle of the Irish against their English overlords. Historian Joe Lee dismisses this idea since it defies logic that anyone would spend so much time preparing just to give their lives in a vain effort.[9] However, there is a difference between sacrifice and suicide. Sacrifice implies that there is a higher purpose, while suicide implies is no higher purpose. The Fenians could very well have known that they were on a mission doomed to fail, but that the most successful they were, the more likely it would be to cause a bigger movement or to inspire the next generation. In that, they were exactly right. The Rebellion did not cause a mobilization of nation, the sacrifice of men and women who fought well and with honor against a centuries old oppressor did. The Leaders of 1916 may have anticipated that their odds of success were slim and that more likely than not they would die on the battlefield or by firing squad, but they also knew that a poorly planned and executed Rebellion would do just as much for their strategic aim as putting a gun on their mouths and pulling the trigger would.

The tradition of sacrifice for the nation stretched back centuries to the Irish resistance against the initial Norman conquest of the island in 1169 under Richard "Strongbow" de Clare and shares many characteristics with the Christian veneration for those who willingly gave their lives for their faith. English intervention in Irish affairs goes back a decade further to a decision made by the English-born Pope Adrian IV to grant lordship of Ireland to the English King Henry II and to authorize the conquest of Ireland. Ironically for a starting point in a clash that is now seen mostly along religious lines, Adrian wrote this papal bull to more fully bring the Irish church under the control of Rome.[10] The parade of martyrs stretched through nearly five hundred years of political, guerilla and massive military resistance that stretched through the crisis of the Pale that culminated in 1515, to the Cess Crisis that caused the Desmond Rebellions 1556-1583, and the Nine Years War of 1594-1603. It is poignant to note that these centuries of conflict and warfare all took place before Henry VIII's polarizing establishment of a new state religion in English Protestantism and the failed gunpowder plot of 1605. This was not originally a religious division. Even to the times present day, the Protestant/Catholic divide is, more often than not, secondary to the nationalist divide in most cases. While the modern perception of the Irish-British conflict is primarily drawn along religious lines, the issues and causes for the strife existed centuries before Henry VIII. While Irish nationalism is in large part tied to Catholicism and Catholicism is an

[9]Helen Litton, 16 Lives: Edward Daly (Dublin, The O'Brien Press, 2013), p. 78.
[10]Alan J Ward, The Easter Rising: Revolution and Irish Nationalism, Second Edition. (Wheelilng: Harlan Davidson 2003), p. 16.

integral part of Irish identity, Irish nationalism existed long before any religious schism on the island.

Theobald Wolfe Tone was one of the most important influences on the leaders of the Easter Rebellion. Furthering the separation of Irish nationalism from being purely a religious conflict. Tone was a Protestant whose mother converted from Catholicism and whose father was a French Protestant whose family fled to Ireland to avoid Catholic religious persecution in Gascony. Born in 1763 into an aristocratic family and educated at Trinity College Dublin, there was little in his early life or upbringing to foreshadow the revolutionary he would become. In 1791 he, along with Napper Tandy and Thomas Russell, founded the Society of United Irishmen, which eventually grew into its own political party. Tone hoped that his party would work on behalf of all Irishmen, regardless of religious affiliation, to advocate to the British government on their behalf, achieve universal male suffrage and quell the conflict between Catholic and Protestant gangs in Ulster. Failure and frustration led Tone to seek out the French, with whom Britain had been at war since the French Revolution began, to raise support and troops for a French-backed expedition to Ireland. This became known as the Irish Rebellion of 1798 and the French forces that participated were known as the Hoche Expedition.

While the Irish Rebellion of 1798 failed in its goals and Tone was eventually hanged for his role in it, this rebellion was just another spike of violence in a continuously contentious relationship between Britain and her vassal. There were dozens of such conflicts across the centuries and hundreds more plots and schemes. While these planned and executed actions are commonly recorded as rebellions, incidents, plots and uprisings they cannot be viewed in isolation either from themselves or from the politics, laws, social and economic circumstances that occurred contemporaneously with them. These minor and major acts of an Irish rebellion, regardless of inspiration and motivation, are parts of the same century's long war. They are more akin to the battles and skirmishes of the generational conflicts between England and France, Rome and Parthia or Christian Europe and the Ottoman Turks than an isolated and spontaneous revolution like America in 1776.

If the Easter Uprising was nothing more than another battle in a long war, why is it given so much more importance than any other clash? It failed in achieving its tactical and operational objectives just as dramatically and decisively as Tone or any other attempt had. It was as - if not more - unpopular with the common Irish person during and immediately after the Rebellion as any of the other Rebellions. The British, for the large part, acted in line with the expectations and proper martial decorum of the time. There is nothing in the writings of Maxwell or his staff to indicate that they thought they were being excessive in their cruelty or taking actions beyond what was required to ensure security on Britain's nearest territory during the largest conflict in the history of the world to that time. Compared to actions in other colonies, including against the white Boers, the British ruled in Ireland with an even gentler hand. Yet, by the end of the Court Martials, executions and mass imprisonments the public opinion and resolve of the Irish people changed dramatically. They were no longer willing to wait for the promise of another Home Rule Bill, no longer to view representation in Parliament as a victory and no longer willing to exist as part of the Empire.

The understanding that the Easter Rebellion was a not a lost war but a sacrificial campaign in a long multigenerational war. The success of Easter Week was not the recognition of a nation, but in achieving the decisive point in centuries of conflict: the unification of the Irish people's will for independence.

Chapter 4: Causes of Rebellion

"Shun the English Army, Navy, and Police forces...the females who keep them company...teach your children to hate and shun them."[1] -NOW political poster

The 1916 Easter Uprising was a generational reaction to the centuries of grievances against British rule in Ireland and the efforts of generations of Irish nationals, who in their recent history began calling themselves Fenians, more than it was a grand culmination of a historical march. In this camp were three distinct types of nationalist: romantic, constitutional and revolutionary. Many of the objectives of each group overlapped and they all worked alongside one another within the Irish Republican Brotherhood, yet there was not a single, unified vision of what a 'free' Ireland would look like.[2]

Ireland had a long tradition of violent revolt against British rule. After the failure of the dominant Irish political party to secure the passage of a Home Rule Bills in 1886, 1893, and 1914 many in Ireland were growing disillusioned at the hope of winning a measure of independence through Parliament. The effects of religious restrictions, class immobility, and the founding of several organizations dedicated to the preservation of Gaelic culture led to the release of repressed Irish nationalism, which preceded the Irish nation.

It is nearly impossible to create and launch an uprising, let alone a successfully one, with a group that does not share a common identity. An Ireland that viewed itself as an equal part of a United Kingdom would have its nationalist leanings split between the common kingdom and its own identity. An Ireland whose arts and cultural contribution were as celebrated in London, Bombay and Bermuda as they were in Dublin would feel culturally aligned with the United Kingdom as it would within itself. These feelings of Irish identity were never homogenous across time, location or religious affiliation. Generally, the Protestants of Northern Ireland who could commonly be categorized as Orangemen were more aligned with the greater identity of the United

[1]NOW, "Poster Against an English Garrison in Ireland" TCDMS 2074 (Political Poster, Dublin, 1916).

[2]Alan J Ward, The Easter Rising: Revolution and Irish Nationalism, Second Edition. (Wheelilng: Harlan Davidson 2003), p. 41.

Kingdom (or in many cases that of England and Englishness specifically) than they were with that of Ireland. The Catholics were the overwhelming majority of the population in the south, but they were also the majority of the population in of the many areas in what would become Northern Ireland. Island wide, the Catholics were the critical population and Catholicism grew into a central component of nationalist identity.

In 1916, many felt aligned with the Empire, especially those with family on the Western Front. Many may have felt the most aligned with the powerful presence of the Catholic Church. Many who felt most closely aligned their island would have still opposed armed revolt in favor of the political process. While others, even those who took up arms on Easter Week, would have felt the greatest association with the International Worker's movement. The strength of the Irish cultural and political identity waxed and waned throughout the history of the English than British sovereignty over Ireland. The British were able to suppress many of the earlier Rebellions due to lack of popular support and factionalism. Before the first bullets could fly, a common Irish identity needed to be re-established – or more accurately popularized and mythologized – to create a coherent people capable of and committed to organized action.

Clashes between sects and dogmas of Christianity are not unique or particular to Ireland. There is nothing in the Irish form of Roman Catholicism or in the Anglican form of Protestantism that necessitates a holy war. While religion used to occupy a much more central place in the daily lives of people from peasant to king and wars between Christian sects have caused wars, battles and purges before the English invasion – which only escalated over the centuries – a clash between Protestant and Catholic was not the single cause issue leading to the separation of the Irish Free State that it is often reduced to. This is in no way to diminish its importance as a proximate cause to the 1916 Easter Uprising, the formation of the Irish Free State or the failure to pass the multiple attempts at a Home Rule Bill. The divisions between Protestant and Catholic became a convenient dividing line between two groups of people and affected the biases of all participants in these conflicts in ways that could never fully be distilled. The divisions this created in Victorian prerogatives, its effect on the reaction to the Potato Famine of the 1840s, the Penal Laws and more were direct causes that were either the purely or partially religiously motivated that lead to the foundation of O'Connell's repeal movement in the mid-1840's and the Young Irelanders to found the Irish Confederation in 1847 to fight against these laws. The Young Irelanders were the first shift towards a more romantic view of Ireland in opposition to England and their thoughts and acts of rebellion were direct influences on Pearse and the other leaders of the 1916 Easter Uprising.[3] Even with these causes, a rebellion in 1916 could not have occurred along purely religious lines. While Catholicism was and continues to be a differentiating feature between the United Kingdom and an Irish Free State, it is only a part – and not necessarily a prerequisite part – of the Irish cultural identity that unified the Fenians.

The resurgence of Irish culture that took place during the late nineteenth century strengthened the reemerging pride of the Irish people, which first manifested itself in the *Gaelic League* (*Conradh na Gaeilge*) founded in 1893.[4] The *Gaelic League* quickly grew to be the most important and influential organization promoting the Irish identity. By 1903 it had over 600 branches throughout the country and had successfully added the Irish language to the curriculum in over 1,300 national schools as well as directly leading to the foundation of Irish focused schools like Pearse's St. Edna's.[5] The League cast a broad, non-exclusive net that welcomed anyone who was interested including Protestants. The fact that the leaders and participants, while overwhelming Catholic, also included devout Protestants and Atheists is a direct lineage of the Gaelic League's policies. For those participants who did not take arms, many of them saw their politic disposition shift more towards a desire for Home Rule. Pearse said of the Gaelic League: "The Gaelic League will be recognized in history as the most important revolutionary influence that ever came into Ireland. The Irish Revolution really began when the seven proto-Gaelic Leaguers met in O'Connell Street…the germ of all future Irish history was in that back room."[6]

Other groups such as the *Gaelic Athletic Association* (*Cumann Luthecleas Gael*) and the *Young Ireland Society* also advanced the preservation of the Irish nation.[7] These groups capitalized on the energy and zeal of the younger generation and created a subculture that was

[3]Alan J Ward, The Easter Rising: Revolution and Irish Nationalism, Second Edition. (Wheelilng: Harlan Davidson 2003), pp.56-57.

[4]Charles Monaghan, "The Revival of the Gaelic Language," *PLMA* 14 (1899) p.xxxiii.

[5]Joseph McKenna, Voices from the Easter Rising: Firsthand Accounts of Ireland's 1916 Rebellion (Jefferson: McFarland & Company, Inc., Publishers., 2017), p. 4.

[6]Joseph McKenna, Voices from the Easter Rising: Firsthand Accounts of Ireland's 1916 Rebellion (Jefferson: McFarland & Company, Inc., Publishers., 2017), p. 4.

[7]Matthew Hoff, "The Foundations of the Fenian Uprising" (Term Paper for History of Great Britain in the Nineteenth and Twentieth Centuries, United States Military Academy, 2006), pp. 1-4.

the vanguard of revolutionary change.[8] Many of the Fenian groups that fought for Irish independence trace their roots back to the league. Sports and arts were the gateway to the nationalist movement. Young Irishmen venerated William Butler Yeats's nationalistic play "Cathleen ni Houlihan" and started joining the Gaelic League to help revive their native language, and began to talk about the reality of Irish independence.[9] These movements revived the Irish national identity; all that was lacking was the mobilization and commitment of the masses to turn this nationalism into something tangible.[10] August Birrell - the British Chief of Staff for Ireland - would write after the revolt that the six causes of the revolt were: "growing doubts about Home Rule, the loss of political influence, the Ulster Rebellion, the prolongation of the war, and the coalition government."[11] While these immediate causes may have sparked the events of Easter Week, the list of Fenian grievances reaches much further back into history.

For the Fenian's, the failure of the Home Rule Bill in 1914 may not have been the single straw that broke the camel's back of the trust in the Redmonite promise for Home Rule. For those Irish nationalists who were already ready to sacrifice themselves for the cause of Irish independence, it made the opportunity provided by the First World War too good to pass up. John Redmond, the most influential Irish politician in Parliament, viewed the struggle for a Home Rule Bill with the same perspective that a general would view a campaign: "Those of us who have been struggling in this cause for thirty years are thankful to feel that at last the fighting is practically over, and that all that remains is to settle the exact terms on which the Treaty of Peace is to be drawn up."[12]

Home Rule would have not only settled the Irish Question, but it would have brought closure to nearly eight centuries of strife and bloodshed between Ireland and England. It may not have instantly solved all wounds and prejudices, but it would have formalized and guaranteed the self-determination that Irish nationalists across the spectrum had de-

---

[8]Benedict Anderson, *Imagined Communities: Reflections on the Origin and Spread of Nationalism* (London: Verso, 1983), p. 119.

[9]Marie O'Brien and Connor Cruise, *Ireland: A Concise History* (New York: Thames and Hudson Inc., 1999), p. 129.

[10]E.J. Hobsbawm, *Nations and Nationalism Since 1780: Programme, Myth Reality* (Cambridge: Cambridge University Press, 1990), pp. 11-12.

[11]"Inquiry into the Rebellion," *The Irish Times*, 20 May 1916.

[12] J.E. Redmond, "What Ireland Wants" (Dublin, 1910), pp. 14-15 (excerpted from Mitchell, Arthur, and O Snodaigh, Padraig, (editors). *Irish Political Documents* 1869-1916. (Dublin: Irish Academic Press, 1989) p. 129.

sired for so long. When British Prime Minister William Gladstone proposed the first Irish Home Rule Bill in 1886, he was not only attempting to rectify centuries of mistreatment and heal the wounds of Potato Famine, but he was trying to set the conditions that would truly integrate Ireland into the United Kingdom. This bill had the potential to tie Ireland as an equal partner to England, Scotland and Wales in the United Kingdom. Ireland was not unique in its history of conflict with London; Scotland's clashes with England may be even more famous. The Home Rule Bills were incredibly forward thinking attempts to unify Britain's nearest colony as well as set the conditions to rectify, atone for and move forward from the religious, nationalist and legal issues that had caused so much conflict. It was never to be. Due to the influence and actions of Protestant Ulster Unionists and the ingrained disdain for the Irish held by the House of Lords, none of the three attempts at passing a Home Rule Bill succeeded.[13]

Before Easter Week, most of Ireland's population – including its nationalist population – did not subscribe to the violent Fenian beliefs.[14] A result of World War One was that a large portion of Ireland was denationalized and supported the war effort.[15] This was in part due to the propaganda and élan of nationalism that naturally sweeps a nation at war. Irishmen had for centuries fought for the crown in the colonies and on the continent. A large section viewed it as their duty to their country as much a Pease and Clarke viewed taking arms against that same crown as their nationalist duty. Many families financially relied on or benefited from their service to Britain. The payment of a private soldier and the pension of a widow were the primary source of income for many on the still largely impoverished island still recovering from the Potato Famine and generation ago. Many also saw the Irish contribution as vital and perquisite blood sacrifice to the passage of a Home Rule Bill. Much like the popular narrative surrounding African-American service during American's twentieth century conflicts, the Irish politicians promised rewards for the oppressed citizenry of the island if they did their part in the Great War.

The man leading this call was the leader of the most dominant

[13]Tim Sullivan, *Irish Home Rule and Resistance, 1912-1916*. (Term Paper, Loyal University. 2003. Available form <http://people.loyno.edu/~history/journal/Sullivan.htm>) Accessed 14 January 2018.

[14]Fenianism is the term to describe those members of the Irish Nationalist Movement that believed in the overthrow of British rule by the means of force.

[15]John Devoy, *Recollections of an Irish Rebel,* (Shannon: Irish University Press, 1969), p. 480.

political party in Ireland: the Irish Parliamentary Party of Sir John Redmond. He was highly popular across the whole of Ireland's political prerogatives and was seen by many as the man who would secure the passage of a Home Rule Bill. In fact, as late as 1915, many members of the ultra-nationalistic Irish Volunteers followed the politics of John Redmond.[16] The question of British support divided the island and symbols of support were widely displayed.[17] Many people believed that a victory for Britain would hasten the passage of Home Rule Legislation which would make Ireland a domestically independent colony and "hoped and prayed" for British victory.[18] This belief coupled with John Redmond's backing of the British war effort led to approximately 150,000 Irishmen serving in the British Army with another 160,000 in John Redmond's pro-British national volunteers.[19]

The motivation for these Irishmen to serve Britain ranged from monetary to nationalistic, but despite their sympathies, and contrary to rebel propaganda, the members of the Royal Irish Constabulary were within the British command for all of Easter Week.[20] Many of the Irishmen who fought for Britain and even against the Rebels might have shared many of the Fenians' complaints and grievances, but to a man they all did their duty and fought well for the crown. Although the Fenians were widely labeled as traitors and their rebellion as unnecessary, their beliefs and desires for Ireland concurred with the popular sentiment.

---

[16] Dan Breen, *My Fight for Irish Freedom* (Dublin: Talbot Press, 1924), p. 24.

[17] Pauline Codd, "Recruiting and the Responses to the War in Wexford," in *Ireland and the First World War*, ed. David Fitzpatrick (Dublin: Trinity History Workshop, 1986), p. 24.

[18] Dan Breen, *My Fight for Irish Freedom* (Dublin: Talbot Press, 1924), p. 25.

[19] W. O'Brien, "An Irish Soldier and the Rebellion," *The Irish Times*, 9 May 1916, p. 25.

[20] Headquarters, Irish Command, "General Maxwell's Report to Field-Marshal, Commanding-in-Chief, Home Forces" (Dublin, 25 May 1916), p. 1.

Left - Daniel O’Connell (1836 Bernard Mulrenin)
Right - Augustine Burriell

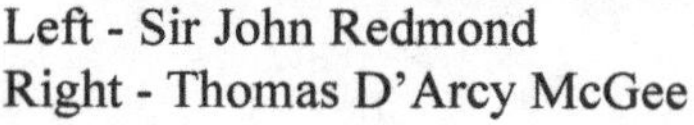

Left - Sir John Redmond
Right - Thomas D’Arcy McGee

Section 2: The Driving Forces and Leaders

Chapter 5: The Fenian Movement

"In victories they were few, yet Fenianism remained a weapon of the Irish poor wherever they were; radical in outlook, fiercely non-sectarian, and because of the anathemas of the bishops—anti-clerical. Fenians shouted defiance from the dock, challenged their jailers and walked erect to the gallows. The rank and file, not the leaders, saved the Fenians." -Sean Cronin[1]

Fenianism was not just the Irish manifestation of the nationalist movements that were sweeping European empires at the turn of the twentieth century, it was a centuries old tradition. While Ireland watched, learned and was influenced by the mid-Nineteenth century rebellions, Fenianism traced its zeitgeist back centuries before the Age of Empire, the Enlightenment and even the Renaissance. Fenianism in 1916 was the extension, throughout Irish history, of a string of mostly failed uprisings against the British. The earliest of these revolts occurred in 1383 by Niall Mor O'Neill. Almost every generation between then and 1916 rose in arms at least once and always unsuccessfully against the British.[2] Differences in religion, the implementation of the discriminatory Penal Code Laws, centuries of wealth disparity, and the ravages Potato Famine created a history of violence and discrimination which made nationalism an innate part of the Irish identity.

The lingering resentment for the oppression of the Catholic populace led to earlier Irish nationalist revolutions. Differences in class and religion forbade the intermarriage and intermingling. Since this melding is a prerequisite to mass assimilation, these laws by de facto and de jury segregated Catholic from Protestant and forced the sustainment of two separate Irish identities. Laws such as the one passed in 1659 that outlawed the practice of the Catholic religion and sentenced priests to death or expulsion reinforced these differences.[3] The disparity in wealth and freedom justified the Fenian claim that throughout most of the British occupation of their island, the native Irishmen and Irishwomen have

[1] Tim Pat Coogan, *1916: The Easter Uprising,* (London: Orion Books Limited, 2001), p. 45.

[2] Sean Duffy and Patrick Power, *Timetables of Irish History*, (London: Worth Press Limited, 2001), p. 22.

[3] Sean Duffy, and Patrick Power, *Timetables of Irish History*, (London: Worth Press Limited, 2001), p. 19.

existed as a persecuted and oppressed race. No one single event, law, practice, or defeat caused Fenianism or Irish defiance. The variety and numerous instances of dividing instances made nationalism almost part of the Irish DNA. On either side of the divide and in both England Ireland, the generational struggle became indistinguishable from Irish identity. More than even a difference in religion, the toll of the centuries of oppression and injustice and the actions of the British Lords and members of Parliament to preserve their hegemony over the island forged the conflict into the very fibers of what it meant to be Irish.

The failed revolutions that the disparity in wealth and freedoms caused did not bring equality or political representation to Ireland, but they were immensely important to keeping the Irish identity separate from the British Empire. The one event that catalyzed nationalism more than any other was the funeral of Jeremiah O'Donnavan Rossa. Rossa was the founder of the Phoenix Society in 1856 and the major intellectual inspiration for the Fenian movement in the 1880s.[4] The crowd of ten thousand that gathered at Patriot's Corner in Glasnevin Cemetery in Dublin for the funeral heard Padraig Pearse eulogize the words that inspired an un-born nation.[5]

> "Life springs from death; and from the graves of patriot men and women spring living nations…the fools, the fools, the fools! - they have left us our Fenian dead, and, while Ireland holds these graves, Ireland unfree shall never be at peace."[6]

John Devoy, the leader of the Clan na nGael, credited these past rebellions and leaders with keeping the spirit of Irish independence alive.[7] He said that the failed revolutions "kept alive the spirit of resistance to that alien rule."[8] The Irish Nationalist groups were growing at an increasing rate throughout the later part of the nineteenth century and these various groups ushered in a new generation of Fenians ready to

---

[4]Matthew Kelly, "Dublin Fenianism in the 1880s: 'The Irish Culture of the Future'?", *The Historical Journal* 43 (2000): 730.

[5]"Rossa Buried in Dublin," *The New York Times*, 2 August 1915, p. 5.

[6]Patrick Pearse, "O'Donovan Rossa's Funeral Address at Graveside." Speech. Glasnevin Cemetery, Dublin, 1 August 1915.

[7]The Clan na nGael is the American branch of the Irish Republican Brotherhood.

[8]John Devoy, *Recollections of an Irish Rebel,* (Shannon: Irish University Press, 1969), p. 479.

act against Britain.

The three failed attempts to pass Home Rule Legislation at the turn of the century caused a decline in number of Irishmen who held hope that Britain would grant Ireland self-determination. Many in Ireland still believed, as James Connolly said, "the British Government has no right in Ireland, never had any right in Ireland, and never can have any right in Ireland."[9] Yet the growth Irish Nationalism was not rapid enough to excite change. The official British inquiry into the Rebellion published in *The Irish Times* stated, "had pro-Irish reforms been earlier exercised, then the movement might have died".[10] While earlier changes in religious toleration, land reforms, and education might have altered the course of history, by the late 1850s Ireland had reached a breaking point and could no longer exist solely as a British vassal.

The Irish Parliamentary Party was the most powerful and popular party in Ireland in the decades preceding the Easter Rebellion. Since its inception under Charles Parnell and Isaac Butts, the sole focus of the party was to secure a Home Rule Bill for Ireland through Parliament.[11] A goal that was never realized.

Sir John Redmond, a Trinity educated Member of Parliament, had been a member of the Irish Parliamentary Party since its inception as the Nationalist Party. He served through the split between Parnellites and anti-Parnellites following Isaac Butts' death and upon the party's reunification in 1900 won the position of chairmen.[12] Redmond was a tremendously popular and influential presence in Irish politics. Redmond's support for the British war effort led many to believe that British victory would mean greater freedom for Ireland. The hope for the passage of the 1914 Home Rule Act and loyalty to John Redmond himself greatly helped to boost British recruiting in Ireland during the war.[13] On the eve of the Rebellion most people in Ireland, including the majority of the Nationalists, followed the politics of John Redmond and had settled for Home Rule legislation.

---

[9] James Connolly, *Labour and Easter Week 1916: A Selection from the Writings of James Connolly,* (Dublin: Sign of Three Candles, 1949), p. 177.

[10] "Inquiry into the Rebellion," *The Irish Times*, 20 May 1916.

[11] Annie Porritt, "The Irish Home Rule Bill," *Political Science Quarterly* 28 (1913): 300.

[12] Paul Bew, "Moderate Nationalism and the Irish Revolution, 1916-1923," *The Historical Journal* 42 (1999): 729.

[13] Pauline Codd, "Recruiting and the Responses to the War in Wexford," in *Ireland and the First World War*, ed. David Fitzpatrick (Dublin: Trinity History Workshop, 1986), p. 21.

The Fenian movement was not a formal organization or a purely reactionary movement against the Irish Parliamentary Party. It can neither be so narrowly nor loosely defined. It was an amalgamation of groups with a common core belief in securing Irish independence and doing so by violent means if necessary. It transcended the well-known friction points of religion (Catholic versus Protestant), economic world view (Socialism versus Capitalism) and national identity (Irish versus English) that served as rallying points for other contemporary rebellions. Fenianism's sole focus was on independence, and, beyond that, there individual members held views that differed significantly from each other.

The Fenian movement may never have materialized if the Irish Parliamentary Party had succeeded in gaining Home Rule. The unrewarded sacrifices and compromises that Redmond made with the British government eventually proved too much for many Irishmen. While the decision to support the Britain's effort in World War I was largely popular, voting with the desires of Westminster to ban the import of arms into Ireland was highly polarizing among the Nationalist community. When the Ulster Volunteer Force was founded, the British government did nothing in terms of legislation or action to restrict them or their efforts. However, when the Irish Volunteers were founded, the British government, with votes from the Irish Parliamentary Party, was able to pass legislation on December 4th, 1913 (just nine days after the first meeting of the Irish Volunteers) restricting the importation of arms into Ireland.[14] This was seen by many, especially in the more radical Irish Republican Brotherhood, as a direct attempt to stymie a potential threat in internal politics and eliminate any alternative to Redmond's preferred Home Rule Bill.

The Fenian leaders were not even united on when and if to use violence. While the names of those who abstained from violent action or who attempt to prevent bloodshed rarely make this history books, there were doubtless men who heard to call of an Irish Free State and chose not to take their place on the barricades despite their beliefs or bravery. The most infamous was Eoin MacNeill and his countermanding order. There were those who no matter how fervently they believed in the cause of Irish independence could never justify the use of violence to achieve it. Besides MacNeill, there were leaders and members of nearly every Sinn Fein and Volunteer organization outside of Dublin who

[14] Joseph McKenna, Voices from the Easter Rising: Firsthand Accounts of Ireland's 1916 Rebellion (Jefferson: McFarland & Company, Inc., Publishers., 2017), p. 28.

chose not to rise. All men and women under this umbrella are Fenians simply because more nuanced definitions did not exist and because public opinion shifted so rapidly following the executions that it is impossible to determine who believed what and how far they were willing to take that belief on Easter Morning.

What did unite the Fenians across the different factions and across the generations was a belief that Ireland was better before the English invasion and always would have been better off without the British Crown's influence and control. The Fenians also had a strong belief in the nobility of martyrdom and the necessity of a representative government for the Irish people. These themes were present in the Easter Proclamation and were also present in the 1867 proclamation of Republican Government during that failed rebellion:

> "The Irish People of the World:
> We have suffered centuries of outrage, enforced poverty, and bitter misery. Our rights and liberties have been trampled on by an alien aristocracy, who treating us as foes, usurped our lands, and drew away from our unfortunate country all material riches. The real owners of the soil were removed to make room for cattle, and driven across the ocean to seek the means of living, and the political rights denied to them at home, while our men of thought and action were condemned to loss of life and liberty. But we never lost the memory and hope of a national existence. We appealed in vain to the reason and sense of justice of the dominant powers. Our mildest remonstrance's were met with sneers and contempt. Our appeals to arms were always unsuccessful. Today, having no honourable alternative left, we again appeal to force as our last resource. We accept the conditions of appeal, manfully deeming it better to die in the struggle for freedom than to continue an existence of utter serfdom. All men are born with equal rights, and in associating to protect one another and share public burdens, justice demands that such associations should rest upon a basis which maintains equality instead of destroying it. We therefore declare that, unable longer to endure the curse of Monarchical Government, we aim at founding a Republic based on universal suffrage, which shall secure

> to all the intrinsic value of their labour. The soil of Ireland, at present in the possession of an oligarchy, belongs to us, the Irish people, and to us it must be restored. We declare, also, in favour of absolute liberty of conscience, and complete separation of Church and State. We appeal to the Highest Tribunal for evidence of the justness of our cause. History bears testimony to the integrity of our sufferings, and we declare, in the face of our brethren, that we intend no war against the people of England – our war is against the aristocratic locusts, whether English or Irish, who have eaten the verdure of our fields – against the aristocratic leeches who drain alike our fields and theirs. Republicans of the entire world, our cause is your cause. Our enemy is your enemy. Let your hearts be with us. As for you, workmen of England, it is not only your hearts we wish, but your arms. Remember the starvation and degradation brought to your firesides by the oppression of labour. Remember the past, look well to the future, and avenge yourselves by giving liberty to your children in the coming struggle for human liberty.
> Herewith we proclaim the Irish Republic.
> The Provisional Government"[15]

The Easter Rebels fulfilled their dreams of keeping this tradition alive and earned their place among the pantheon of Fenian martyrs. They rose, fought and gave their lives. And as their forbearers before them, they did it in vain. At the end of Easter Week, there was no mass rising in the country, no German reinforcements and no Irish Free State. What was left of the movement was martyrs, soon to be martyrs and those who would carry the fight into the Irish Civil War to come.

In Fenian circles, men had dreamed about and advocated for an armed rebellion even as the ashes of previous attempts still glowed. A speech by Padraig Pearse marked the turning point from a theoretical dream to active planning. Before the Easter Rising one of the most catalyzing moments occurred at O'Donovan Ross' funeral. Padraig Pease marked inspired this transition when he stated: "The fools, the fools, the fools! – they have left us our Fenian dead, and, while Ireland holds

[15] Joseph Lee, *The Modernization of Irish Society* (Dublin: Gill and MacMillan Ltd, 2008), p. 58.

these graves, Ireland unfree shall never be at peace."[16] This quote foreshadowed the Fenian's true end state for the Easter Rebellion – to offer a human sacrifice to show themselves, the nation and the British that they were willing to fight and die for their independence. The Fenians were an inherently fragile and fractured coalition. While united in their cause against the British, it is impossible to imagine how a party organized around one goal and with fundamentally opposed views on every other aspect of governance could have governed. The likelihood of their coalition surviving a success was as much of a longshot as Regiments of the Kaiser's troops landing on Irelands shores to join them in arms.

Fenianism was most useful to the Irish as a narrative ideal; tying the current generation's struggles and beliefs back through their ancestors all the way to the generation who witnessed and resisted the Norman invasion. It set the conditions and that reinvigorated repressed Irish culture, brought various factions of nationalism together and created an ideal of a lost historical paradise that all nationalist myths rely on. While few would have primarily identified as a Fenian in lieu of a more specific designation, all Irish participants in the Uprising would have recognized themselves as members in its tradition.

[16]Patrick Pearse, "O'Donovan Ross's Funeral Address at Graveside." Speech. Glasnevin Cemetery, Dublin, 1 August 1915.

Chapter 6: The Political Faction

"Our work henceforward must be done less and less through the Gaelic League and more and more through the groups and the individuals that have arisen, or are arising, out of the Gaelic League"[1] -Padraig Pearse, 1913

There are often similarities between oppressed societies that peacefully remain in bondage and those that rise violently against their masters. Some of the most common similarities are: a shared cultural identity, a somewhat organized (and often ineffective) nascent political structure, a history of rebellion (even if it is glorified and largely exaggerated) and extraneous conditions that make the success of another such rebellion appear feasible. That Ireland had all of these traits in 1916 is due in large part to two organizations that grew out of the earlier Fenian movement. The Fenian movement was the spark that reignited interest and pride in Gaelic identity. The Gaelic League and Irish Parliamentary Party were the kindling that led to war. While much of this was circumstantial and inadvertent, the dreams and promises that the Irish Parliamentary Party fought hard and fruitlessly for helped drive the leaders of Easter Week to a violent rebellion.

The Irish Parliamentary Party retained its monopoly on Irish politics partly due to a lack of competition. There was a plethora of competing nationalist groups in the wake of the dissolution of the Gaelic League and the multiple factions were unable to unify into a competing organization around a set agenda or organization. As a movement, the foundation of the Irish Volunteers was an attempt to reconcile all the groups, Fenian and otherwise, that wanted more self-determination for Ireland. The Irish Volunteers, founded in 1913, served primarily as the Home Rule response to the Unionist Ulster Volunteers led by Sir Edward Carson.[2] The foundation of the Irish Volunteers was driven by members of the secret Irish Republican Brotherhood to provide a less radical, popular front for its activities. The Irish Republican Brotherhood held the primary allegiance of its members, and its sole purpose

---

[1]Padraig Pearse, "The Coming Revolution," *An Claidhamh Soluis,* 8 November 1913, p. 6.

[2]F.X. Martin, ed., *The Irish Volunteers 1913-1915: Recollections and Documents* (Dublin: James Duffy & Co. LTD., 1963), p. vii.

was one thing: rebellion.[3]

At the founding of the Irish Volunteers in the Rotunda Rink in central Dublin on 25 November 1916, the excitement from the mostly young attendees was high. While many of the young men in attendance were motivated to join by nationalism and in response to the formation of the Protestant Ulster Volunteer Force (UVF). Eoin MacNeill was very clear that the new organization was not founded solely in opposition to the UVF and that it was to be a purely defensive outfit.[4] Each enrollee was handed a green membership card with the three objectives printed on the back. These objectives were: "1. To secure and maintain the rights and liberties common to the people of Ireland. 2. To train, discipline, and equip for this purpose and Irish Volunteer Force. 3. To unite, in the service of Ireland, Irishmen of every creed, and every party and class."[5]

Almost all the Nationalists in Ireland, including the Fenians, believed that the passage of the Home Rule Act would occur in their near future. However, it was a promise that seemed to be perpetually just over the next hill. No Irish nationalist organization held enough sway or influence to be capable of forcing the hand of the British Parliament into passing the Home Rule Bill or seriously advancing the legislation. On November 25, 1913, the Irish Volunteers met for the first time at the Rotunda in Dublin.[6] All Nationalist groups from the Irish Republican Brotherhood to the Irish Parliamentary Party were present at this meeting. Although John Redmond demanded that his personal appointees run the committee, Tom Clarke's violently revolutionary Irish Republican Brotherhood was able to take firm control of the organization by ensuring that his supporters filled the key positions within the organization.[7]

Eoin MacNeill became the first leader of the Volunteers, and this was a double-edged sword. Known as the Professor, he was a powerful Republican intellectual presence who had influenced many members

---

[3] Thomas Coffey, *Agony at Easter: The 1916 Irish Uprising* (London: George G. Harrap & Co, LTD, 1969), p. 15.

[4]Joseph McKenna, Voices from the Easter Rising: Firsthand Accounts of Ireland's 1916 Rebellion (Jefferson: McFarland & Company, Inc., Publishers., 2017), p. 15.

[5] Joseph McKenna, Voices from the Easter Rising: Firsthand Accounts of Ireland's 1916 Rebellion (Jefferson: McFarland & Company, Inc., Publishers., 2017), p. 16.

[6] Tim Pat Coogan, *1916: The Easter Uprising* (London: Orion Books Limited, 2001), p. 51.

[7]Ed Moloney, *A Secret History of the* IRA (New York: W.W. Norton & Company LTD., 2002), p. 309.

of the Irish Republican Brotherhood through his educational work in preserving Gaelic culture and provided a tangible link to the earlier, cultural nationalist movements. While his countermanding order tarnished his legacy amongst the Irishmen and historians most interested in glorifying the events of Easter Week, his influence as shown it the number of Fenians that heeded his order, and the effects of his cultural work cannot be forgotten. MacNeill, more than anyone, revived the cultural link that was able to create a separate identify. The geographical distinction of being a separate island was not enough to spark a rebellion. There was not enough oppression since the revocation of the penal laws and in the wake of the Irish diaspora to foment a rebellion in the early twentieth century. There was not even enough of an economic or class divide to cause a rebellion. There was not a single current issue or grievance that the aspiring revolutionaries could rally around. The Fenians who rose crossed religious, political, and geographic lines and took up arms in defiance of the popular perception of the imminent of the passage of a Home Rule Bill because they were united as an Irish people. The Easter Rising was a nationalist rising and Eoin MacNeill's work, more than that of any other man, created and defined who the Irish people were in the early Twentieth century.

Although the Brotherhood hoped that he would join with them once the Rebellion began, MacNeill was staunchly against violence as a means to win freedom. In an effort to prevent the issuance of a rogue order to revolt, MacNeill insisted that he countersign all orders for revolution. Since there was no coherent plan for a nationwide uprising, it is a stretch to say that MacNeill's countermanding order was the sole or even primary cause for the Fenian failure.[8] Pearse's efforts to rescind and override the order were futile. Despite the best efforts of the mostly female messengers, who included James Connolly's daughters among their ranks, almost all of the Battalions outside of Dublin decline to take up arms.[9] The shock and feeling of betrayal among the Fenian was palpable, but they did their best to hide it from both the rank and file and the from the citizenry of Dublin. The Rebellion proceeded with Dublin alone.

While the common and most simplistic explanation for the failure of the of the Rebels to achieve their operational and strategic ob-

[8] Michael Tierney, *Eoin MacNeill: Scholar and Man of Action 1867-1945* (Oxford: Clarendon Press, 1980), p. 183.

[9] Nora Connolly O'Brien, *The Irish Rebellion of 1916 or, the Unbroken Tradition.* (New York: Boni and Liveright, 1918), 100-103.

jectives is the countermanding order, it is a 'lost cause' myth. The state of the Great War and the troops that the British had at their disposal were so disproportionate to what the Fenians had in their ranks that it is doubtful that even if a German expeditionary force landed to support the Fenians that it would have changed the outcome. The Irish Volunteers provided the means that unified the Fenian groups. They never had the chance to fulfill its original purpose as the defense against Unionism, but it did serve as the vanguard for Irish self-determination. The Volunteers served as the vehicle for the Fenians to combine their manpower and efforts and take a chance on a revolution.

The Irish Volunteers were a hodgepodge organization without a clear organizational structure or intent. The Volunteers were an intermediary step in the transition of Gaelic organizations from benign cultural preservation movements to radical military organizations. Padraig Pearse correctly believed that "The Gaelic League has brought into Ireland not peace, but a sword."[10] While the Fenian cultural movement begat a recreational organization that begat a political movement it did not have a unified ideology or plan or even goal. It contrasted sharply from its contemporary movement Communism that had a singular view of history, goal and even strategy all codified and widely distributed by its universal founder Karl Marx. Even if the Irish Volunteers had not risen against the British, it is very likely that they would have eventually taken arms against anti-Home Rule groups like the Ulster Guards or even themselves. The Irish Volunteers were always strange bedfellows untied more by the same enemy than by common cause. Catholic and Communist, worker and aristocrat, pacifist and revolutionary could never peacefully coexist with themselves or their enemies for long.

The signers of the *Poblacht Na H Eireann* (The Easter Proclamation) should have known that the base of popular support needed to wage an effective revolutionary war simply did not exist in Ireland. They may have been in denial about the effects of the countermanding order, but to them the launching of a rebellion was more important than it succeed. If the writings and the remembrances of the survivors are correct, and the leaders support that they were so committed to the belief of a blood sacrifice that they would have rebelled despite knowing the consequences and inevitability of their defeat.

Wrought with mistakes and missed opportunities, the short-lived rebellion lasted from April 24th to 30th. Due to Eoin MacNeill's

[10]Padraig Pearse, "The Coming Revolution," *An Claidhamh Soluis,* 8 November 1913, p. 6.

countermanding order canceling the rebellion a mere two days prior to commencement, only 1,200 of the nearly 10,000 Volunteers mustered to fight the British on Easter Monday.[11] In one instance, only two members of an entire company gathered at Saint Stephen's Green.[12] In his Tuesday proclamation, Pearse proclaimed that: "Dublin, by rising in arms, has redeemed its honour….It has redeemed an honour forfeited in 1803 when it failed to support the rebellion of Robert Emmet."[13]

The rebels achieved all of their goals for the first day, but they made their most costly mistake by not seizing the undefended Dublin Castle - the center of British government in Ireland - when they had the chance.[14] Diverting forces away from other, less consequential objectives like the Four Courts or nearly impossible positions to defend positions like St. Stephen's Green, would have been a much better choice. Some citizens of Dublin hardly noticed the rebellion occurred at all and went about their routine.[15] Others harassed and threw things at the rebels.[16] The Volunteers greatly overestimated the willingness of the countrymen to commit to an open and violent revolution. All of the Battalions outside of Dublin failed to revolt. This manifested itself during Easter Week when the unsupportive public reaction to their long-awaited revolt surprised many of them.

The arrival of reinforcements under Sir General John Maxwell on Friday eradicated all Fenian resistance by the early afternoon on Sunday.[17] Additional forces, even a large landing of substantial German forces, would have only prolonged the conflict. To the rebels holding out in Jacob's Factory "the word of surrender came as a bit of a surprise", but the British had routed every other Fenian citadel.[18] In Dublin the rebellion was over. In the rest of Ireland there was too much dissent

[11]Tim Pat Coogan, *The IRA* (New York: Palgrave, 2002), p. 18.

[12]Peader O Cearnaigh, *Reminiscences of the Irish Republican Brotherhood and Easter Week 1916,* TCDMS 3560/1, 2.

[13]Thomas Coffey, *Agony at Easter: The 1916 Irish Uprising* (London: George G. Harrap & Co, LTD, 1969), p. 111.

[14]Max Caufield, *The Easter Rebellion* (New York: Holt, Rinehart, and Winston, 1963), p. 20.

[15]"The Sinn Fein Rising. Scenes and Incidents in Dublin Streets. A Citizen's Diary," *The Irish Times*, 2 May 1916, p. 4.

[16]Peader O Cearnaigh, *Reminiscences of the Irish Republican Brotherhood and Easter Week 1916,* TCDMS 3560/1, 5.

[17]Tyler Toby, "Exemplary Violence Used in British Colonial Policy: One Explanation for General John Maxwell's Violent Reaction to the Easter Rising of 1916" (Masters diss., University of Massachusetts Boston, June 1997), p. 1.

[18]Thomas Pugh, *Bureau of Military History, 1913-1921,* p.397.

and confusion for it to have even begun.[19] Letters to the *Irish Times* and blasé reaction of the citizens of Dublin indicates that the people were far from inspired.[20] The Fenian cause, and movement died with the surrender of their headquarters at the General Post Office on Sackville Street. The movement and rebellion were most likely doomed from the start. However, the feat of even giving it life was remarkable when so many of their countrymen opposed it.

---

[19]Michael Brennan, *The War in Clare 1911-1921: Personal Memories of the Irish War of Independence* (Dublin: Irish Academic Press, 1980), p. 15.
[20] "The Proclamation of the Republic," The Irish Times, 6 May 1916.

Chapter 7: General Sir John Maxwell

"I wish to draw attention to the fact that, when it became known that the leaders of the rebellion wished to surrender, the officers used every endeavour to prevent further bloodshed; emissaries were sent in to the various isolated bands, and time was given them to consider their position.

I cannot imagine a more difficult situation than that in which the troops were placed; most of those employed were draft-finding battalions, or young Territorials from England, who had no knowledge of Dublin."[1] *-General Sir John Maxwell*

The responsibility for both the successes and the failures of the British Army during and after Easter Week rest on the shoulders of British General Sir John Maxwell. Even though General Lowell was responsible for most of the tactical and operational level fighting and the initial response, Maxwell bears the burden for the treatment of the Fenians during the trials and for a large amount of the devastation caused during the fighting. In a sense, Lowe won the battle while Maxwell lost the peace.

The vast majority of those who have studied the Rebellion place the blame of all British follies squarely on his decisions. In this regard, his generalship and his reputation suffer from the same fate as his contemporaries who fought on the Western Front. These men were the best trained and most competent military professionals that Britain could offer: the officer elite of the Victorian Army who saved Europe from the menace of Napoleon a short century before. Yet, for all of their accolades, elitism, higher breeding and experience against native uprisings these aristocratic generals failed to grasp and react to the rapid evolution in warfare occurring right in front of their face.

Ensconced in the British military aristocracy, General Maxwell was eminently qualified for his post as the General Officer Commanding His Majesty's armed forces in Ireland. General Sir John Maxwell's lineage, upbringing, education and experience met the standards of the British military aristocracy of the time. Born to a Scottish Protestant family in Liverpool, a young John Maxwell saw action in several conflicts before assuming his post in Ireland. Educated at Sandhurst, dec-

[1] "Official Report by General Sir John Maxwell on the Easter Rising, April 1916", Source Records of the Great War, Vol. IV, ed. Charles F. Horne, National Alumni 1923

orated for valor in combat as a young officer and a notable role in the Sudanese War that caught the eye of his superiors. His list of campaigns includes the Mahdist War in the Sudan, Wolseley's expedition during the Anglo-Egyptian War of 1882 and the First and Second Boer Wars. Ireland was not even his first stint as a military governor. He served as the military governor of Nubia, then Omdurman, the Pretoria and the Western Transvaal. He was also the commanding officer of British forces in Egypt on two separate occasions.[2]

Fifty-six years old at the time of the Rebellion, General Maxwell had a lifetime of experience fighting and winning against colonial revolutions. During the course of his distinguished service in the face of the enemies of the Empire earned him high awards including: the Order of the Bath, Companion of the Order of St Michael and St George, Commander of the Victorian Order and Distinguished Service Order.[3]

It would be almost impossible to find an officer with a better pedigree for the task that General Maxwell faced in Dublin. Not only did he come from a class and station that fostered trust from Lord Asquith's government, but he had a nearly spotless martial record and reputation. Further, he had experience with this kind of warfare.

With the exception of the urban environment and for Ireland in particular, Maxwell had not only successfully suppressed rebellions, but had experienced the aftermath of such a suppression with white colonials who were only marginally loyal to or openly hostile towards the British crown. The lessons learned in the Sudan and South Africa would have provided him with an invaluable firsthand education and set of experiences. Unlike many of his peers, the delicate racial and social distinctions between the handling of white and "native" subjects should have been clear to Maxwell. While it is clear from his subsequent actions and their results, it should have been clear to Maxwell that the heavy hand that the British were able to apply in places like India or the Sudan needed a more delicate touch in southern Africa to be successful. Maxwell should have realized that in Ireland, with its well-established press, large diaspora and active Home Rule movement that his handling of the situation would require kid-gloves that the Empire was unaccus-

---

[2] Eunan O'Halpin, "A History of Ireland in ten Englishmen (7): General Sir John Maxwell – The Man Who Lost Ireland?", June 2015 [RGS History] Available from < https://rgshistory.wordpress.com/2015/06/02/a-history-of-ireland-in-ten-englishmen-7-general-sir-john-maxwell-the-man-who-lost-ireland/>; Accessed 21 March 2018.

[3] Peter De Rosa, *Rebels: The Irish Rising of 1916* (New York: Fawcett Books, 1990), p.1.

tomed to wearing.

General Maxwell was not the only officer in the British Army with these experiences. In fact, most members of the pre-War British Army would have cut their teeth in low intensity conflicts in some far-flung corer of the Empire. The Victorian British Army did not possess the institutional professionalism that modern armies maintain in terms of training, professional journals and advanced courses. There was no formal organization tasked with compiling, distilling and disseminating vignettes, best practices and lessons learned. However, the close-knit and highly social nature of Britain's aristocratic officer class would have fostered an informal collective of knowledge. Maxwell, his peers, subordinates and superiors would have all been the beneficiaries of informal discussions on the nature, martial and political, of the various reaches of the Empire. So, while this would have been Maxwell's first sojourn to Ireland, he would not have been unfamiliar with the situation that he was entering.

It may seem surprising that in an Army full of officers that had largely made their careers in Ireland, held close connections to the island or were even more culturally and ethnically aligned with the majority of Ireland that the British government would choose a man who was a relative neophyte on peculiarities of the island. In fact, Asquith wrote to Lord Kitchener specifically extolling the virtues of someone without much previous experience in Ireland compared to an officer with a history in Ireland: "I think on the whole it would be better to not send [General Sir Ian Hamilton]…to Dublin. There is a good deal of bitterness in Ireland about Suvla, etc., to which Redmond gave expression in the House this afternoon….It is desirable to send a competent man who so far as Ireland is concerned has no past record."[4] Compared to the officer in question, who had commanded a large number of Irish soldiers during a failed operation at the Suvla Bay during the Gallipoli Campaign, would have been a known and highly unpopular choice, there were other officers who in normal times that may have performed better. These were not normal times and the priority for the Empire was on the Western Front. While it was urgent to contain the fighting in Dublin, it would have been unthinkable to divert a capable officer from the Western Front. Choosing an officer with little history or reputation in Ireland, who was capable and was not currently assigned to a specific fight was the most logical and timely choice that Asquith had available.

[4] Kitchener Papers PRO 30/57/55; see also Asquith to King George V, 27 April in PRO Cab37/146 and cabinet discussion in PRO CAB41/37.

Maxwell also had the advantage of having seen firsthand, albeit briefly, that the world was witnessing another major revolution in warfare. He served a brief stint on the Western Front and commanding British forces in Egypt before returning to Britain to assume his next assignment. His most notable achievement during his command in Egypt was successfully resisting an Ottoman Raid on the Suez Canal.

The Easter Uprising diverted those plans and sent him to Dublin after hostilities had started and the British forces had ceased back the momentum from the Rebels. General Maxwell had almost every advantage that commander entering such a challenging situation could have: he was given the authority to unify the British combatant forces, he reported directly to the Prime Minister Lord Asquith, he had experience with this type of conflict, he had seen how the advances in military technology were changing the face of modern warfare, his experience and formal military education qualified him as a competent strategist and tactician, and his informal military education would have acquainted him with the unique challenges of the 'Irish Question'.

Not even the harshest critics of General Maxwell considered him to be barbaric in the execution of his duties nor would they consider him grossly incompetent in the execution of his tasks. There is no documentation, recollection or personal correspondence yet found to indicate the Maxwell was assigned the task of suppressing the Dublin rising primarily due to a lack of confidence in his ability to perform in France. While surely there was some deliberation on which general should be sent to Dublin, the decision lacked controversy or conflict. If Maxwell was considered exceptional or critical, other officers would have taken the role in Dublin and his previous posting in Egypt. On the onset, his task was simple and straightforward: end an unpopular rebellion by a small minority in Dublin and return the city and the remainder of Ireland to normal activities in support of the war effort as quickly as possible.

Whether by haste, ignorance or the desire to quash the embers of uprising for good, Maxwell despite or because of his experiences and education ordered arrests and executions that turned the majority of the people of Ireland away from supporting remaining in the Empire to supporting a violent revolution. Later in life it appears that he regretted his decision to order the executions, it is clear from his reports and writings that he took no pleasure and there was no masochism in the harsh treatment of the Fenians that occurred in the wake of the Uprising.[5] Further, he ignored the advice of Prime Minister Asquith and the resigning administration from Dublin Castle to show leniency.[6] Some historians have depicted his actions to be either bumbling or incompetent, but more likely, he was just trying to make it clear that the British presence was there to stay and had the power to act with impunity. While they did not meet his desired end state and more likely caused more harm than good, his decisions and orders fell in line with the best practices of the day, reflected the lessons he learned fighting in the Colonial British Army, and it is doubtful that any besides the most enlightened of his peers would have acted any differently.[7]

Maxwell arrived four days into the fighting. While he would not have been wholly unfamiliar with the Irish situation, in those four days a tremendous amount about the island had changed. There was a tremendous amount of information for Maxwell to getting process when he assumed command: the operations on the ground, the movement and disposition of both his forces and the Rebel forces as well as the feelings and reactions of both his forces and of the citizens of Ireland. Further, Maxwell would have relied on his previous experience in more far-flung colonies. The more racist dispositions of the Victorian era would have viewed the rights and inherent worth of those darker skinned subjects differently than that of the Irishmen, even if they were "Papist" Catholics. While this would not have been a surprised to a well-connected Britain, especially one with experience with the Boers in South Africa, Maxwell's understanding of and fluency in Irish politics and history is unknown.

During the course of Easter Week, General Maxwell's forces suffered significant loses. The men under his command ranged from mostly green recruits diverted from their original destination on the Western Front and a plethora of the Crown's representatives in Ireland ranging from unarmed constables to firemen. Many units suffered losses, but all had some casualties. In total his command suffered losses of seventeen

[5] Vivienne Clarke, "Maxwell did not like ordering 1916 executions, says great grandson", March 2016 [The Irish Times] Available from <https://www.irishtimes.com/culture/heritage/maxwell-did-not-like-ordering-1916-executions-says-great-grandson-1.2585599>; Accessed 3 January 2018.

[6] Helen Litton, *16 Lives: Edward Daly* (Dublin, The O'Brien Press, 2013), p. 169.

[7] Ronan McGreevy, "General who had Easter Rising leaders shot was 'able, level-headed and clear-sighted'", March 2015 [The Irish Times] Available from <https://www.irishtimes.com/news/ireland/irish-news/general-who-had-easter-rising-leaders-shot-was-able-level-headed-and-clear-sighted-1.2127915>; Accessed 3 January 2018.

officers and forty-six wounded along with eighty-nine killed and two hundred and eighty-eight wounded among the other ranks. Maxwell reported proudly on the brave conduct and behavior of this men as well as the grace which with they accepted the surrender of the Rebels.[8]

Regardless of whether General Maxwell earnestly believed the whitewashing of the British response or if he was trying to justify the destruction and collateral damage wrought on Ireland's principal city during the bombardment, Maxwell stated that: "I wish to emphasize that the responsibility for the loss of life, however it occurred, the destruction of property and other losses, rests entirely with those who engineered this revolt, and who, at a time when the empire is engaged in a gigantic struggle, invited the assistance and cooperation of the Germans."[9] General Maxwell understood the concept and ramifications to excessive collateral damage upon both his reputation and end state. In his official report, he specifically justified the application of indirect fires: "Artillery fire was only used to reduce the barricades, or against a particular house known to be strongly held. The troops suffered severe losses in establishing these cordons, and, once established, the troops were subjected to a continuous fire from all directions, especially at night time, and invariably from persons concealed in houses."[10] He also was very clear to point out that he was personally aware of and actively investigating any and all allegations of misconduct committed by British forces and was "glad to say they are few in number, and these are not all borne out by direct evidence."[11] General Maxwell was not, by the standards of the day and his peerage, overly cruel or incompetent. However, his failures to grasp the nuances that made Ireland in 1916 different from the Transvaal or Sudan caused the failure of his plan.

[8]"Official Report by General Sir John Maxwell on the Easter Rising, April 1916", Source Records of the Great War, Vol. IV, ed. Charles F. Horne, National Alumni 1923

[9] Ibid.

[10] Ibid.

[11] Ibid.

Chapter 8: The Fenian Leaders

Most casual understandings of the Easter Rebellion and the Irish Civil War divide the conflict along clearly down religious lines. While the Protestant-Catholic divide is the clearest demarcation and at the root of centuries of laws, injustices and insubordinations that grew into an Irish Free State it was not so clear in April of 1916. While the Protestant side was equally nuanced and played just as large of a role in the following years, this was a side of the British Empire. Regardless of feelings on Home Rule, independence or the maintenance of the status quo, it is possible to summarize the common position of the Protestant side as pro-unity, pro-British war effort in World War I and anti-armed rebellion on Easter Week.

On the other hand, the Catholic side was split. Before and during Easter Week in 1916, the majority of Catholics were against the Uprising and pro-British war effort. Whether motivated by pensions, patriotism or the imminence of Home Rule, the vast majority of Catholics did not initially support the Republic proclaimed on Easter Week. There is no need to rely on an accurate poll to determine how the Catholic side felt. The overwhelming dominance of the Irish Parliamentary Party and a long history of both repression and failed rebellions put most in Catholic Ireland, including leading Fenians like Eoin MacNeill, strongly in favor of Home Rule by peaceful means.

It may come as a surprise that even within the Fenian movement, there were wildly different opinions and goals. The Fenians were the most radical and violent Irish Independence group. All of the men and women who bore arms or rose to support the call to arms by other means during the Rebellion were inherently anti-Union. Their opinions, however, diverged on the use of force, the timing of the Rebellion, and their beliefs on the ethics (not to mention viability of) using Germany as an ally. Disharmony on these fundamental beliefs and strategies was exacerbated by the lack of anything even remotely resembling a coherent chain of command and the cults of personalities surrounding each of the primary and subordinate leaders.

Fundamentally, what separated the Fenians from other factions that supported a more independent Ireland was the opposition to Home Rule. While many, including O'Neill and Pearse initially welcomed and openly and vociferously advocated for the 1914 Home Rule Bill arm in arm with John Redmond, a split occurred after the failure for the Bill to pass.[1] The camp aligned with Redmond believed that time and continued Irish contribution to the glory of the Crown would guarantee the bill's passage, especially with the sacrifices being made by Ireland's sons on the Western Front. The other camp believed that this was another empty promise leaving Redmond and his compatriots to be the latest to abandon the true Irish cause at a decisive hour.

Pearse opposed the continuing alliance with Redmond after the failure of the 1914 Home Rule Bill saying: "The leaders in Ireland have nearly always left the people at the critical moment; they have sometimes sold them. The former Volunteer movement was abandoned by its leaders; O'Connell recoiled before the cannon at Clontarf; twice the hour of the Irish revolution struck during Young Ireland days and twice it struck in vain, for Meagher hesitated in Waterford, Duffy and McGee hesitated in Dublin. Stephens refused to give the word in '65; he never came in '66 or '67. I do not blame these men; you or I might have done the same. It is a terrible responsibility to be cast on a man, that of bidding the cannon speak and the grapeshot pour"[2]

The split from Redmond's camp separated and isolated a smaller, more radical group that was preparing for war. The Irish Volunteers "soon found that it was impossible to arm and prepare men for revolution against a government, while paid servants of that government were still amongst them."[3] This group was far from homogenous. In fact, the only thing that unified them was their rejection of Home Rule as being insufficient and the belief in Irish independence. They were not unified by economic theory, religion or even in their belief in and approach to the application of force as a means to achieve their ends. One of the fundamental requirements necessary for a successful military or political organization is unity. This is especially true in a military organization, where unity of command is one of the ten fundamental principles of war. The Fenians were an amalgamation of not only several different ideologies, but several different organizations. While a charismatic, competent leader could have rallied this hodgepodge into a cohesive unit, the man ostensibly in charge of *The Rising*, Padraig Pearse was not up to the task.

---

[1]Michael Foy and Brian Barton, *The Easter Rising (*London: Sutton Publishing, 2004) pp. 7–8.

[2]Seán Cronin, *Our Own Red Blood* (New York: Irish Freedom Press, 1966), pg.15

[3]Nora Connolly O'Brien, *The Irish Rebellion of 1916 or, the Unbroken Tradition.* (New York: Boni and Liveright, 1918), vii-viii.

While Pearse was well-liked and respected, he was not a commander. He was an intellectual; an idealist and fiery orator who made a tremendous political and ideological leader. However, no matter how eloquent his funeral orations, his Easter Proclamation and his other lectures and speeches, he did not exert any command authority over the organization or his lieutenants. This inability to establish a unified command manifested itself in the infamous countermanding order. It is in fact surprising that his orders to surrender were obeyed by the commands at the Four Courts and Jacob's Biscuit Factory where the Fenians had bloodied the British more than they had received. Pearse was responsible more than anybody else for the Fenians adopting a bad strategy and executing it poorly.

Beyond a unified rejection of Home Rule, there was not much to unify the objectives and opinions of the Fenians. To truly determine their motivations, performance and legacy, it is necessary to look at each of the key players as an individual. More than any tactical or ideological failure, the inability to unify and control their subordinate commands outside of Dublin doomed the Fenians to failure. While the British had a traditional command structure that clearly fell in line with centuries of military best practices, it is impossible to say who the true leader of the Irish military forces was or where the ultimate allegiances of the subordinate commanders and independent commanders lay.

Chapter 9: Padraig Pearse

"This man was a member of the Irish Bar and was Principal of a college for boys at Rathfarnham, Co Dublin. He had taken an active part in the volunteer movement from its inception, and joined the Sinn Fein or Irish Volunteers when that body became a separate organisation (sic). He was a member of the Central Council of the Irish Volunteers and a regular attendant at the meetings of that body. He was one of the signatories to the Declaration of Irish Independence which document contains the following passage "... She now seizes that moment and fully supported by her exiled children in America and by gallant allies in Europe ... she strikes in the full confidence of victory ... ". He was "Commandant General of the Army of the Irish Republic" and "President of the Provisional Government", and as such, issued a Proclamation to the people of Ireland which was printed and distributed in Dublin and elsewhere."[1] - General Sir John Maxwell

Padraig Pearse was the unifier and leader of the Fenian movement before, during and until his execution in the aftermath of the 1916 Easter Rebellion. He was an unlikely Rebel leader, especially for the Irish. His family was originally of English lineage and had originally spelled its name Pierce.[2] He was a true romantic nationalist whose views on Irish independence were highly inspired by the revolutions of the previous century. The need to Gaelicize both his first and last name, his slight lisp and total lack of military experience would normally have disqualified him as a candidate to lead a new nation. Pearse, however, had the earnest commitment to the cause and the natural air of a leader.

He was only thirty-six years old when he stood on the steps of the GPO as the Commander-in-Chief and President of the Provisional Government to declare the new, free Irish Republic. Rebellions, like most of world history, tend to gravitate towards one man. Irish rebellions tended to follow this trend as well. While Pearse was to be remembered

---

[1] General Sir John Maxwell. Transcript of Court Martial. May 1916. Available from <http://www.aoh61.com/history/easter_trials.htm>.

[2] Max Caufield, *The Easter Rebellion* (New York: Holt, Rinehart, and Winston, 1963), p. 34.

as the Easter Rising's Wolfe Tone, his control over the forces under his command and that of his fellow founders was far from complete. While tasked as the overall commander and organizer of the Rebellion, Pearse was not a founder with the experience, capabilities or disposition to lead such a movement. He was not a George Washington or Simon Bolivar. Pearse was more of a bookish intellectual like Thomas Jefferson whose contribution to the new Republic would have been better served with the pen then with the sword. While he may have been the only man in the Fenian organization who could have united the various revolutionary factions, his shortcomings were a detriment to the execution of a successful military operation.

Few men can be both the master of the battlefield and the congress. Augustus had Agrippa, Justinian had Belisarius and the Fenian leader had no one. While there were more martially inclined members of his organization, there were no true experts. Especially when compared to the leaders on the British side, the Fenian leaders were all total amateurs and pretenders. The Fenians did the best they could with the men and resources they had available and had not choice, in their minds, but to fight the British with the army they had. Pearse knew that his revolution required intellectuals to become generals and workers to become soldiers and the metamorphosis of the former proved much more difficult than the later.

Pearse was born on 10 September 1879 in Dublin, the first son of an English monumental sculptor. He is yet another example of an Irishmen whose lineage conflicts with the archetypical Irish nationalist. His English blood was never brought into question not only because of his conviction but because it was a trait that so many of his peers in the Fenian movement also shared.

Pearse's most notable accomplishment prior the Rebellion was the establishment of St. Enda's, a school based on the glories of Ireland's past. Pearse took great lengths to ensure that the Gaelic ideal permeated everything in the school. From paintings of Irish folk heroes like Cuhulainn on the walls to the teaching of a then dying language. The establishment of this school and the propagation of these ideals coincided with Pearse's joining of the IRB in 1914. As time wore on, the school became more and more of a training ground for you men indoctrinated in the arguments for rebellion.[3]

---

[3]Max Caufield, *The Easter Rebellion* (New York: Holt, Rinehart, and Winston, 1963), p.37.

There is evidence that as early as 1915 he was both dedicated to a military revolution and had accepted the fact not only would it fail, but that he would give his life in that failure.[4] Pearse was not the sole driving force behind the Rebellion, but he stood confidently and convinced that this was the right course of action. During the course of the fighting, Pearse stayed focused on the strategic needs of the new state rather than focusing on the operations and the tactics. For a man with no experience and little inclination towards martial affairs, allowing his subordinates to run the fight as they saw fit was a wise decision.

Pearse's main contributions during Easter Week were the issuance of proclamations and boosting morale. While ultimately fruitless, without these proclamations and other communications, there would have been no hope of gaining international recognition or support. Not only from German forces, but from the large and politically active Irish diaspora population in neutral countries – namely America. Further, the Countermanding Order eliminated a key part of the Fenian strategy: creating a nationwide revolt that would create multiple fronts, stretch British logistical and combat power and relieve pressure from the main objective at the GPO in Dublin. These communications and proclamations were a failed attempt to mobilize the units that followed MacNeill's order. This is precisely what the de jure and spiritual leader of the Irish forces should have focused on at this point in the conflict.

Pearse's performance during the fighting was a far cry from that of a George Washington or a Simon Bolivar. However, given his competencies and the strategic and tactical situation, it is hard to propose any way he could have better applied his time and talents during Easter Week. Following the Rebellion, his actions and words during the court martial trials did much to galvanize the righteousness of the Irish position and improve the public's perception not only the cause, but the men who fought for it.

One of the more regrettable consequences of Pearse's role as the leader of the *Rebellion* was the execution of his brother Willie. Willie Pearse was Patrick's younger brother. Throughout his life, he shared a close connection with the more accomplished Patrick and was by his side for most of his most important moments. Prior to the *Rebellion*, Willie had some achievement as an artist.

During the *Rebellion*, he took up a post as a Volunteer at the GPO. He bore no leadership responsibilities and was hardly a driver for the *Rebellion*. Much to everyone's surprise, he was found guilty in his

[4]*IBID*, 37.

court martial and sentenced to death. Despite the appeals that other men who had a greater role in the fighting were not condemned to death. On the 3rd of May he was granted permission to visit his brother one last time, but Patrick was executed before Willie could see him. On the 4th of May, he was shot and killed in Kilmainham Gaol. They were the only two brothers executed for their role during Easter Week.

These two executions helped turn public opinion against the British response. Patrick's execution was understandable based on his role in the Rebellion. However, he remained a popular and sympathetic figure for his idealism and nationalism. The execution of Willie was seen as crossing a line. He was executed primarily for who his brother was instead of what he did during or leading up to the fighting. Following the executions, Willie was unfairly characterized as being mentally handicapped or less intelligent than the average man. While this was not true, Willie may have paled in comparison to his brother's intellect but there is no indication that he was below average, it painted the British response as even more unusually cruel than already was.

In an organization with as many larger-than-life figures as were present in the Fenian ranks, it is noteworthy that Padraig Pearse rose to be the first among peers. Even wielding enough influence to launch a rebellion in the direct defiance of their de jure leader and several of his key lieutenants. Pearse knew and never tried to act as the leader of the fighting force. He knew that his destiny was to be the leader of a new government and to take advantage of whatever time the fighting volunteers could afford him to gain legitimacy for an independent Ireland. He correctly focused his efforts on giving the Irish Free State an air of legitimacy and to mobilize the battalions that adhered to the countermanding order. Despite the fact that all of his efforts to establish an Irish Republic quickly failed. His legacy as the father of an independent Irish Republic is indisputable.

Chapter 10: Tom Clarke

Of all of the men associated with the Fenian leaders of the 1916 Easter Raising, Tom Clarke was the most revolutionary. A firebrand and a socialist organizer, Clarke and his faction, the Irish Republican Brotherhood, operated out of Liberty Hall and were the most vehement advocates for an Irish revolution. Clarke was comparatively technically and tactically competent and his subordinates generally took the martial aspects of their organization more seriously than their peers in other Battalions. Clarke was a true believer in the Fenian cause and had dedicated his life to its efforts. He was also determined that he would dedicate his death to it as well.

Clarke was actively involved in the movement from an early age. He joined the secret and outlawed Irish Republican Brotherhood in 1878 at the age of twenty.[1] The Irish Republican Brotherhood was founded by James Stephens in 1858 and was the principal organization behind the Fenian Uprising (also known as the Fenian Bombing Campaign) and was one of the more militant and most vocal advocates for armed uprising within the Fenian organization.

Ironically for such a staunch Irish nationalist, Clarke was born in Hampshire, England to a Sergeant of the British Army. His family later moved to County Tyrone, Ireland where young Tom spent his youth. Clarke's beliefs, organizational skills, strength of conviction and the cult of personality that developed around him were major reasons that the countermanding order had less of an effect on halting the mobilization of his Irish Volunteers compared to the other Rebels.

Tom was engaged in a violent form of Fenianism far before Easter Week and truly believed that a violent uprising was the only means by which his island could gain and guarantee its freedom. At the young age of twenty-five, Clarke had received training on basic explosives and espionage from Irish separatists on Long Island, New York. In 1883 he was sent to England along with a case of liquid explosives with designs to blow up a major landmark – the Houses of Parliament or London Bridge primarily. The British authorities discovered him almost immediately and given a life sentence, of which he served fifteen years. During this time, he shared a cell with his future comrade in arms John Daly,

[1] Peter De Rosa, *Rebels: The Irish Rising of 1916* (New York: Fawcett Books, 1990), p. 23.

eventually marrying his niece, Katherine.[2] Although just one amongst many an Irishmen who attempted and failed to enact violence upon their British overlords, by the time Tom Clarke left prison his bona fides as a revolutionary and his willingness to personally sacrifice for Ireland had been well established. Prison did little to cool his revolutionary zeal and Clarke used the next eighteen years to establish and build an organization around himself that was deeply committed to revolution.

Tom Clarke was often seen as stern and austere by those who knew him, but around his family and close associates he could be jovial and was even known to play practical jokes.[3] There is no doubt that Clarke and his acolytes were the main drivers in pushing the Finian's towards rebellion. They were the most militant faction within the organization and even without any support from any of the other factions, the Irish Volunteers would have risen before the war was over.

During his court martial, General Sir John Maxwell was adamant in his damnation of Clarke's role in the rebellion: "This man was a signatory to the Declaration of Irish Independence. He was one of the most prominent leaders in the Sinn Fenn *movement in Dublin. He was present* with the rebels in the GPO, Sackville Street, where some of the heaviest fighting took place and was proved to have been in a position of authority there. On 20 May 1885, under the name of Henry H. Wilson, he was sentenced in London to Penal Servitude for life for the felony of treason and was released on license *on the 20 September 1898. He exercised a great influence over the younger members of the* organization with which he was connected."[4]

This attestation of Clarke's role was corroborated by a British officer, 2nd Lieutenant S.L. King of the 12th Royal Enniskillen (Inniskilling) Fusiliers, who was taken prisoner outside the GPO. "Between 10 and 11am Tuesday 25 April 1916 I was in Sackville Street, 2 men rushed across from the direction of the Post Office and took me prisoner, taking me into the main entrance of the Post Office. While I was detained there, I often saw the prisoner. He appeared to be a person in authority although he was not in uniform. Some of the men obtained a key from him at different times and some wore uniform. I have no doubt that he was one of the rebels."[5]

---

[2]Ibid.

[3]Helen Litton, *16 Lives: Edward Daly* (Dublin, The O'Brien Press, 2013), p. 37.

[4]General Sir John Maxwell. Transcript of Court Martial. May 1916. Available from <http://www.aoh61.com/history/easter_trials.htm>.

[5]S.L.King.Transcript of Court Martial. May 1916. Available from <http://www.aoh61.

If Pearse was the figurehead of the Revolution, Clarke was the heart. His passionate calls for Rebellion, the early and comparatively professional martial training and organization of the Volunteers and the role that those in his circle played in the rebellion cannot be understated. He had little care for the chances of success for the Irish Free State and viewed his sacrifice as almost a family obligation. Clarke involved everyone in his orbit in the Rising all the way down to his daughter Nora who was sent on a last-ditch effort to help mobilize the north of Ireland shortly before the hostilities began.

Clarke's greatest contributions came prior to the Rising. During the actual fighting he did little tactically or strategically to further the Fenian efforts. While he was present at almost all pivotal points in the GPO during Easter Week, he was not the key player. However, before the fighting, he was the main driver in many of the conversations, discussions and actions that lead to a Rebellion. His direct influence was present in many of the decisive points and battalions throughout Dublin. Clarke was never the sole voice that drove the Fenians towards Rebellion, but the groundwork that he laid and the mid-level leaders he mentored and influenced were essential to the Fenian plans and his influence would go on to affect Irish nationalists throughout the Civil Wars and the Troubles.

com/history/easter_trials.htm>.

Chapter 11: Countess Markievicz

Constance Georgine Markievicz, known as the Countess Markievicz due to her marriage to a Polish aristocrat, was one of the most striking and historically lasting figures of the Easter Rebellion. Born in 1868 in London to a famous arctic explorer and Baronet, she was yet another Irish nationalist with deep connections to England and a family legacy with ties to supporting the established order. Her father, Sir Henry William Gore-Booth, 5th Baronet, was a famous arctic explorer.

The Countess was one of the most unlikely, but most committed Revolutionaries of Easter Week. Her high class, English Protestant background and upbringing was the antithesis of the socialist, Irish nationalist cause that she fought so hard for. From the time she went to study at the Slade School of Art in London she became politically active, initially joining the cause of women's suffrage joining the National Union of Women's Suffrage Societies (NUWSS). She later moved to Paris where she met her future husband Casimir Markievicz, from whom she would acquire the title Countess. Although there is, and has always been, some doubt regarding the validity of the title.

In 1903 she moved to Dublin and settled into the artistic circles. These cliques eventually led her to the Gaelic League. While she was still apolitical at this time and the Gaelic League was far from a revolutionary organization, it was her introduction to the historical plight of the Irish. This plight gradually became more of a focus of intertest until in 1908 when she joined Sinn Féin and Inghinidhe na hÉireann (Daughters of Ireland), a revolutionary woman's movement founded by the actress and activist Maud Gonne, muse of W. B. Yeats. The Countess and Maud Gonne became fast friends and collaborators. Partnering on several plays at the newly established Abbey Theater and becoming increasingly more involved with the Suffrage movement.

In 1909 she co-founded the Fianna Éireann, a paramilitary nationalist scouting organization along with Bulmer Hobson. This was more martial and extremist than any other organization which she had participated in, going so far as to that instructed teenage boys in the use of firearms. Many of these boys would grow into the men who fought on the streets of Dublin. While this was not the only scouting revolutionary nationalist organization that Baden Powell's model and used it as a means of training and radicalizing the youth, the early and prominent involvement of women at its head was unique.

During this time, the Countess oversaw a kitchen for women. After noticing that the women would typically take the food home and distribute it amongst their families without saving any for themselves, the Countess changed the operation so that the women would have to eat at the kitchen before being allowed to take any food home to feed their families.[1]

Her involvement with revolutionary organizations was not limited to women and the youth. In partnership with Tom Clarke, she founded the Irish Citizen Army and fired one of the first deadly shots of the Rebellion at St. Stephen's Green. She also founded the Cumann na mBan, which were some of the most influential organizations in shaping Irish public opinion towards an acceptance of nationalism. The Cumann na mBan was the Irish women's paramilitary operation. Their members were at nearly every position during the Easter Rebellion serving as nurses, couriers, cooks and they performed other support operations. Especially with the lack of manpower due to the countermanding order, these women were absolutely essential to freeing up the manpower to allow the Fenians to fight for as long as they did. Their members were also critical to the popular opinion campaign that turned the Rebels into martyrs and the British into villains and murders.

During the Rebellion she was the de facto co-commander alongside Michael Mallin, a British Army veteran who had served in India, at St. Stephen's Green.[2] While there a few records to suggest that she was the decision authority in any of the Battalion's tactical or operational decisions, the Countess was essential for morale and was incredibly brave in close combat. She made a great show of being among the fighting and leading the often-leaderless men in individual fighting positions. In function, she acted as the squad leader for all of the Rebel's at St. Stephen's Green. Constantly moving to the point of action and never hesitating to pull the trigger.

Following the Rebellion, she was sentenced to death, which was granted a reprieve because the British government did not want to execute a woman. She then became the first woman elected to the United Kingdom's House of Commons winning 66% of the vote against her opponent William Field, which she then declined in accordance with Sinn Fein's policies at the time. After that, she was arrested. She was in Holloway Prison when the first Irish Dail sat 1918 and she was listed

---

[1]Nora Connolly O'Brien, *The Irish Rebellion of 1916 or, the Unbroken Tradition.* (New York: Boni and Liveright, 1918), p. 2.

[2]Annie Ryan, *Witness Inside the Easter Rising* (Dublin: Libertas Press, 2005) pp 105.

as "imprisoned by a foreign enemy" when her name was called at role.[3] She was present at the second and third Dials. She became the Minster of Labor from April 1919 and also held the rank of Cabinet Minster. She was only the second women in Europe to hold the title of government minister. She was the only Irish women Cabinet Minister until 1979.

In 1922 she stood alongside Eamon de Valera and several others in leaving the government in protest to the Anglo-Irish Treaty. She again took up arms and participated in active combat on the front lines during the Irish Civil War. She helped to defend Moran's Hotel during a pivotal battle. Following this battle, she toured the United States raising sympathies for the Republican cause, was reelected in the 1923 election, refused her seat and was jailed again.

The Countess was one of the most remarkable participants and leaders of the Easter Rebellion. Her stay of execution afforded her the opportunity, alongside De Velara and some of the other survivors or Easter Week, to continue the Republican movement and to change the perception of Fenianism in Irish public opinion. Alongside other women, the Countess was a leading driver in shaping the fighting during Easter Week as a heroic sacrifice for Irish Freedom.

The Countess struck an imposing figure. After the Rebellion she would be viewed with the same mythology as Boudica, the Queen of the British Iceni tribe who lead a Rebellion against Rome. She had worked as hard as anyone else in the Fenaian movement to get to this point and she carried herself, acted and dressed as a commander on a full peer footing with the male Fenian leaders. Nora Connolly said of her uniform for the Rebellion that she "looked like a Field Marshall."[4] During the fighting "she had on a dark green woolen blouse trimmed with brass buttons, dark green tweed knee britches, black stockings and high heavy boots. As she stood, she was a good advertisement for a small arms factory. Around her waist was a cartridge belt, suspended from it on one side was a small automatic pistol, and on the other a convertible Mauser pistol-rifle. Hanging from one shoulder was a bandolier containing the cartridges for the Mauser."[5]

Of all of the main characters in the Easter Rebellion, the Countess saw the most direct action. She did not shy from the thick of the

---

[3]John McGuffin, "Internment – Women Internees 1916–1973". Irish Resistance Books. (1973) Available from <http://www.irishresistancebooks.com/internment/intern6.htm >.

[4]Ibid p. 39.

[5]Ibid p.38.

fighting and actively engaged with British forces. Twice during the initial fighting, she temporarily silenced British machine gun file with her Mauser rifle-pistol and she showed no aversion or hesitation to move under fire to give orders to the Fenians.[6] In cold blood, she shot and killed Dublin Metropolitan Police Officer Police Michael Lahiff at Stephen's Green on April 24, 1916 when he refused to hand over the keys.[7] This killing was far more aggressive than the actions of the other battalions and much more aggressive than how the men under Mallin's command treated the Dublin citizenry. Officer Lahiff did not offer an attack, only a refusal to surrender to what was at the time an unqualified threat.

The Countess was eager to prove herself on the battlefield. A motivating factor for this aggressiveness could have come from her strong suffrage beliefs. She may have known that the bigger her legend the more sway she would have in shaping the legal treatment of women in the new Republic and that if she proved herself as valuable of a fighter as any man then her comrades would be more willing to accept women as political equals when the dust settled. More likely, any justifications or desired outcomes from her actions were secondary to her desire to fight. The Countess was a revolutionary and a fighter until the day that she died and regardless of the optics or outcomes, she would have been in the thick of the fighting.

Unlike most of her peers, the Countess' legacy extends beyond her role in the Easter Uprising. Her work and accomplishments after the Rebellion have had a much greater and longer lasting impact. The Easter Rebellion was her coming out party. Rapidly elevating her prestige and notoriety from a minor nobility and curiosity in the Dublin social scene who was deeply involved with a niche section of fringe and extremist movement to an internationally known name whose actions had real impact on Irish and British politics. Without her active role in the Easter Rebellion and the decision to pardon her death sentence, the Countess may never have become the trailblazer that she became. Her role in the fighting, while most likely exaggerated to some extent, became a keystone for arguments for gender equality in the new Irish state and gave her the legitimacy as a true leader that commanded respect from all genders and classes. Her role in the Easter Rising went beyond direct combat, organizing the female participants who motivated

---

[6]Max Caufield. *The Easter Rebellion* (New York, Holt, Rinehart and Winston, 1963), p. 153.

[7]https://www.thesun.ie/archives/irish-news/154954/was-countess-markievicz-a-hero-or-a-cold-blooded-killer/

the fighters and supported the leaders, provided all of the medical and service support functions, organizing the Fenian scouting organization that shaped many of the future fighters in the Rising and later during the Irish Civil War.

Chapter 12: James Connolly

Constance Markievicz's tribute to James Connolly, May 1916:

You died for your Country my Hero-love
In the first grey dawn of spring;
On your lips was a prayer to God above
That your death would have helped to bring
Freedom and Peace to the land you love,
Love above everything.[1]

"The cause of labour is the cause of Ireland, the cause of Ireland is the cause of labour. They cannot be dissevered. Ireland seeks freedom. Labour seeks that an Ireland free should be the sole mistress of her own destiny, supreme owner of all material things within and upon her soil. Labour seeks to make the free Irish nation the guardian of the interests of the people of Ireland, and to secure that end would vest in that free Irish nation all property rights as against the claims of the individual, with the end in view that the individual may be enriched by the nation, and not by the spoiling of his fellows."[2] -James Connolly, 8 April 1916

"This man has been a prominent leader in the Larkinite *or Citizen Army for years. He was also a prominent supporter of the Sinn Fein movement. He held the rank of Commandant General of the Dublin Division in the rebel* army, and had his headquarters at the GPO from which place he issued orders. On the 24 April he issued and signed a general order to "The Officers and soldiers in Dublin of the Irish Republic" stating that " *... the armed forces of the Irish Republic had everywhere met the enemy and defeated them.» This man was also a signatory to the Proclamation of Irish Independence."*[3] -General Sir John Maxwell

---

[1] http://lissadellhouse.com/countess-markievicz/

[2] James Connolly, "The Irish Flag," *The Irish Times*, 8 April 1916.

[3] General Sir John Maxwell. Transcript of Court Martial. May 1916. Available from <http://www.aoh61.com/history/easter_trials.htm>.

Another foreign-born Fenian who sacrificed his life for his adopted island, James Connolly saw the casting off of the British yoke for Ireland as one in the same with as the worker's revolutions that he and his Marxist comrades believed were about to spring forth across Europe. A Scotsman by birth, Connolly was serving as a Union organizer at the Irish Transport and General Workers Union before the Rebellion.[4] He was born on June 5th, 1858 to deeply Irish immigrants.[5] Connolly was a fiery writer and orator who saw Ireland's struggles as long and but a part of the larger conflicts between races and classes within the British Empire: "The power which holds in subjection more of the world's population than any other power on the globe, and holds them in subjection as slaves without any guarantee of freedom or power of self-government, this power that sets Catholic against Protestant, the Hindu against the Mohammedan, the yellow man against the brown, and keeps them quarreling with each other whilst she robs and murders them all – this power appeals to Ireland to send her sons to fight under England's banner for the cause of the oppressed. The power whose rule in Ireland has made of Ireland a desert and made the history of our race read like the records of a shambles, as she plans for the annihilation of another race appeals to our manhood to fight for her because of our sympathy for the suffering, and of our hatred of oppression."[6]

Connolly's early life did not indicate that he would grow into such a militant Irish nationalist. He followed his elder brother John into the Army served with the Royal Scots Guards and following his term followed John again, this time into Socialism.[7] James' history of activism started in Scotland, eventually rising to succeed his brother as the secretary of Scottish Socialist Federation before moving to Dublin to take the post of secretary for the Dublin Socialist Club.[8] Poverty forced him to move to America for seven years where he gained further expe-

[4]Peter De Rosa, *Rebels: The Irish Rising of 1916* (New York: Fawcett Books, 1990), p. 34.

[5]Hamish MacPherson, "James Connolly – The Scot Who Died for Ireland and Irish Freedom" [The National] Available from: <http://www.thenational.scot/news/16240567.James_Connolly_the_Scot_who_died_for_Ireland_and_freedom/>; Accessed 29 May 2018.

[6] James Connolly, "The Irish Flag," *The Irish Times*, 8 April 1916.

[7]Hamish MacPherson, "James Connolly – The Scot Who Died for Ireland and Irish Freedom" [The National] Available from: <http://www.thenational.scot/news/16240567.James_Connolly_the_Scot_who_died_for_Ireland_and_freedom/>; Accessed 29 May 2018.

[8]Ibid.

rience organizing Trade Unions. In 1910, Connolly moved back to Ireland and formed an unlikely partnership with "Big" Jim Larkin. While the two were never friends, they jointly formed the Irish Labor Party in 1912.[9]

Following the Lockout of 1913, Connolly partnered with Captain Jack White to form the Irish Citizen Army.[10] Captain White was a Sandhurst educated veteran of the Boer War who had won the DSO for his service to the crown in that action. His formal drilling was the most professional training that any Fenian organization had. This became the core for what would become the Fenian forces during the Easter Rebellion. Their training and organization were the most formal of any of the Rebels leading up to Easter Week.

Connolly, more than any of his comrades, had grown frustrated and nervous that the plans for the Uprising were taking too long. He feared the Dublin Castle would grow wise to the Fenian plans and would preempt it by arresting the leaders or seizing the weapons. At this critical juncture, even the slightest action by the British government could have nipped the Rebellion in the bud. Rebels would be less likely to rebel and any disruption to their already meager arms and supplies would devastate their combat power.

While naturally one of the most inclined towards launching the Rebellion, Connolly was also fearful of that preemptive raid by the British government would rob them of their only opportunity for revolt. He believed that an immediate uprising would catch the British unprepared and in doing so, it would force the IRB and the Volunteers into immediate action as well as inspiring the wider separatist movement. He was anxious to launch at the first possible moment and his daughter Nora recalls him walking around his quarters singing "we've got another saviour now, and that saviour is the sword."[11]

Connolly was one of the most committed of his peers to rebellion. A large part of the credit for the materialization of the Rebellion must come from his years of campaigning for it through speeches and writings. He was also a foundational member of the Irish Citizen Army. While not alone in its creation, all of its officers and men were vetted

[9]Ibid.

[10]Ibid.

[11]Nora Connolly O'Brien, *The Irish Rebellion of 1916 or, the Unbroken Tradition.* (New York: Boni and Liveright, 1918), p. 96.

by him and he created its structure and organization.[12] While draconian in his demand for discipline, this behavior that was better drilled into his men than marksmanship was fundamental to winning over the hearts and minds of Dublin citizenry. The Citizen Army was respectful of property, careful with the citizenry (even when being jeered and harassed) and fought bravely against an insurmountable enemy.

On March 22, 1914 the Irish Citizen Army launched printed a pamphlet called "Reasons Why You Should Join The Irish Citizen Army" as a call for men to join its ranks and adopted a constitution with very progressive principals. These principals were:

> "1. The first and last principal of the Irish Citizen Army is the avowal that the ownership of Ireland, moral and material, is vested of right in the people of Ireland.
> 2. That the Irish Citizen Army shall stand for the absolute unity of Irish nationhood and shall support the rights and liberties of the democracies of all nations.
> 3. That one of the objects shall be to sink all differences of birth, property, and creed under the common name of the Irish people.
> 4. That the Citizen Army shall be open to all who accept the principal of equal rights and opportunities for the Irish people.
> 5. Before being enrolled, every applicant must, if eligible, be a member of his trade union, such union to be recognized by the Irish Trade Union Congress."[13]

While tactically, this plan was even less likely to succeed since it would have allowed the British the time to defeat the various rebel bodies piecemeal, it does show Connolly's serious commitment to martyrdom at any cost. Following two police raids at his store in late 1915 where the police searched for contraband publications, Connolly and Markievicz called out the Irish Citizen Army on a brazen demonstration march. The Volunteers left their places of work, grabbed their rifles and bandoleers and marched through Dublin signing towards Liberty Hall

---

[12]Michael Foy and Brian Barton, *The Easter Rising (*London: Sutton Publishing, 2004) p. 158.

[13] Joseph McKenna, Voices from the Easter Rising: Firsthand Accounts of Ireland's 1916 Rebellion (Jefferson: McFarland & Company, Inc., Publishers., 2017), pp.12-13.

singing their Citizen Army marching tune:

"We've got guns and ammunition, we know how to use them well,
And when we meet the Saxon we'll drive them all to Hell.
We've got to free our country, and avenge all those who fell,
And our cause is marching on.
Glory, glory to Ireland.
Glory, glory to our sireland.
Glory to the memory of those who fought and fell,
And we still keep marching on"[14]

With fears of further interference in mind, Connolly made it known at Liberty Hall that he was planning to take his two-hundred-man strong Irish Citizen Army and launch his men into action as early as January. While Pease, Clarke and others were able to talk Connolly out of this plan over a three-day conference – whether or not Connolly's attendance was voluntary, or the result of a kidnapping is the stuff of legend – his independence as a separate was another indicator that the command and control over the Fenian forces was nearly nonexistent.[15]

Despite being wounded in the fighting, Connolly remained one of the most steadfast sources of hope in the GPO. On Friday morning, the fifth day of the Rising when all hope seemed lost and Maxwell's noose was tightening around the starving Rebels, he issued a proclamation praising the Rebels and predicating that victory would soon be theirs. Pearse had issued a similar proclamation earlier in the day, and while positive in outlook in tone, it at least acknowledged the possibility of defeat and the effect of the countermanding order on the turnout of troops.

Connolly's message had not even the slightest tinge of negativity, but even he was beginning to waiver at this point.[16] Whether from self-imposed delusion to keep his own spirits up or the willful intention to lie to support the morale of the beleaguered and besieged Rebels, Connolly continued to push the false narratives of German intervention

[14]Nora Connolly O'Brien, *The Irish Rebellion of 1916 or, the Unbroken Tradition.* (New York: Boni and Liveright, 1918), p. 36.

[15]Connor O'Malley. "The Secret Meeting: Setting the date for the Easter Rising." [Century Ireland.] Available from <http://www.rte.ie/centuryireland/index.php/articles/the-secret-meeting>. Accessed 29 March 2018.

[16]Thomas Coffey, *Agony at Easter: The 1916 Irish Uprising* (London: George G. Harrap & Co, LTD, 1969), p. 196.

and a support coming from outside of Dublin: "Not a day passes without seeing fresh postings of Irish soldiers eager to do battle for the old cause. Despite the utmost vigilance of the enemy, we have been able to get information telling us how the manhood of Ireland, inspired by our splendid action, are gathering to offer up their lives, if necessary, in this same holy cause."[17] More than any other speech that week, Connolly's had the most positive affect on the garrison's morale. His juxtaposition of the failure of the same British Army whose exploits on the Western Front were "for ever having dinned into our ears" made the admittedly amateur Army feel optimistic for their future efforts and proud of what they had already accomplished.[18]

Connolly believed that new Republic could only solve Ireland's problems through economic as well as political reforms. He told the Irish Citizen Army that after the Rebellion was successful that: "The odds against us are a thousand to one. But if we should win, hold on to your rifles because the Volunteers may have a different goal. Remember we are not only for political liberty, but for economic liberty as well. So hold on to your rifles."[19] Connolly's economics had gain increasing influence with Pearse over the preceding few years. While Pease conceptually agreed with large parts of Connolly's thesis that Ireland was "the people-exploited, under-paid, badly housed, and badly nourished thanks to a greedy, unfeeling establishment, which was not altogether English."[20]

Too wounded to stand for his execution, he was tied to his bed and shot. Father Alyious, the Priest who tended to him while in jail and witnessed his execution recounted his execution to Connolly's wife and children: "They carried him from his bed in an ambulance stretcher down to a waiting ambulance and drove him to Kilmainham Jail. They carried him from the ambulance to the jail yard and put him on a chair… He was very brave and cool…I said to him. 'Will you pray for the men who are about to shoot you?', and he said 'I will say a prayer for all the brave men who do their duty'…His prayer was, "Forgive them for they

[17]Max Caufield, *The Easter Rebellion* (New York: Holt, Rinehart, and Winston, 1963), p. 108.

[18]Michael Foy and Brian Barton, *The Easter Rising (*London: Sutton Publishing, 2004) pp. 7–8.

[19]Thomas Coffey, *Agony at Easter: The 1916 Irish Uprising* (London: George G. Harrap & Co, LTD, 1969), p. 33.

[20]Thomas Coffey, *Agony at Easter: The 1916 Irish Uprising* (London: George G. Harrap & Co, LTD, 1969), p. 33.

know not what they do'…And they shot him."[21] Heroic stories like this did much to lionize the men and turn their deaths into martyrdoms.

Connolly's legacy is that of a man who did so much to make a Rebellion happen, but at its commencement was too weak and wounded to do anything other than offer emotional support and encouragement to the forces fighting. While an avowed Socialist, he knew that his allegiances were always with Ireland; "The Socialists will never understand why I am here [in prison awaiting execution]. They will forget I am an Irishman".[22] Connolly, like Pearse, was an instigator, organizer and planner of the Rebellion, but during Easter Week did little for the cause. In fact, his presence was probably more of burden on the fighters than anything else since he needed to be tended to throughout the entire week. His overly optimistic reports to the fighters was a double-edged sword. While his false reports of German and American landings bolstered morale at the beginning, it only made the crash all the more painful when defeat became apparent. Connolly was one of the most integral figures in setting the conditions among the Fenians to make the Rebellion happen, but once the fighting began his actions did more harm than good.

[21]Nora Connolly O'Brien, *The Irish Rebellion of 1916 or, the Unbroken Tradition.* (New York: Boni and Liveright, 1918), p. 190.

[22] Joseph McKenna, *Voices from the Easter Rising: Firsthand Accounts of Ireland's 1916 Rebellion* (Jefferson: McFarland & Company, Inc., Publishers., 2017), p. 307.

Chapter 13: Eoin MacNeill

"There will be no waste of lives for which I am directly responsible. I will not allow a half-armed force to be called out. I can promise you this; I will do everything I can to stop a Rising – everything, this is short of ringing up Dublin Castle."[1] -Eoin MacNeill to Padraig Pearse on Good Friday Morning

"There'll be no waste of lives for which I am directly responsible. I'll not allow a half-armed force to be called out. I can promise you that this: I'll do everything I can to stop a rising – everything, that is, short of ringing up Dublin Castle."[2] -Eoin MacNeill's confrontation with Padraig Pease the evening of April 23rd

Eoin MacNeill earned his position as the president of the Volunteers as a result of his strong and well-known beliefs in pacifism. In the whole group he was the last person the British would suspect of being a violent revolutionary. Had someone who was more of a "practical revolutionary" and less of an academic been made president, it would have brought far more suspicion upon the group.[3] MacNeill was an avowed and committed pacifist, but because of the rise of the Ulster Volunteer Force (UVF) and the tacit British support of the anti-Home Rule actions MacNeill began to believe that having an armed nationalist force was necessary to achieve balance. He wrote an article in the Gaelic League's newspaper *Claidheamh Soluis* (*The Sword of Light*) which attracted the attention of the more radicalized elements of the Irish Republican Brotherhood.[4] While the intention was for MacNeill to be the civil pres-

---

[1]Joseph McKenna, *Voices from the Easter Rising: Firsthand Accounts of Ireland's 1916 Rebellion* (Jefferson: McFarland & Company, Inc., Publishers., 2017), p. 52.

[2]Max Caufield, *The Easter Rebellion* (New York: Holt, Rinehart, and Winston, 1963), p. 46.

[3]Nora Connolly O'Brien, *The Irish Rebellion of 1916 or, the Unbroken Tradition.* (New York: Boni and Liveright, 1918), pp. 194-195.

[4] Joseph McKenna, Voices from the Easter Rising: Firsthand Accounts of Ireland's 1916 Rebellion (Jefferson: McFarland & Company, Inc., Publishers., 2017), p. 9.

ident and for Pearse to serve as commander in chief, that may be an invention by the Fenians to justify how the countermanding order came to be and an attempt to keep MacNeill from becoming seen as a Judas to the movement. The fact is that most of the Volunteers nationwide were more than happy to obey MacNeill's order. Not every Fenian was as committed to martyrdom and the fact that it coincided with a major holiday made it easy for many Volunteers, including the Belfast Volunteers that Nora Connolly chastised, more than happy to comply with the order to stand down.[5]

MacNeill and Michael O'Rahilly, known as 'the O'Rahilly' due to his position as the head of a County Kerry clan, did everything they could to prevent the Rising.[6] While the capture of the Aud convinced them that any hope for a successful rebellion was doomed, it further spurred the pro-Rising Sinn Feinners to action.[7] Once ten o'clock passed on the 22nd without hearing a reply from Pearse, MacNeill issued the infamous countermanding order to all Volunteers: "Volunteers completely deceived. All orders for special action are hereby canceled, and on no account will action be taken. Signed: Eoin MacNeill, Chief of Staff."[8] Following the issuing of the order, The O'Rahilly took off like an anti-Paul Revere driving through six counties to quash any movement before ending in Limerick. Despite his efforts to prevent the Rebellion, by Easter Monday The O'Rahilly resigned himself that the Rising was inevitable, and that he would take up arms with his fellow Fenians. As the fighters were embarking from Liberty Hall, he proclaimed to the Countess Markievicz: "It is madness, but it is glorious madness!"[9]

Even more devastating was that MacNeill went directly to the papers, publishing in the Dublin Sunday paper: "Owing to the very critical position, all orders given to Irish Volunteers for tomorrow, Easter Sunday, are hereby rescinded and no parades, marches, or other movement of Irish Volunteers will take place. Each individual Volunteer will

---

[5] Nora Connolly O'Brien, *The Irish Rebellion of 1916 or, the Unbroken Tradition.* (New York: Boni and Liveright, 1918), pp. 110-111.

[6] Thomas Coffey, *Agony at Easter: The 1916 Irish Uprising* (London: George G. Harrap & Co, LTD, 1969), p. 48.

[7]Max Caufield, *The Easter Rebellion* (New York: Holt, Rinehart, and Winston, 1963), p. 54.

[8]Max Caufield, *The Easter Rebellion* (New York: Holt, Rinehart, and Winston, 1963), p. 55.

[9]Michael Foy and Brian Barton, *The Easter Rising* (London: Sutton Publishing, 2004), pp. 54.

obey this order strictly and in every particular."[10]

This very public proclamation coupled with the capture of the Aud to make the threat of the Rebellion very real to Lord Wimborne and Colonel H. V. Cowen, the commander of British troops in Dublin. As the men contemplated a preemptive raid on Liberty Hall, the lack of any artillery in Dublin and the difficulties faced by the dispersion of Fenian forces.[11]

In Kent's Battalion, out of a possible one hundred and twenty men, only around showed seven up.[12] While the countermanding order cannot bear the full burden for this, it no doubt had a tremendous affect. Volunteers may have failed to muster for a variety of reasons, but many of them had a dubious commitment to the cause in the first place. Men grow cowardly when the time finally comes, and the plague and the pleas of family members may have caused the better sense of many of the Volunteers.

Eoin MacNeill is often depicted as a traitor to the Fenian cause. A man whose decision doomed the Rebellion at worse and whose weakness as a leader and lack of true commitment to the cause fostered the conditions that allowed for a shadow chain of command within his own organization. He has derisively been castigated as the Irish Benedict Arnold, unlike Arnold he was never a traitor to the cause as he saw it. MacNeill believed in pacifism as the mechanism for Irish self-determination and that an armed insurrection was doomed to do more harm than good towards that end. MacNeill was committed to the Irish nationalism long before the Rebellion; he and Douglas Hyde co-founded the Gaelic League on July 31st, 1893 with the goal to preserve the Irish language and to use the Education act of 1870 to further the reestablishment of Gaelic as a means of de-anglicizing Ireland.[13] This group was instrumental in setting to conditions in Ireland to create a movement and culture that would allow the Irish Volunteers to form and rise.

[10]Eoin MacNeill, "Countermanding Order" The Irish Times, 23 April 1916.

[11]Max Caufield, *The Easter Rebellion* (New York: Holt, Rinehart, and Winston, 1963), p. 59.

[12]Max Caufield, *The Easter Rebellion* (New York: Holt, Rinehart, and Winston, 1963), p. 65.

[13]Joseph McKenna, Voices from the Easter Rising: Firsthand Accounts of Ireland's 1916 Rebellion (Jefferson: McFarland & Company, Inc., Publishers., 2017), p.4.

Chapter 14: Ned Daly

"Men of the First Battalion, I want you to listen to me for a few minutes, and no applause must follow my statement. Today at noon, an Irish Republic will be declared, and the Flag of the Republic hoisted. I look to every man to do his duty, with courage and discipline. The Irish Volunteers are now the Irish Republican Army. Communications with other posts in the city may be precarious, and in less than an our we may be in action."[1] -Ned Daly's address to the First Battalion

"The reason I pleaded 'Not guilty' was because I had no dealings with any outside forces. I had no knowledge of the insurrection until Monday morning April 24. The officers including myself when we heard the news held a meeting and decided that the whole thing was foolish but that being under orders we had no option but to obey." -Ned Daly during his Court Martial[2]

John Edward "Ned" Daly was the youngest leader amongst the Fenians on Easter Week. Born in Limerick, Ireland in 1891 he was just 25 years old when he was executed for his role in the Easter Uprising. One of ten children, Ned owed much of his position of prominence within the Fenian movement to his close relation with his older sister Kathleen and her husband Tom Clarke. His rank was not a case of mere nepotism. Daly served as the Commandant for the First Battalion of the Irish Volunteers during the Easter Uprising a position that he earned through his pre-Uprising study and performance and proved his worth

[1]Desmond Ryan, *The Rising, The Complete Story of Easter Week*, Golden Eagle Books Limited (1957 ed.), pp. 203-4.
[2]Ned Daly. Transcript of Court Martial. May 1916. Available from <http://www.aoh61.com/history/easter_trials.htm>.

during the fighting. This unit saw the most intense combat during the Easter Rebellion and Daly established himself as the shrewdest and most competent tactician in the Fenian ranks.[3] Although much younger than his peers, Daly's battalion was stationed at the Four Courts area which housed Ireland's courts of courts of the Chancery, King's Bench, Exchequer and Common Pleas. Located at the Church Street/North King Street/North Brunswick Street area, this position was located just over a mile (1.7km) from the main Fenian post at the General Post Office.

Irish nationalism ran in his blood. Both his father and uncle were prominent members of the Irish Republican Brotherhood. His uncle was even rumored to be a participant in the Fenian Bombing Campaign of 1881 and 1885 and served twelve years in prison for the possession of explosives.[4] Fenianism was truly a family affair for Daly. The Daly's were truly one of the most staunchly Fenian families in Ireland, with his Uncle John being described as "the most relentless Fenian of his generation". [5] Daly's uncle John Daly maintained his position as the family's patriarch throughout his life. Besides his involvement in Fenian activities, he and the entire Daly clan were active in Irish politics well past the Civil War. In fact, John Daly had the distinction of being elected Limericks' first Nationalist Mayor in 1899.[6] Uncle John loomed so large of Ned Daly's life that among the few items in Ned's possession at the time of his imprisonment was a partial train stub from his last trip to Limerick.[7] His sister Kathleen was the wife of Tom Clarke and Ned had moved in with her and Tom when he moved to Dublin in 1912.[8] The influence of Clarke and the views of his family only further reinforced Daly's commitment to and belief in the cause.

Daly followed in the footsteps of his father, uncle and brother-in-law joining the Irish Republican Brotherhood and later the Irish

---

[3]Charles Townsend, *Easter 1916: The Irish Rebellion.* Allen Lane (2005), p. 204

[4]National Library of Ireland. "The 1916 Rising: Personalities and Perspectives", February 2018. Available from <http://www.nli.ie/1916/exhibition/en/content/executed/edwarddaly/index.pdf>; accessed 11 February 2018.

[5]Dermot McEvoy, "Easter Rising Leader Executed in 1916: Edward Daly", May 2017 [Irish Central] Available from <https://www.irishcentral.com/roots/history/easter-rising-leader-executed-in-1916-edward-daly>; accessed 5 March 2018.

[6]Helen Litton, *16 Lives: Edward Daly* (Dublin, The O'Brien Press, 2013), p. 31.

[7]Helen Litton, *16 Lives: Edward Daly* (Dublin, The O'Brien Press, 2013), p. 62.

[8]Dermot McEvoy, "Easter Rising Leader Executed in 1916: Edward Daly", May 2017 [Irish Central] Available from <https://www.irishcentral.com/roots/history/easter-rising-leader-executed-in-1916-edward-daly>; accessed 5 March 2018.

Volunteers in November of 1913. It is unknown at what age Daly joined the IRB, but it can be assumed that he gained membership as soon as the organization would accept the youth as a member.[9] Daly took his task within the Irish Republican Brotherhood seriously, vigorously studying military strategies and tactics. It is believed that Daly was able to commit to the Volunteers full time due to financial support from his Uncle John.[10] In an amateur and part-time organization his dedication and self-education paid dividends. His personal studies and ambition took over as the most important factor in his life, surpassing even his love of Gilbert and Sullivan musicals.[11] He quickly became the de facto subject matter expert for the organization and his performance during the landing of arms at Howth in July of 1914 impressed his superiors within the IRB enough that he was named Commandant of the 1st Battalion in March of 1915.[12] One of his more impressive feats that night was to personally approach the King's Own Scottish Boarderer's that were positioned at the Howth Road Junction. His calm handling of the British forces allowed the Fenians to disappear with or hide the rifles and prevented an intervention that would have nipped the Rebellion in the bud.[13]

Accounts from both the men under his command and his British adversaries report that Daly handled his Battalion very well and that the performance of his battalion at the Four Courts were amongst the most tactically sound of any of the Rebellion's redoubts.[14] According to the recollections of those who served under him, Daly exhibited the air of a Victorian officer. Acting aloof and reserved in front of his men, most of which were considerably older and more experienced with him.[15] The Four Courts, geographically speaking, may have been the most operationally important piece of terrain that the Rebels held. While their main

---

[9]Dermot McEvoy, "Easter Rising Leader Executed in 1916: Edward Daly", May 2017 [Irish Central] Available from <https://www.irishcentral.com/roots/history/easter-rising-leader-executed-in-1916-edward-daly>; accessed 5 March 2018.

[10]Helen Litton, *16 Lives: Edward Daly* (Dublin, The O'Brien Press, 2013), p. 75.

[11] Helen Litton, *16 Lives: Edward Daly* (Dublin, The O'Brien Press, 2013), p. 41.

[12]Ibid.

[13]Helen Litton, *16 Lives: Edward Daly* (Dublin, The O'Brien Press, 2013), p. 55.

[14]John Dorney, "Book Review – Crossfire, The Battle of the Four Courts 1916", February 2013 [The Irish Story] Available from <http://www.theirishstory.com/2013/02/18/book-review-crossfire-the-battle-of-the-four-courts-1916/#.WnB1K6inHIU>;accessed 30 January 2018.

[15]Helen Litton, *16 Lives: Edward Daly* (Dublin, The O'Brien Press, 2013), p. 48.

battle plans placed a higher importance on seizing more politically symbolic landmarks such as Dublin Castle and the General Post Office. The Four Courts (while still holding political significance) sat astride several important intersections in Dublin. The Four Courts effectively served as a blocking position that could interdict or disrupt the movement of British reinforcements from the barracks located to the west of the city to the main Rebel positions in the city's center.

Easter Monday, Daly led the 260 men of his Battalion against the Four Courts. His mission was to capture the courts, hold them against British attacks and disrupt the movement of British forces moving from Marlborough Cavalry Barracks in the Northwest and Royal Barracks in the West against the main rebel position at the General Post Office.[16] By noon that Daly, the 1st Battalion had accomplished its mission. Daly did not let his men rest on their success. Instead, he quickly transitioned them into a defensive posture. Quickly and effectively barricading the streets to restrict British movement, concealing their fighting positions and deliberately burning the Linenhall Barracks of the Metropolitan Police to the ground to deny the British a convenient base of operations. He assured fair and humane treatment to the twenty-five policemen found hiding in the basement.[17]

Shortly after noon approximately fifty Lancers of the 6th Cavalry Regiment (5th and 12th Lancers) arrived at the North Quays.[18] Further British forces would also arrive to reinforces the Lancers during the week. Fighting against both the green South Staffordshire Regiment and the veteran Dublin Fusiliers who were home on leave from a tour in France, the men under Ned Daly's command held their own against these troops. In fact, when Pearse formally surrendered on the Saturday of Easter Week the men of the First Battalion continued to hold their positions until Sunday. This was due in part to the time it took to communicate the message, but when the First Battalion did finally raise the white flag, it was with great reluctance and with more defiance than defeat.

Daly's Battalion inflicted significant casualties on the British forces, including the Commander of the South Staffordshire Regiment

---

[16]Dermot McEvoy, "Easter Rising Leader Executed in 1916: Edward Daly", May 2017 [Irish Central] Available from <https://www.irishcentral.com/roots/history/easter-rising-leader-executed-in-1916-edward-daly>; accessed 5 March 2018.

[17]Ibid.

[18]Paul O'Brien, Crossfire: The Battle of the Four Courts, 1916 (Dublin: New Island, 2012), p. 19.

Major Sheppard.[19] Over the course of the fighting over 40 British men and officers became casualties in narrow streets of the Four Courts. Daly and his men made effective use of the terrain in the area, turning the short, narrow streets into kill boxes. This defensive use of terrain was so effective that the British forces resorted to breaking through the walls between the buildings in order to avoid being obliterated by the effective fire of the Irish.[20] British forces were unable to discern the location of their Irish adversaries due to the echoing effect that the firing of high powered Maxim guns made when against the stone walls.[21] The most foolish and fatal action taken by the British was a frontal bayonet assault by the Staffordshire's that cost fifteen lives, and left their commander, Major Sheppard, wounded.

Effectively dispersing his troops into smaller, mobile elements and taking advantage of the urban terrain created a three-dimensional battlespace that no one in the British Army had any experience confronting before. To their credit, the British were able to effectively adapt to the challenges. Boring through walls to move through the buildings instead of through the dangerous open areas and by improvising an armored car that allowed them to finally maneuver along North King Street.[22] While the First Battalion inflicted casualties and outlasted any of their peers, this was not intended as a permanent defensive position.

Daly and his command are often held up as the most successful and competent of the Fenians at Easter Week. The British officer in charge of the area said, "This whole neighborhood was strongly held by the rebels, who had elaborately prepared and fortified it against the military with barricades across the street, and by taking out house windows and sandbagging them, etc."[23] Among the forces of the Free Irish State, they may have been the most prepared for the Rebellion. Much is often made of the Rebels being untrained civilians who rose to a cause and performed admirably. That is not entirely true or uniform across the command. Many of the Rebels, especially those in the Irish Volunteers,

---

[19]John Dorney "The North King Street Massacre, Dublin 1916" April 2012 [The Irish Story] Available from <http://www.theirishstory.com/2012/04/13/the-north-king-street-massacre-dublin-1916/#.WpW3g6inHIW >; accessed 27 February 2018.

[20]Ibid.

[21]Ibid.

[22]Ibid.

[23]Dermot McEvoy, "Easter Rising Leader Executed in 1916: Edward Daly", May 2017 [Irish Central] Available from <https://www.irishcentral.com/roots/history/easter-rising-leader-executed-in-1916-edward-daly>; accessed 5 March 2018.

had been training for the Uprising for months.[24] While they may have had some drill and training, the difference and competencies of a force of amateurs lead and trained by amateurs is substantial.

An excellent comparison for this is the performance and casualties taken by the hastily trained and mobilized South Staffordshire Regiment whom the British diverted to Dublin while they were on the way to France versus that of the veteran Fusiliers at the Four Courts. While South Staffordshire's lost 14 men in a pointless frontal assault on fortified positions on North King Street and killed 15 civilians – whose participation in the Rebellion were dubious at best – in revenge. The Fusiliers, by comparison, suffered very few casualties and contained the resource scare Rebels just as effectively as the more aggressive Staffordshire's and with far less collateral damage.

An even better comparison may be the two unit's treatment of the civilians they encountered. While the Staffordshire's have gone to live in infamy for their killing of fourteen unarmed civilians, Daly and his Battalion had the good judgement to leave Monk's Bakery open despite the barricade.[25] This not only alleviated some of the disruption and negative effects of the Rebellion on the civilian populace, but it also ensured that by comparison they would be viewed in a favorable light after the cessation of hostilities.

The performance of the First Battalion of the Irish Volunteers mirrored the Staffordshire's more than it did the Fusiliers. While it would be incorrect to call the Battalion untrained, being trained is a far cry from being competent, experienced or prepared for war. They executed their initial assault with vigor (and probably excessive violence of action), they made good use of the terrain of the Four Courts and prepared fortifications to create effective kill zones and a well-executed defensive operation. The performance of the First Battalion shows that the tactical objectives may not have all been far-flung dreams. With just a modicum of training, strong leadership and some common sense the First Battalion was able to secure their objective past the end of hostilities. While they would never have been able to hold out indefinitely

[24]John Dorney, "Book Review – Crossfire, The Battle of the Four Courts 1916", February 2013 [The Irish Story] Available from <http://www.theirishstory.com/2013/02/18/book-review-crossfire-the-battle-of-the-four-courts-1916/#.WnB1K6inHIU>;accessed 30 January 2018.

[25]John Gibney. "Sites of 1916: The Four Courts and Church Street", 2016, [Century Ireland] Available From https://www.rte.ie/centuryireland/index.php/articles/the-four-courts-and-church-street; Accessed May 2018.

without relief, this action, it demonstrates what could have been for the Fenians.

Ned Daly leadership during the First Battalion's seizure and subsequent defense of the Four Courts cannot be overly glorified. While they fought well, especially when his age and experience are taken into consideration, there were mistakes and actions that lead to excessive collateral damage committed by the Battalion and its leaders. Both sides were guilty of killing when they could not have, leaving behind unnecessary corpses. Daly's force had the advantage of the defensive, meaning that history would judge their competency by their reactions rather than their decisions. Daly personally handled his forces well. His forces held their ground against both an inexperienced and an experienced force. In a short-lived and long romanticized rebellion, it is surprising that Daly and his force get less attention than the other actions. While they were the only Rebel force to meet their tactical objective – secure the Four Courts area and disrupt British movements into Dublin – it ultimately had no effect on the larger operation.

This lone and underappreciated redoubt held onto the belief in the Fenian cause longer than their comrades were able to hold onto their positions. Many of the men who fought with Daly would live to fight another day during the Irish Civil War. Ned Daly might be better remembered had he stood in defiance and delivered a memorable speech before the British Court Martial. Instead, he denied that he knew about the specific date for the Rebellion in advance and spent the majority of his final words on his family and praising the men of his Battalion. There was no incantation of 'liberty or death' nor anything that even came close to the eloquent notions of self-sacrifice of Pearse. For his Fenian upbringing, connections and education, Ned Daly gave a matter-of-fact soldier's plea of not guilty in his court martial. He had surrendered out of logic and as a soldier following orders instead of going down in a romantic blaze of glory. But he sacrificed his life, nonetheless.

In a memorandum to Prime Minister Asquith, General Maxwell condemned Daly as one of the worst offenders against the Crown: "This man was one of the most prominent extremists in the Sinn Fein organization (sic). He held the rank of Commandant and was in command of the body of rebels who held the Four Courts where heavy fighting took place and casualties occurred (sic). He admitted being at the meeting of officers which decided to carry out the orders of the executive council and commence the armed rebellion."[26] Despite pleading not guilty on the basis that he was just following orders; Daly did not call any witnesses. The verdict was a foregone conclusion; when Daly surrendered, he was in uniform and clearly in charge of his forces. He had also interacted as the leaders of Rebel forces in the Four Courts with at least two British Lieutenants whom he had taken prisoner.

He was among the executed Fenians, and probably more due to the family ties of his father, uncle and brother-in-law than to any specific action of his. Ned Daly lived the life that he had envisioned for himself. A soldier and a Fenian patriot. He died the death of a traitor to the crown, unceremoniously shot on May 4th between 4 and 4:30 a.m.[27] His end was as anticlimactic as the actions and surrender of his Battalion. His burial place next to Tom Clarke as overshadowed as his role in the struggle for Irish independence had been - a mere footnote of what could have been a remarkable chapter.

[26]Ned Daly. Transcript of Court Martial. May 1916. Available from <http://www.aoh61.com/history/easter_trials.htm>.

[27]John Dorney, "Book Review – Crossfire, The Battle of the Four Courts 1916", February 2013 [The Irish Story] Available from <http://www.theirishstory.com/2013/02/18/book-review-crossfire-the-battle-of-the-four-courts-1916/#.WnB1K6inHIU>;accessed 30 January 2018.

Chapter 15: Eamon de Valera

Eamon de Valera's legacy in the fight for Irish independence had its most significant moments after the Easter Uprising. De Valera lived until 1975 and rose to the position of the President of Ireland and he still holds the record as the longest serving *Taoisearch* (the head of the Irish government). During the Civil War, his record was highly divisive. Leading the anti-treaty faction of Sinn Fein, his staunch Republican beliefs may have prolonged the fighting by years and helped create the conditions that lead to 'The Troubles" – the period of low-level civil war and IRA bombings that continued until the Good Friday Accords. De Valera became a mainstay and focal part in Irish politics for the greater part of the 20th Century largely due to how stiffly he held to his Fenian beliefs. While his role in the Easter Uprising was minimal compared to that of Connolly and Pearse and the fighting at his command was less than that seen by Daly, de Valera was alone in his position as a senior Fenian leader who was able to carry the fight into the next phase.

The American-born de Valera was a math teacher in his mid-Thirties before becoming a member of the Irish Republican Brotherhood.[1] This American birth and the British desire to persuade America to enter World War I on the side of the Allies granted him a stay of execution during the Court Martials the followed the Fenian surrender. By the time of the trails, the war still had no end in sight. The disaster at Gallipoli was still less than six months in the past and the offensives on the Western Front were at a standstill. Britain was actively working to bring American manpower into the war. To make the dependency even worse, Britain was critically dependent on materials and food from the United States to sustain its populace and the war effort. At the height of the U-Boat campaign in the North Atlantic and almost a year after the sinking of the Lusitania, Britain could not risk any decision that would jeopardize its relationship with America or the American people's willingness to continue to supply the island.

After being appointed to as a Battalion Commandant in March 1915, he committed himself fully to the cause becoming practically a full-time resident at the battalion headquarters on Great Brunswick

---

[1]Michael Foy and Brian Barton, *The Easter Rising (*London: Sutton Publishing, 2004), p. 71.

Street.[2] During the preparation for the Rebellion, de Valera's efforts were overshadowed by those of the principal signers of the Proclamation. Like he fellow Battalion Commandants, he drilled the 3rd Battalion and prepared them as best he could with their limited Fenian resources, knowledge and experience.

The 3rd Battalion was tasked with seizing and controlling the area around Boland's Bakery. The plan called on the Battalion to control a large swatch of area using various outposts and redoubts in order to disrupt British logistics and transportation and to interdict any movement from the area against the GPO. This area controlled some of the most important transportation nodes in Dublin: The Grand Canal Dock and Ringsend including the gas works, a dispensary, Boland's Mills and Bakery, a railway workshop, the Dublin Distillery and the Guinness Granary stores. This also include an important stretch of the River Liffey.[3]

The British relied on their artillery advantage against to fix and destroy 3rd Battalion. The Fenians were largely defenseless. One of their most effective measures was to place a makeshift Irish flag on top of pike on a water tank of the tall Irish Distillery building. This created a reference point that was too good to ignore for the British artillery observers and caused the British to assume that de Valera's command was using this building as their headquarters. Fourteen shots from the H.Y.M Helga hit this target and other members of the Battalion claimed to have counted over seventy-five shots being fired at this location.[4] The Irish were, of course, unable to respond.

Had the conflict ended there, de Valera would be a minor footnote in Irish history mostly known for commanding the battalion that saw ancillary actions at an isolated position during Easter Week. Many of the leaders of the Fenian Rebellion were not natural born Irishmen. Many were even born across the Irish Sea in England. De Valera was born in New York City and this American birth granted him citizenship of the still neutral United States whom Britain still relied on for the sup-

---

[2]Michael Foy and Brian Barton, *The Easter Rising (*London: Sutton Publishing, 2004), p. 71.

[3]Alva Macgowan, "Boland's Bakery and 1916". May 2016 [The Archaeology of 1916] Available from <https://thearchaeologyof1916.wordpress.com/2016/05/05/bolands-bakery-and-1916/>; accessed 18 February 2019.

[4]Alva Macgowan, "Boland's Bakery and 1916". May 2016 [The Archaeology of 1916] Available from <https://thearchaeologyof1916.wordpress.com/2016/05/05/bolands-bakery-and-1916/>; accessed 18 February 2019.

plies, sustenance and financing that allowed it to maintain its war effort.

To de Valera's personal benefit, The British grand focus and strategy was rightly pointed on the war against Germany at the sacrifice of all else. Every decision and action had to be couched with how it would affect the war on the Western Front. Whether or not the Rebellion was seen as a German plot, the actions and reactions of the British government treated the Rebellion as if it were a failed attempt by Germany to open up a new front, just like the British had failed to do in Turkey hardly a year before.

Britain desperately needed to get America into the war and the Empire's war machine was even more desperate for continued American support and supplies. The British knew that they could not risk the American public opinion backlash that would occur if General Maxwell executed de Valera alongside his Fenian comrades. This decision to spare his life made him the highest ranking male Fenian to survive the Easter Rising. Along with the Countess Markiewicz, they were the only two people who held leadership of a battalion and with name recognition to survive the Rebellion. Unlike the Countess who due to the customs, laws and norms of the time could not have led the continued Fenian efforts, de Valera was perfectly positioned to take up the torch and to emerge as the leader of Sinn Fein going into the Irish Civil War.

Chapter 16: Thomas MacDonagh

> *"This man was a M.A of the National University in Ireland and a tutor in English Literature in the University College Dublin. He took an active part in the Sinn Fein movement since its inauguration and was a prominent officer and Director of Training. He was also a signatory to the Declaration of Irish Independence. He signed a document headed "Army of the Irish Republic" which set out the various "Commands" and described himself there as "Commandant General and member of the Provisional Government of the Irish Republic". He was in command of the party of the rebels who occupied and held Jacob's Biscuit Factory from the* neighbourhood of which the British troops were fired on and numerous casualties occurred."[1] -General Sir John Maxwell

Thomas MacDonagh was another intellectual who, under normal times and circumstances, was not the archetype of a violent revolutionary. Born in Cloughjordan, County in Tipperary in 1878, MacDonagh developed a deep interest in the traditional Irish language and culture that British laws had repressed for generations. That interest led him to join the Gaelic League where he met Padraig Pearse and to follow him as a teacher and co-founder of St. Edna's School. While interest in language and culture can lead to nationalism and nationalism can lead to radicalization, it is hard to say if MacDonagh's radicalization would have occurred without the influence of Pearse. Regardless, the imposition of the unfair Penal Laws made Irish culture a conduit for nationalism and revolution. The shortsighted aims of Anglicization turned the very culture and language inherent to Ireland into a recruiting tool for revolutionaries.

In his early life, MacDonagh trained to be a priest, but eventually decided not to pursue that career and to follow in his parents' footsteps as a teacher instead. He attended Rockwell College and published his first book of poetry: *Through the Ivory Gate* in 1902. Like many of

---

[1]General Sir John Maxwell. Transcript of Court Martial. May 1916. Available from <http://www.aoh61.com/history/easter_trials.htm>.

his Fenian peers, MacDonagh had a deep interest in the arts, especially the native artistic traditions of Ireland. He was a notable playwright and poet. The arts and nationalism were completely intertwined. His posthumously published *Literature in Ireland* shows that even up to the point of revolution he held his role as a champion of Irish culture in near equal importance to his role as a commander in the Irish Republican Brotherhood.

MacDonagh's path toward radical nationalism was very similar to that of the Countess Markievicz. It started with an interest in Gaelic culture and arts, moved towards equal rights for the genders and finally into Fenianism. MacDonagh played an active in the feminist movement in Ireland, helping to set up the Irish Women's Franchise League in 1911. This predated his membership in the Irish Republican Brotherhood, which he did not join until April of 1915. Though he maintained a close relationship with Pearse, he did not join the military counsel until April of 1916, making him one of the last members to join. While he probably played little to no role in the planning of the Rising, he applied his skills as a poet and from his time as a lecturer in English at University College Dublin to help in the writing of the Easter Proclamation.

MacDonagh had a history of depression that was often recorded in his works. 1914 was a high point of his personal life; he was a happily married man with a new son when the British Conservative Party blocked the passage of Home Rule.[2] This incensed a man who would have otherwise remained happily as an academic with a myriad of interests in Irish culture. This blockage of the long overdue bill was the tipping point for the inwardly gloomy man that led to the fulfillment of the death wish that he often wrote about in his poems.

A professor of English at the National University and a dramatist and poet of minor renown, MacDonagh added an air of romanticism to the Irish movement.[3] Despite his lack of martial training and prowess MacDonagh was given a major command in the IRB organization. Being a late addition to the group means that he most likely did not participate in any of the planning. Fortunately for his Battalion, while marching to Jacob's Biscuit Factory they happed to run into the longtime Fenian Major John MacBride who had fought for the Boers against the British. MacBride took over as second in command from Michael

[2]Max Caufield, *The Easter Rebellion* (New York: Holt, Rinehart, and Winston, 1963), p. 32.

[3]Ibid

O'Hanrahan.

Even more fortunately for the Battalion, they saw very little fighting during Easter Week. This did not spare MacDonagh personally. Though he was not the most competent, senior or influential member of the IRB, but he was executed as a signatory, nonetheless. His prominence during Easter Week shows how the Fenians valued idealism and connections over military competence. Though this was largely driven by the overwhelming scarcity of actual experience. In the end, MacDonagh was an intellectual and a culturally important Irishmen whose execution meant more for the ideal of the blood sacrifice and did more to disrupt the status quo than any tactical objective his Battalion could have achieved.

Chapter 17: Sean MacDermott

"This man signed the Declaration of Irish Independence. He was one of the most prominent of the leaders of the Irish Volunteers and attended at the meetings of the Executive and Control Councils. He wrote and sent despatches and mobilisation orders for and to the rebels during the rebellion and he surrendered with a body of rebels in Sackville Street with whom he had been operating for the previous week."[1] -Memorandum sent by General Sir John Maxwell to the then British Prime Minister, Herbet Asquith

One of the youngest members of the military council, Sean MacDermott or Mac Diarmada, followed the familiar path to radical Fenianism as his contemporaries. Born in County Leitrim on January 27th 1883, MacDermott's initial curiosity with Gaelic revivalism lead to the Gaelic League, the Ancient Order of Hibernians and eventually to a close association with Tom Clarke. His father Donald McDermott was a member of the IRB and a friend of John Daly.[2]

Deeply Catholic, he originally refused to join the IRB because it was condemned by the Catholic Church. Bulmer Hobson eventually intervened and convinced him to join. He rose to the position of Secretary and became a member of the Military Council.[3] MacDermott was also an active member in the Irish literary scene. In 1910, he began managing the radical *Irish Freedom* newspaper that Bulmer Hobson and Dennis McCullough founded. This became a natural extension of his role as an IRB organizer throughout the country.

The junior partner of the pair, MacDermott and Clarke were the most vocal advocates and active planners for an armed insurrection. As the Great War dragged on and the paranoia of a primitive strike by the British against their plans for a rebellion grew, Clarke and MacDermott became the main diverging voices for arguing for immediate rebellion.

---

[1]General Sir John Maxwell. Transcript of Court Martial. May 1916. Available from <http://www.aoh61.com/history/easter_trials.htm>.

[2]Brian Feeney, *16 Lives: Sean MacDiarmada* (Dublin: The O'Brien Press, 2014). p. 36.

[3] Ibid.

At one point, they had serious plans to have their factions rise with or without the support of the rest of the Volunteers. Without Clarke and his "zealous pupil" Sean MacDermott, there most likely would never have been an Uprising on April 25th 1916.[4]

MacDermott had been born with the demeanor and all the physical trappings of a natural military leader until a bout of polio left him near crippled and forced him to walk very slowly and with the aid of a walking stick.[5] If not for the polio, MacDermott would have most likely served as one of the principal commanders during the Rebellion, but during Easter Week he was among the governing body at the General Post Office and had no direct task or purpose besides supporting Clarke and serving in a nominal role in the Provisional Republican Government.

Executed along with the rest of co-signatories, MacDermott felt no remorse for the fighting and was fully content with his role in the 'blood sacrifice' writing: "I feel happiness the like of which I have never experienced. I die that the Irish nation might live!"[6]

Author Fearghal McGarry described MacDermott as the mind behind the Easter Rising.[7] While MacDermott had been a central figure in the Military Council, it is unknown just how much of the actual strategic or tactical planning he was directly responsible for.[8] He was fully bought into the concept of the 'blood sacrifice' telling Volunteer Sean Murphy while being marched to captivity: "Sean, the cause is lost if some of us are not shot."[9] This is not to conflate his beliefs in sacrifice and a generational struggle with a tangible plan for a multiphase conflict that would take shape during the Irish Revolutionary and Civil Wars. It just shows his commitment to give his own life and the lives of others

---

[4]Max Caufield, *The Easter Rebellion* (New York: Holt, Rinehart, and Winston, 1963), p. 31.

[5] Michael Foy and Brian Barton, *The Easter Rising (*London: Sutton Publishing, 2004), p. 4.

[6]Gerard MacAtsaney, Sean MacDiarmiada, The Mind of A Revolution, Drumlin, 2004, p137

[7]Fearghal McGarry, The Rising, Ireland, Easter 1916, Oxford University Press, 2010, p117

[8]John Dorney, "'Slaves or Freemen?' Sean McDermott, the IRB and the psychology of the Easter Rising", April 2011 Available from <http://www.theirishstory.com/2011/04/23/%e2%80%98slaves-or-freemen%e2%80%99- sean-mcdermott-the-irb-and-the-psychology-of-the-easter-rising/#.XX6EBChKiUk>; accessed 15 September 2019.

[9] Murphy, Sean, *Bureau of Military History, 1913-1921.* p. 204.

to Irish nationalism and a belief in Ireland's eventual victory. Without the Polio, MacDermott surely would have commanded a major position during the Rebellion. While his contributions and role as a signatory on the Easter proclamation were not insignificant, they were just a fraction of what he could have done.

Chapter 18: Joseph Plunkett

Joseph Mary Plunkett was born to one of the most noble and renowned families in Ireland. His father was member of the Papal Court and the Director of the National Museum. Blessed Oliver Plunkett was the Roman Catholic Archbishop of Armagh and Primate of All Ireland who was the last victim of the Popish Plot.[1] He was beatified in 1920 and canonized in 1975. Sir Horace Plunkett reorganized Irish agriculture at the beginning of the 20th century. As a young boy he and his brother often played with toy soldiers and studied tactics. Legend says he worked out the strategy for the Easter Rebellion as a younger man in his drawing room, although that is highly doubtful.[2]

Plunkett had a more difficult start to the Rebellion than most. Having had surgery for glandular tuberculosis just three weeks before the commencement of the Rebellion, Plunkett barely completed the route march to the GPO with the main body of Fenians.[3] Despite his frail state and the fact that he "looked like a man pointing out possible routes for his own funeral cortege" more than a general planning a complex operation, Plunkett was determined to stay with fighters.[4]

He was the chief planner of the Easter Rebellion despite having no military background. Much like the rest of his peers, he was a poet and a journalist more than anything else. While he had an extensive formal education that included time studying Arabic literature and language in Algiers, studying at the Catholic University Schools, and under the Jesuits at Belvedere College in Dublin. He did have some limited formal military training from his time in the Officers' Training Corps at Stonyhurst College in Lancashire, England.

---

[1] The Popish Plot was a conspiracy that caused wide-spread anti-Catholic hysteria in both England and Scotland between 1678 and 1681. Tituss Oates invented the conspiracy when he alleged that there was an extensive network of Catholics who were plotting to assassinate King Charles II. This directly led to the execution of twenty-two men and was the catalyst for the Exclusion Bill Crisis.

[2] Max Caufield, *The Easter Rebellion* (New York: Holt, Rinehart, and Winston, 1963), p. 32.

[3] Thomas Coffey, *Agony at Easter: The 1916 Irish Uprising* (London: George G. Harrap & Co, LTD, 1969), p. 12.

[4] Thomas Coffey, *Agony at Easter: The 1916 Irish Uprising* (London: George G. Harrap & Co, LTD, 1969), p. 12.

His involvement in Irish Nationalism began innocently enough when he joined the Gaelic League. He quickly befriended and began studying with Thomas MacDonagh, with whom he joined the Irish Volunteers and enjoyed a mutual interest of theater and poetry.

At some point in 1915, he joined the Irish Republican Brotherhood and traveled to Germany to meet with Sir Roger Casement in an attempt to get the Kaiser to commit to providing military support to the Rebellion. As Casement was not formally a member of the Irish Republican Brotherhood, he was not an official emissary. Plunkett's mission was an attempt to bring Casement's freelance activities and popularity into the fold of the official plan. Casement had won international renown and a knighthood for his exposure of colonial atrocities and enslavement in the rubber harvests in Belgian Congo and Putumayo region of the Brazilian rainforest. He had grown increasingly anti-colonial and viewed the Irish as "white Indians" and stated that the colonial abuses of Ireland had turned improvised Galway into the "Irish Putumayo".[5] While the pair was able to secure a shipment of arms, it was generally a fruitless endeavor.

During Easter Week, Plunkett was mostly a passive observer as his plan unfolded and failed. Due to a recent surgery on his neck earlier in the week, most of the activity was directed by Clarke and Pearse. Although he was able to stay abreast due to the efforts of Michael Collins, his aide de camp who would find fame as a principal leader during phases of the conflict.

Plunkett was executed along with his fellow signatories following surrender. His death was far more notable than his role in the fighting. Shortly before the execution, he was allowed to marry his fiancée Grace Gifford in the prison chapel. As further proof that the Rebellion was not strictly drawn along religious lines, Gifford was a Protestant who converted to Catholicism (as was her sister who did the same to marry Thomas MacDonagh).

Joseph Plunkett was a well bread, highly influential member of the Irish upper class. His family that survived the Rebellion went on to play important roles in the founding of the Irish Republican Army and during the Civil War. He, like the majority of his peers, had their interests in traditional culture and the arts transformed into violent, radical nationalism. His role as a planner and emissary could have been deci-

[5] Adam Hochschild, King Leopold's Ghost (New York: Mariner Books, 1998), p. 270.

sive in Easter Week, but in both his planning of the Rebellion and his mission to Germany, he could not achieve the objectives of his mission.

Left - John Devoy
Right - James Connolly

Left - Padraig Pease
Right - Eion MacNeill

Left - Tom Clarke
Right - John Maxwell

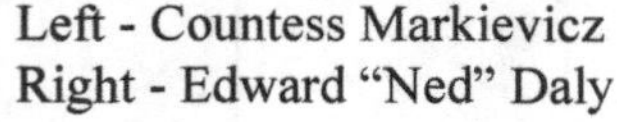

Left - Countess Markievicz
Right - Edward "Ned" Daly

Left - Eamon de Valera
Right - Thomas MacDonagh

Left - Sean MacDermott
Right - Joseph Plunkett

Section 3: The Battle

Part 1: The Beginning (Sunday – Monday)

Chapter 19: Events Prior to Sunday April 24th, 1916

Prior to the call to muster, only a select few people in the Irish Volunteers were aware of the plan. The existence of paramilitary organizations within the Irish Volunteers who were actively participating in drills and vague preparations for the event of a rebellion was publicly known. There were public marches, well-known songs and published propaganda. However, the seriousness, timing and specifics of plans to initiate a rebellion was known only to a select few within the military counsel. Most importantly, Eoin MacNeill, the Volunteer's Chief of Staff, knew nothing of the plans for the Rebellion. While MacNeill stayed true to his pacifist beliefs and did not join with the Rebellion after it began, the same cannot be said for Michael Joseph O'Rahilly, known as 'the O'Rahilly' for his position as the head of his clan. The O'Rahilly worked at a breakneck pace to stop the Rebellion after it had been made known to him, but in the end, he joined in the fighting.

The planners of the Rebellion understood that a preemptive raid by the British authorities would easily nip the Rising in the bud. Some on the ranks, like Clarke, were anxious to start the Rebellion as quickly as possible regardless of how complete the plans and preparations were. In order to prevent Clarke's Irish Citizen's Army from prematurely launching their own, independent Rebellion, Pearse and the military counsel agreed in early April that orders for parades and maneuvers beginning on Easter Sunday would serve as the commencement for the revolution.

The secret military counsel consisted of Padraig Pearse, Eamonn Ceannt, Joseph Plunkett, Tom Clarke and Sean McDermott. James Connolly was later convinced to join the counsel.[1] Eventually the military counsel made Eoin MacNeill aware of their plan and since the majority of the men on the counsel held high positions in the Irish Volunteers and because it became obvious that the more radical factions would fight alone if necessary, MacNeill relented and agreed to the plans for the Rebellion.[2]

In order to make sure the Rebellion was sufficiently armed, Sir

[1]Paul O'Brien, *Blood on the Streets: 1916 and the Battle for Mount Street Bridge* (Dublin: New Island, 2012), p. 15.

[2]Paul O'Brien, *Blood on the Streets: 1916 and the Battle for Mount Street Bridge* (Dublin: New Island, 2012), p. 16.

Roger Casement had arranged for Germany to send 20,000 rifles, one million rounds of ammunition and explosives to Ireland aboard a ship flying a Norwegian flag and going by the name *Aud*.

As the *Aud* was sailing, a rumor began to circulate among the Volunteers that the British authorities were about to arrest the leaders of the Irish Volunteers, Sinn Fein and the Gaelic League. While this purportedly leaked document proved fake, the "Castle Document" had the desired effect of putting the Fenians on a war footing and to brace them for real action. This document originated on April 19th from an Alderman and Sein member named Tom Kelly.

On Good Friday, April 21st, 1916, the *Aud* was captured off the coast of Cork. The news of this capture caused MacNeill to issue the infamous "countermanding order" through both individuals such as The O'Rahilly and in the *Sunday Independent* newspaper.[3] While small groups did mobilize throughout the country, most quickly disbanded as it appeared that most of the Volunteers were obeying MacNeill's command. With only 1,500 men, women and teenagers mobilizing and at that only in Dublin, the military counsel had to quickly adjust their plans. To them, calling off the Rebellion after the capture of the *Aud* was not an option. The element of surprise was lost and raids on Fenian meeting spots and leaders would defeat the Rebellion before it could start and lose Ireland its opportunity to strike while Britain was the most vulnerable.

---

[3]Paul O'Brien, *Blood on the Streets: 1916 and the Battle for Mount Street Bridge* (Dublin: New Island, 2012), p. 16.

Chapter 20: The Plan Sunday April 24th, 1916

For such an amateur and loosely controlled force, the plan was far too complicated and ambitious. Especially given the manpower constraints caused by the countermanding order. Simply put, the Fenian plan was to seize and hold several key positions and avenues of approach in Dublin and to fight a barricaded defense that would inspire some vague and unplanned or prepared for subsequent actions that would lead to the formal recognition of an Irish Free State. The end state of the Easter Week operations was that the Fenians in Dublin would have inspired enough of the other Battalions and populace in Ireland that the Rebellion would spread like a wildfire throughout the country and exhaust British resources forcing them to grant independence for the sake of the fight on the Western Front. Dublin would remain the main objective – it was the only objective the military counsel planned for – and actions throughout Ireland were largely uncoordinated and unplanned for past the initial phase. Dublin, in and of itself, was probably enough to achieve the Fenian aims. It was the political, cultural and symbolic center of gravity for the country. It also held a large portion, though not a majority of the population. The command-and-control center for the Sinn Feiners would stay at the General Post Office, but there would be a large amount of operational autonomy outside of the city. Concentrating the leadership in Dublin alone was a mistake that allowed the British to easily contain the Rebellion and ensure that it could not spread throughout Ireland.

A dispersed command structure would have been a major advantage to the Fenians as it was in the later civil war and in almost every successful insurgency. The presence of the likes of Tom Clarke or even a lesser figure like Ned Daly could have outweighed the nerves and the effects of the countermanding order in Battalions that had prepared for action, but did not rise like those in Belfast, Cork or Galway. While Clarke unsuccessfully sent his daughter Nora to help ensure Belfast rose, his personal presence in that city could have made a tremendous difference.

The Fenian plan was to occupy four separate positions and multiple redoubts throughout the center of the city. These headquarters and the seat of the Provisional Government was at the General Post Office

(GPO) on Sackville (modern O'Connell) Street. The 1st Battalion under Commandant Ned Daly would occupy the Four Courts which would directly block the movement of British troops from the Royal Barracks. Commandant MacDonagh's 2nd Battalion would occupy Jacob's Biscuit Factory in order to block movement from the Portobello and Richmond Barracks on the southern part of the city. The 3rd Battalion under Commandant de Valera would occupy Boland's Bakery close to the Beggar's Bush Barracks and near the Kingstown Road and rail routes which would be the main avenue of approach for British reinforcements coming from England. Commandant Ceannt's 4th Battalion would occupy the South Dublin Union and would focus on occupying British forces from the Richmond and Islandbridge Barracks as well as seizing key railway stations that ended rail lines from the south that they hoped would bring in reinforcements and supplies from the south and west and control key telegraph and telephone stations.[1]

The specific plan for Easter Monday was as follows:

1. The IRB Military Council was to seize and occupy the General Post Office on Sackville [now O'Connell] Street and there establish the Headquarters of the Provisional Government. This task assigned to a combined force of the Volunteers and Citizens Army under James Connolly. Although the presences of almost all the signatories of the Easter Proclamation and the O'Rahilly neutralized any unity of command that Connolly may have hoped to enjoy.
2. City Hall in Dame Street, facing Dublin Castle, was to be seized in order to delay British movement against the GPO for as long as possible. This would allow enough time to establish the command center at the GPO and establish communications with the other Battalions.
3. The First Battalion under Edward (Ned) Daly was to occupy the Four Courts and the necessary outposts.
4. The Second Battalion commanded by Thomas MacDonagh was the seize and hold Jacob's Biscuit Factory.
5. Eamon de Valera's Third Battalion was to seize and hold Boland's Bakery in order to block the main road lead-

[1] Michael Foy and Brian Barton, *The Easter Rising* (London: Sutton Publishing, 2004) p. 26.

ing from Kingstown Harbor to Dublin. This position would also block the railway line from Lansdowne Road to Westland Row. This would block both the main avenue of approach for British Troops landing by ship from England/Wales and troops being repositioned from the north of Ireland to Dublin.

6. The Fourth Battalion commanded by Eamonn Ceannt was to seize and hold the Kingsbridge Station. This was the end of the railway that came to Dublin from the South.
7. Con Colbert, a Company Commander in the Fourth Battalion was detached to seize Roe's distillery. Other, smaller sections were detached to occupy supporting positions like the South Dublin Union.
8. The Irish Citizen's Army was to seize and establish defensive positions (mostly ineffective trenches) at St. Stephen's Green. This detachment was under the command of the ICA's Chief of Staff Michael Mallin and the Countess Markievicz as second in command.
9. Units of the Cumann na mBan were attached to each battalion for medical, courier, scouting and logistical support.[2]

[2] Joseph McKenna, Voices from the Easter Rising: Firsthand Accounts of Ireland's 1916 Rebellion (Jefferson: McFarland & Company, Inc., Publishers., 2017), p. 67.

Chapter 21: The Beginning Monday April 25th, 1916

Even before the beginning of the Easter Rebellion, the British forces, especially the leaders in Dublin Castle, were aware that a rebellious faction Fenians movement existed and harbored intentions to act against the British government. They did not know specifics but suspected that there was a strong possibility of a hostile action in Dublin. The capture of the *Aud* only reconfirmed these beliefs. However, the British wildly underestimated the scope and severity of the Rebellion and the Rebel surprise would have been even more overwhelming had it not been for the countermanding order. Even as a Rebel company was marching up O'Connell Street, a group of British officers standing in front of the Metropole Hotel remarked: "Will these bloody fools never tire of marching up and down these streets?"[1]

British forces in Dublin at the beginning of the Rebellion would have had more than a three to one advantage over the Fenian forces. While not all these men were fully trained and prepared, the 120 officers and 2,265 enlisted would overwhelm the Sinn Feiners even without a heavy weapons and artillery advantage. These forces were dispersed throughout the city. At Marlborogh Barracks in Phoenix Park the 6th Cavalry Regiment had 35 officers and 851 other ranks. The 3rd Royal Irish Regiment had 21 officers and 650 other ranks at Portobello Barracks. Finally, at the Royal Barracks, there were 37 officers and 430 other ranks of the 10th Royal Dublin Fusiliers.[2] This was also supplemented by the Officer Training Corps (O.T.C) at Trinity College and the mostly elderly men of the Home Defense Force knows and the Georgius Rex – or as irreverently called by Dubliners, the Gorgeous Wrecks.[3] While insignificant in the action, both groups helped alleviate some of manpower constraints of securing the largest city in Ireland. The O.T.C did secure Trinity College, although unopposed, which stood at a key crossroads between Rebel positions.

---

[1]Thomas Coffey, *Agony at Easter: The 1916 Irish Uprising* (London: George G. Harrap & Co, LTD, 1969), p.4.

[2]Max Caufield, *The Easter Rebellion* (New York: Holt, Rinehart, and Winston, 1963), p. 91.

[3]Max Caufield, *The Easter Rebellion* (New York: Holt, Rinehart, and Winston, 1963), p. 125.

Other sources cite a lower number of British forces available. With just 111 officers and 2,316 other ranks available. These forces were available as:

Marlborough Barracks, 6th Cavalry Regiment – 35 officers and 851 other ranks
Portobello Barracks, 3rd Royal Irish Rifles – 21 officers and 650 other ranks
Richmond Barracks, 3rd Royal Irish Regiment – 18 officers and 385 other ranks
Royal Barracks, 10th Royal Dublin Regiment – 37 officers and 430 other ranks
Total – 111 officer and 2,316 other ranks[4]

Fenian forces were shockingly low during the Rebellion. According to Lieutenant Ruaidhri Henderson's best analysis the Fenian forces were as follows:

GPO – approximately 135
Four Courts – 320
Jacob's Factory – 70
Boland's Mill – 170
South Dublin Union – 200
St. Stephen's Green – 137
Total – 1,132[5]

Regardless of the numbers available, the British forces in Dublin had an overwhelming manpower advantage over the Fenians. Standard military thought dictates that an attacking force must have a three to one advantage to successfully attack a well-entrenched force. However, this does not account for the lack of provisions for the Fenians – they could have been starved out in about a week – or the tremendous differences in firepower from both direct and indirect weapons. The British may not have had the manpower on hand to immediately assault and dislodge all positions, but they did have the manpower to easily contain and isolate the Fenian positions. Which would have then allowed them to move

[4] Joseph McKenna, Voices from the Easter Rising: Firsthand Accounts of Ireland's 1916 Rebellion (Jefferson: McFarland & Company, Inc., Publishers., 2017), p. 68.
[5] Ibid, p. 68.

from objective to objective easily defeating them in detail.

The Rebels mitigated this by creating a defense in depth from their headquarters at the General Post Office. Multiple defensive positions, redoubts, and observation posts coupled with targeted acts of sabotage to turn Dublin into a complicated urban fortress. While the Fenians lacked the manpower to execute on their plan due to the large number of men who failed to muster, they were able to adjust and concentrate to create a very difficult and unfamiliar operating environment for the British.

Fenian failures to execute limited the advantage of surprise. One of the most impactful instances was the failure to destroy the telephone exchange. The inability to complete this mission allowed the Dublin police to alert both Dublin Castle and the military headquarters at Parkgate.[6] The British were quick to mobilize in response. Not only by diverting troops destined for France, but by quickly calling in units from outlying areas after the realization was made that the areas outside of Dublin fully failed to mobilize and moving infantry from as far away as Belfast.[7]

At 4pm, the first trains carrying troops from outside of Dublin began arriving. This train traveled through some rifle fire and carried men for the 3rd Reserves Cavalry Regiment.[8] While they left their gun carriages and horses behind, they still carried a significant amount of firepower and manpower. By 5:30pm they had begun their advance on Dublin Castle to help secure it from further attacks.[9] The Rebels has missed a golden opportunity, in his report to the Commission of Inquiry into the Rising, Major Ivor Price, The British Army's Chief Intelligence Officer in Ireland, stated that "Twenty-five determined men could have done it [taken the castle]. I think there was only a corporal's guard there at the time."[10]

---

[6] Max Caufield, *The Easter Rebellion* (New York: Holt, Rinehart, and Winston, 1963), p. 91.

[7]Ibid, p. 92.

[8]Ibid, p. 130.

[9] Ibid, p. 130.

[10] Michael Foy and Brian Barton, *The Easter Rising* (London: Sutton Publishing, 2004), p. 55.

Chapter 22: The Countermanding Order

If the full potential of the Fenian forces rose during the Rebellion, the results of the Easter Uprising, and possibly World War I, could have been dramatically different. Had the total number of Irish Volunteers had mobilized, there would have been over ten thousand Fenians under arms.[1] This alone would have been tantamount to a separate front for the British fighting the Great War, especially considering that these forces would have been dispersed across the entirety of the island, making massing against them and organizing the logistics a significant feat. Standard doctrine states that an attacker needs a 3:1 advantage. To further enhance the danger posed by a second front in the rear of the British lines, this front would have manifested without much prior warning, isolated the large reserve of British manpower training and recovering in Ireland, disrupted the flow of critical war supplies and made American intervention on the side of the Entente powers more complicated and politically difficult. While the lack of artillery and other constraints may have nullified some of this need, the potential to require the diversion of over twenty-thousand troops would have been one of the most significant events in World War One.

Further, once the Rebellion had begun, it might have been a catalyst for some of the more moderate groups. There was further potential that Redmond's National Volunteers would also join in if the Fenians had achieved significant momentum. This would have brought the total number under arms to over one hundred thousand.[2] While still lacking machine guns, artillery and other necessities of modern warfare, this large of an insurrection would have forced Britain to sue for peace with either Ireland or Germany. Germany would surely have taken greater efforts to support the Rebels than some minor gun running. To what extent they would have been willing to risk the fleet prior to the Battle of Jutland is hard to determine, but it is certain that they would have exerted much more effort to support the Sinn Feiners. Had the nation rose, the entire course of the war would have been shifted.

---

[1]Max Caufield, *The Easter Rebellion* (New York: Holt, Rinehart, and Winston, 1963), p. 38.
[2]*Ibid.*

Prolonged warfare in Ireland would have also risked Britain's relationship with America due to the large Irish population there. Few politicians in isolationist America would have been willing to lose votes over the preservation of an English colony. The combination of the voting power of the Irish, German and Europeans from lands under Austrian control could have either forced American neutrality or possibly even shifted American allegiances.

Eoin MacNeill's order killed this dream before Easter Week even began.

Chapter 23: Phoenix Park

Barely a week before the commencement of hostilities on Palm Sunday Paddy Daly brought a bold plan to the IRB Council (Clarke, McDermott and MacDonagh). With a force of twenty men and knowledge he gained working as a carpenter in the fort, he would seize and destroy a major supply depot and secure for the Fenians some much needed supplies and ammunition.[1] At Nine in the morning on Easter Monday Paddy Daly woke up his friend Gary Holohan to prepare for the opening shot of the Rebellion. While there was some confusion on the time – Holohan thinking that it would not start until the evening and Daly knowing that it would commence at noon and still others clueless as to the actual start time – by five past eleven only five of the men had managed to make their way to Liberty Hall. The contingent received additional support from the Battalions already mustered and made their way in three separate groups (two by tram and one by bicycle) to Pheonix Park. Daly, who had been in the employee of a staff member there, served as the leader of the group since he had the most intimate knowledge of the magazine.[2]

At 12:17 Daly led the party inside. They made their way through a long passageway and into the guardroom. Holohan demanded the first guard they encountered to surrender. The guard did not comply and was shot twice in the leg. The Rebels quickly overpowered and captured the remaining guards they encountered, taking them and Ms. Isabel Playfair (the wife of the fort's commander) prisoner along with her children. The Fenians showed mercy to both, allowing Playfair six minutes to evacuate the fort.[3]

At this point, the plan was to set explosives and to blow the fort using the munitions stored in the high explosives room. In the first of what would become a string of unlucky breaks, the key to that room was not at the fort that day, but in the possession of the Officer in Charge who was away at the Fairyhouse.[4] The Fenians improvised by stacking

---

[1]Joseph McKenna, Voices from the Easter Rising: Firsthand Accounts of Ireland's 1916 Rebellion (Jefferson: McFarland & Company, Inc., Publishers., 2017), p. 69.
[2] Max Caufield, *The Easter Rebellion* (New York: Holt, Rinehart, and Winston, 1963), pp. 61-62.
[3] Max Caufield, *The Easter Rebellion* (New York: Holt, Rinehart, and Winston, 1963), p. 64.
[4] *Ibid*

belts of ammunition from the small arms room on top of a bag of gelignite next to the door of the munitions room. Playfair's son attempted to run back into the fort to warn its inhabitants but when the Rebels saw this, he was shot and killed after being warned to stop.

Chapter 24: Harcourt Street Station

A section from the Irish Citizen's Army including both men and women departed from Liberty Hall around 11:30 in the morning and marched towards City Hall and the Harcourt Station.[1] Under the command of Captain Richard McCormack, the detachment was to seize the rail station, which was the end of the line for the Dublin and South Eastern Railway and thus the most likely avenue of approach for British forces that would be moving to Dublin from Curragh.[2] With only 45 men in the detachment and a few boys from the Boys' Corps of the ICA, the plan to hold the station for the duration of the fighting was already unraveling. The adjustment was to hold the station long enough so that the main Irish Citizen's Army force at St. Stephen's Green would have enough time to establish itself and fortify its position.

The detachment quickly seized the railway station and even took an off duty British officer, Lieutenant M. Kelly, as their prisoner.[3] They began the work to build their defenses and to seize surrounding buildings to create redoubts. Three men under Sergeant Joe Doyle seized Davy's public house on the bridge over the Grand Canal. These were the first forces from the Irish Citizen's Army to see action against the British. The small contingent was discovered en route to their objective by a pair of mounted soldiers.

At about 1:30, the ICA men saw a small, loose contingent from the Royal Irish Rifles and upon the order from Captain McCormack began to fire on them. The British brought in reinforcements and machine guns and launched an attack on the ICA position.[4] By this point, Doyle and his men had already withdrawn from Davy's and McCormack had received the word that the position at St. Stephen's Green was established and the detachment was making preparations to withdrawn and rejoin the main body.[5] A secondary objective to destroy the telephone and telegraph cables at the nearby telephone exchange was unsuccessful due to a lack of expertise and manpower.[6]

[1]Joseph McKenna, Voices from the Easter Rising: Firsthand Accounts of Ireland's 1916 Rebellion (Jefferson: McFarland & Company, Inc., Publishers., 2017), p. 73.

[2] Ibid

[3] Ibid.

[4] Joseph McKenna, Voices from the Easter Rising: Firsthand Accounts of Ireland's 1916 Rebellion (Jefferson: McFarland & Company, Inc., Publishers., 2017), p. 74.

[5] Ibid.

[6] Ibid.

Chapter 25: Dublin Castle

At 12:04 in the afternoon on Easter Monday Constable James O'Brien of the Dublin Metropolitan Police waved off a half-joking question from a passing nurse. He dismissed the rumors that the Sinn Feiners were going to assault Dublin Castle.[1] At approximately the same time, H.S. Doig the editor of the Dublin Mail and Express looked up from his work to see that the Fenians from the Citizen Army, clad in dark green uniform and Boer-style slouch hats pinned with a Red Hand badge to represent their Union, marching down towards the castle in spite of Eoin MacNeill's order.[2] Suddenly and with an unexpected and cold blooded shot that killed a policeman, the Rising had begun.

The scene was chaos. The first shot was fired as the top British authorities in Ireland, including the Under Secretary for Ireland and the Military Intelligence Officer, were meeting to create their plan to arrest the political leaders. While these men were aware of the potential for a revolt, and how could they not with the public marches and provocative articles published from Liberty Hall, the consensus was it would probably not amount to much more than either a strike or a few homemade bombs.[3]

A sentry inside the gate fired into the air to alert his comrades.[4] The Fenians shoved past the barricades and stormed the castle, sporadically firing. A priest ran to Constable O'Brien to administer his last rites. The remainder of the six guards were making lunch when the fighting began. The Rebels were firing and throwing homemade bombs. Despite catching the Guards by surprise and the castle without reinforcements, the attack proved unsuccessful.[5] John Connolly, the leader of the Rebel contingent, surrendered the initiative, split his forces and retreated from the Castle. With this initial success and almost immediate self-inflicted failure, the Easter Rebellion had begun.

The Rebels failed to capitalize on taking the British by surprise at Dublin Castle. Some think Connolly retreated because of fears of concentrated British forces inside Dublin Castle. To launch a half-hearted raid on the most defensible position and the government's center of

---

[1] Max Caufield. *The Easter Rebellion* (New York, Holt, Rinehart and Winston, 1963), p. 1.

[2] Ibid, pp. 1-4.

[3] Ibid, p. 28.

[4] Ibid, pp. 5-6.

[5] Ibid, p. 6.

gravity in Dublin makes no sense. Surely the objective was to seize the Castle. This assault was a failure.

Meanwhile, at Liberty Hall, Pearse, Connolly and Plunkett formed their troops and began the march in a column of orthodox fours towards the General Post Office. Amongst their ranks stood nameless soldiers awkwardly carrying not one, but two rifles. Equally unprepared were a future president of Ireland (Sean T. O'Kelly) and the most notable figure of the future civil war Michael Collins.[6] Many in their ranks thought they were participating in a routine march; few had any idea of the fight that awaited them.

The rebels were armed with a hodgepodge of equipment ranging from smuggled rifles, shotguns and homemade bombs fashioned from old tobacco tins to crudely manufactured six-foot pikes.[7] The Rebels efficiently stormed the scarcely guarded GPO and took quick work to setting up barricades and laying communication lines. Part of the appeal of the GPO was that it was a communications hub for the city and came with telegraphists who could be impressed into service. Captain Michael Collins made sure that the prisoners were treated with dignity by the men under his command.[8]

For all of the fears and rumors of German actions, nothing more than a few Zeppelin attacks and a small, four ship naval sortie in the North Atlantic materialized.[9] In England, Field Marshall Lord French was excited to finally have some action as the Commander in Chief of the Home Forces after six months of busy work after being replaced by Sir Douglas Haig.[10] He quickly ordered blackouts, mobilized home defense units and recalled troops from leave. Units diverted to Ireland included the 59th (North Midland) Division and the 178th Infantry Division. The first movement of the 59th was to move to two different railheads so that they could rapidly move to counter a German landing in Britain.[11]

That the British were overly focused on German actions is understandable. The Irish never posed a real conventional threat with the strategy that they adopted. While the effort to seize Dublin Castle was

[6] Ibid, pp. 8-11.
[7] Ibid, p. 12.
[8] Ibid, p. 14.
[9] Ibid, p. 150.
[10] Ibid, p. 146.
[11] Ibid, p. 147.

a tactical failure, the Rebels could have adopted a guerilla strategy and turned that into a very successful raid on the heart of the British administration in Ireland. Neither side was prepared for an insurgency and thankfully for the British forces the Fenians decided to stand and fight.

Chapter 26: The South Dublin Union

At eleven thirty-five in the morning on Monday Commandant Eammon Kent lead a party of ten men by bicycle along a back route to the Dublin Union. The Vice-Commandant Cathal Brugha lead the main party. Only one hundred and twenty men of the possible seven hundred had mustered for the Rebellion. Kent believed that if it had not been for the countermanding order, he would have had at least five hundred.[1] As they made their way, smaller parties dispersed to occupy redoubts that would disrupt any counterattack. Captain James Murphy and twenty men occupied the Jameson Distillery. Con Colbert and his party took Watkin's Brewery. Captain Tomas MacCarthy took Roe's Distillery on James Street. These positions also allowed the Rebels to control movement along the Liffey quaysides, Kingsbridge Railway, the Royal Hospital, Kilmainham.[2] Since this was the main terminal that British troops moving from the main British Army camp in Curragh would have to use, securing this area would essentially block the movement by rail of British forces into Dublin.

At noon, once the other positions were secured, Kent moved to the back entrance of the Union at the Rialto Bridge and with little resistance secured the key from a porter and opened the door for Brugha and the main party.[3] With the Union secured, defensive preparations promptly began. Kent had only about a quarter of the troops available that he planned on. While the men got to work knocking down walls to create internal lines of movement to enable them to better shift to mass against an attack, the lack of manpower must have felt overwhelming. Kent quickly set about setting out listening and observation posts designed to make first contact and alert the main body of any British movements. Brugha also made the decision to consolidate the main body in the Night Nurse's House, the most sturdy and defensible building in the compound.

The first signs of a British response did not appear until twelve twenty-five when one of these observation posts, who had previously been occupied in a shouting match with women whose husbands were serving in France, noticed a small contingent of British soldiers dressed

[1]Max Caufield. *The Easter Rebellion* (New York, Holt, Rinehart and Winston, 1963), p. 66.

[2] Ibid, p. 66.

[3] Ibid, p. 67.

in khaki marching towards them.[4] Soon, two hundred men under the command of Major Edward Warmington and Lieutenant Alan Ramsay of the Royal Irish Regiment began their assault on the Rialto Bridge and on other outlying buildings that were occupied by the Rebels.[5] The British initially had mixed success. While they had an advantage in manpower and machine guns, the confusion of urban warfare and the Fenian defensive network stymied the initial British thrust.

[4] Ibid, p. 69.
[5] Ibid, pp. 98-102.

Chapter 27: Jacob's Biscuit Factory

At Jacob's Biscuit Factory the men under Commandant MacDonagh's 2nd Battalion which included, the former Boer Army Major John MacBride who was a leader in the commando Irish Brigade, occupied the factory which was located nearly adjacent to St. Patrick's Cathedral and a few blocks away from Dublin Castle.[1] Major MacBride was the most experienced fighter among the Volunteers. In his court martial, General Maxwell described him as: "This man fought on the side of the Boers in the South African wars of 1899 and held the rank of Major in that Army, being in command of a body known as the Irish Brigade. He was always one of the most active advocates of the anti-enlistment propaganda and the Irish Volunteer movement. He was appointed to the rank of Commandant in the rebel army, and papers were found in his possession showing that he was in close touch with the other rebel leaders and was, "issuing and receiving despatches (sp) from rebels in various parts of the city. He voluntarily stated at his trial that he had been appointed second-in-command of portion of the rebel forces and considered it his duty to accept that position. He was accompanied by over 100 men at the time of his surrender. He had great influence over the younger men in the associations with which he was connected"[2]

The purpose of this position was to primarily protect the western flank of the garrison at St. Stephen's Green and the College of Surgeons. The secondary purpose was to provide much needed food to the other Fenian positions. The women of the *Cumann na mBan* were to play a critical role in moving these supplies to the other positions.[3] If not for the shortage in manpower, members of this positions were to play a supporting role in the attack on Dublin Castle by capturing the Ship Street Barracks. This was ultimately abandoned due to a lack of manpower.[4]

MacDonagh's plan was to seize this critical position and lure General Lowe into launching a costly attack against a defended posi-

[1] Michael Foy and Brian Barton, *The Easter Rising (*London: Sutton Publishing, 2004), p. 89.

[2]General Sir John Maxwell. Transcript of Court Martial. May 1916. Available from <http://www.aoh61.com/history/easter_trials.htm>.

[3]Joseph McKenna, Voices from the Easter Rising: Firsthand Accounts of Ireland's 1916 Rebellion (Jefferson: McFarland & Company, Inc., Publishers., 2017), p. 110.

[4] Ibid, p. 109.

tion. His men quickly got to work fortifying the position, using sacks of flour to act as sandbags.[5] General Lowe did not take the bait and instead allowed his cordon and low intensity sniping to do the work of wearing down the Rebels.[6] Due to the proximity of the nearby houses to the bakery, the British found it difficult to access the rooftops to establish their artillery and machine gun positions. With this difficulty, General Lowe decided not to attack and rather to just isolate this position.[7] Throughout the week, fighting here was minimal, with a few exceptions where the Fenians were able to attack scatterings of British troops. The positions at the Biscuit Factory and the other outposts spread throughout the South Dublin Union area were surprised and dismayed to find out about the surrender.

[5] Ibid, p. 109.

[6]Michael Foy and Brian Barton, *The Easter Rising (*London: Sutton Publishing, 2004), p. 92.

[7] Joseph McKenna, *Voices from the Easter Rising: Firsthand Accounts of Ireland's 1916 Rebellion* (Jefferson: McFarland & Company, Inc., Publishers., 2017), p. 110.

Chapter 28: The Battle – The Four Courts

The Fenians, for all their tactical flaws, were smart about establishing dispersed defensive positions throughout the city to restrict and disrupt British movement against their main position at the General Post Office. A great example of this is the actions of Ned Daly's First Battalion. The First Battalion mustered at the 11:00am at the Colmcille Hall, Blackhall Place and after a speech from Daly began its movement to its positions.[1] The battalion established itself at the Four Courts and would see some of the most significant fighting. Second in command to Daly was Vice-Commandant Piaras Beaslai, who came to the Volunteers via the Gaelic League and had once founded the Gaelic Writers Society and *An Fainne*, a newspaper. [2] The primary purpose of this location was to disrupt the movement of British forces in the city.

While the seizure of the Four Courts went off relatively easy, seizing territory was not the purpose of the 1st Battalion. Unlike the units at the GPO and St. Stephen's Green, Daly's mission was to disrupt the movement of British forces. Wisely, he decided to disperse his extremely limited forces to several smaller objectives.

A Company under the command of Captain Dennis O'Callaghan was originally tasked with occupying the Broadshire Railway Station, which was located at the ending station for the Midland Great Western Railway. Due to his limited forces, he made the decision instead to occupy some tenement buildings along North King Street. There, he used materials from nearby construction sites to fortify his positions and to make one of the most challenging defensive obstacles that the British would face.

One of the tasks given to the First Battalion at the beginning of hostilities was to arrest Bulmer Hobson to ensure that he did not have the opportunity to continue to send out conflicting messages to the Fenian forces.[3] Hobson was critical in influencing MacNeill to issue the countermanding order. It was an awkward, but necessary task to detain

---

[1]Paul O'Brien, *Crossfire: The Battle of the Four Courts, 1916* (Dublin: New Island, 2012), p. 5.

[2] Paul O'Brien, *Crossfire: The Battle of the Four Courts, 1916* (Dublin: New Island, 2012), p. 6.

[3]Helen Litton, *16 Lives: Edward Daly* (Dublin, The O'Brien Press, 2013), p. 93.

someone who had been so critical to the Fenian movement, but Daly and his men handled it and Hobson with dignity and restraint.

Company B under the command of Captain Jim O'Sullivan had one of the most important tasks of the entire Battalion. Nested into the mission of disrupting British movement through Dublin, Company B moved to the railway bridges at the North Circular and Cabra roads. By this time, Britain was already mobilizing its reserves against the Fenians in Dublin. As O'Sullivan's command was busy at work, the British had already moved in a brigade from Curragh Camp in Kildare and the transports for newly trained 59th North Midlands Division was diverted from France to Dublin – much to the surprise of the men.[4] With all of these forces converging from outside Dublin, the sabotage efforts and defensive positions became all the more vital for the preservation of the Rebel headquarters in the GPO.

During this operation, the First Battalion's restraint again became the stuff of legend. The men of Company B showed tremendous discipline and did have any response or reaction when they were pelted with rotten fruit and vegetables by 'separation women' as they moved up Constitution Hill.[5] While this incident is relatively obscure, had the Fenians reacted it would have shown them to be no better than the British they were fighting against. Simple acts of restraint like this not only swayed the citizenry that were involved or observed the action but denied the British of a propaganda counterpoint that could have derailed the moral advantage that the Fenians had. Ultimately, the efforts to disrupt British movements were fairly successful. The destruction of the bridges did delay British movement, but the weight of British forces and industry was a tidal wave that could not be stopped by the forces available to the British. More effective, the lack of Fenian action in the conduct of their duties denied the British important propaganda tools that could have countered the Fenian narrative.

Daly stayed with C Company, where Captain Frank Fahy and Lieutenant Joseph McGuinness commanded the Volunteers. The seizure was easily accomplished by relieving one lone guard of his keys.[6] The Volunteers got to quick work fortifying their position and unfurling an Irish tricolor over the Four Courts complex.

---

[4] Helen Litton, *16 Lives: Edward Daly* (Dublin, The O'Brien Press, 2013), p. 115.
[5] Helen Litton, *16 Lives: Edward Daly* (Dublin, The O'Brien Press, 2013), p. 116.
[6]Paul O'Brien, *Crossfire: The Battle of the Four Courts, 1916* (Dublin: New Island, 2012), pp. 8-9.

Daly had the foresight to send 'D' Company under the command of a young Sean Heuston to occupy the Mendicity Institute.[7] This action was intended to only last for a few hours to give Daly time to establish his position at the Four Courts. Heuston and his men would and did attack any British forces moving along the North Quays.

This position was only meant as a temporary redoubt, but Heuston decided to hold onto the position until Tuesday. Unfortunately for Heuston, the British also realized the importance of the location and it became the site of intense fighting. The original force of twelve was eventually reinforced to twenty-six, but this mattered little against the overwhelming odds that the British had at their disposal.

Company F under Captain Fionan Lynch, took positions along Church Street and began to dig in. Their primary position was located at the intersection of the Quays and Church Street. They also had a second position that was based around a low brick wall. This redoubt's primary purpose was to slow any British advance.

Commanded by Captain Nicholas Laffan, Company G occupied buildings on North King and Brunswick Street and erected a barricade on the eastern end of Brunswick Street.[8] The most notable part of this barricade was the men used material seized from the Jameson Distillery to fortify their position.[9]

One of the fighters under Heuston recalled of the battle: "Our tiny garrison of twenty-six had battled all morning against three or four hundred British troops. Machine-gun and rifle fire kept up a constant battering of our position. Seán visited each post in turn, encouraging us. But now we were faced with a new form of attack. The enemy, closing in, began to hurl grenades into the building. Our only answer was to try and catch these and throw them back before they exploded. Two of our men, Liam Staines and Dick Balfe, both close friends of Seán's were badly wounded doing this. We had almost run out of ammunition. Dog-tired, without food, trapped, hopelessly outnumbered, we had reached the limit of our endurance. After consultation with the rest of us, Seán decided that the only hope for the wounded and indeed, for the safety

[7] Paul O'Brien. "Heuston's Fort – The Battle for the Mendicity Institute, 1916", August 2012 [The Irish Story] Available from < http://www.theirishstory.com/2012/08/15/heustons-fort-the-battle-for-the-mendicity-institute-1916/#.Ww6tk0gvzIW >; accessed 30 May 2018.

[8] Paul O'Brien, Crossfire: The Battle of the Four Courts, 1916 (Dublin: New Island, 2012), p. 10.

[9] Ibid, p. 11.

of all of us, was to surrender. Not everyone approved but the order was obeyed, and we destroyed as much equipment as we could before giving ourselves up…"[10]

[10]Paul O'Brien. "Heuston's Fort – The Battle for the Mendicity Institute, 1916", August 2012 [The Irish Story] Available from < http://www.theirishstory.com/2012/08/15/heustons-fort-the-battle-for-the-mendicity-institute-1916/#.Ww6tk0gvzIW>;accessed 30 May 2018.

Chapter 29: Boland's Bakery

Under the command of New York born, thirty-four-year-old mathematics teacher and future President of the Irish Republic Commandant Eamon de Valera established a headquarters in a single-story building facing Grand Canal Street. Secondary positions were also established at nearby locations such as the Clanwilliam House.[1] Other positions were established at the Ringsend Distillery, Westland Row Railway Station and railway-level crossing at Landsdowne Road, Horan's Fort and the Mount Street Bridge.[2] De Valera, brandishing a sword, had his position occupied by twelve thirty and like many of his comrades, the seizure of these positions met stiffer resistance from upset noncombatants than from any British force. The Fenians had yet another opportunity to show that they were just fighting for independence when they secured six gold sovereigns in a locked drawer and leaving a note.[3] Stories like these would gain more publicity than most of the actual fighting in the aftermath of the Rebellion.

As de Valera's subordinate Lieutenant Simon Donnelly and his men were busy erecting a gangway from the Bakery to the main Dublin-Kingstown tracks to allow movement from the headquarters to the outpost one of the sentries was confronted by a British soldier. After a brief standoff, Tom Walshe, a member of "B" Company fired his first shot and killed the man on the spot.[4]

There was also a plan conceived to occupy positions along the Grand Canal near the Mount Street Bridge to prevent British reinforcements from entering the city from Kingstown.[5] Originally, the Volunteers planned to occupy five posts along the route to prevent the British from being able to enter the city. The first of these positions was the Crisbrooke House at the junction of Pembroke Road and Northumberland Road. Next was at 25 Northumberland Road, which would cover

[1] Max Caufield. *The Easter Rebellion* (New York, Holt, Rinehart and Winston, 1963), p. 76.

[2] Joseph McKenna, *Voices from the Easter Rising: Firsthand Accounts of Ireland's 1916 Rebellion* (Jefferson: McFarland & Company, Inc., Publishers., 2017), p. 110.

[3]Max Caufield. *The Easter Rebellion* (New York, Holt, Rinehart and Winston, 1963), p. 77.

[4]Ibid, pp. 78-79.

[5] Joseph McKenna, *Voices from the Easter Rising: Firsthand Accounts of Ireland's 1916 Rebellion* (Jefferson: McFarland & Company, Inc., Publishers., 2017), p. 115.

not only the road, but the main gate of the Beggars Bush barracks. The third position was a parochial hall and the fourth was a schoolhouse, both of which were redoubts for 25 Northumberland Road. The fifth position was the Clanwilliam House, which would cover the Mount Street Bridge, Northumberland Road and canal bank.[6]

The Volunteers under the command of Lieutenant Michael Malone from Company C, 3rd Battalion occupied seven separate positions spread along the canal. Like all of the other occupations around Dublin, the Volunteers met some indignation but little real resistance as the seized property. While the Volunteers would not hold these positions for very long, they could have proven a significant obstacle for the British had they chosen to heavily utilize this avenue of approach.

At the same time, other members of "B" Company under the command of Lieutenant John Quinn had seized Westland Row terminus and were doing their best to prevent the 12:15 train to Kingstown from departing.[7] Again, despite the fact that the Fenians were armed with rifles, most of the population that they encountered were far from intimidated by their presence and had no issues verbally confronting them. While the main party attempted to hold up the train at gunpoint, others in the company tore up the rail lines.

At 4:00 in the afternoon, the first shots in this sector were fired. Members of the local militia defense force (the Georgius Rex), who had been on maneuvers near Kingstown. Having heard word of the beginning of the Rebellion, they returned from their maneuvers and split into two groups. One reinforcing Trinity College and the other moving to the Beggars Bush barracks. While they carried no ammunition with them, the extra men and rifles – even if there was no ammunition for the Italian rifles – were a welcome addition to the defenders.[8]

Overnight, the Volunteers stationed in the Clanwilliam House took their own initiative to moved back to the main headquarters.[9] Abandoning this post had no immediate affect and the Rebels been able re-occupy the position before the British could exploit this. However,

---

[6] Paul O'Brien, *Blood on the Streets: 1916 and the Battle for Mount Street Bridge* (Dublin: New Island, 2012), p. 18.

[7]Max Caufield. *The Easter Rebellion* (New York, Holt, Rinehart and Winston, 1963), p. 79.

[8]Paul O'Brien, *Blood on the Streets: 1916 and the Battle for Mount Street Bridge* (Dublin: New Island, 2012), p. 23.

[9]Max Caufield. *The Easter Rebellion* (New York, Holt, Rinehart and Winston, 1963), p. 159

this clearly displays how lax the command over these outposts were and amateurish the Fenian volunteers were.

Chapter 30: St. Stephen's Green

The Irish Citizen Army under the command of Commandant Michael Mallin and the Countess Markievicz were charged with securing St. Stephan's Green. Michael Mallin was considered to be one of the most capable men in the Citizen Army and was one of the only ones with any real military experience, having served as a British soldier.[1] The most likely avenue of approach for British forces was from the Portobello Barracks towards the Green. The Fenian forces knew that they would need time to fortify the low-lying area, so they occupied several structures to serve as strong points and disrupt British movement. While Mallin was in charge, there is no doubt the flamboyantly dressed Countess was the spiritual leader despite the fact that the forces organized under her direct control consisted of only Boy Scouts and women who would serve in the aid station.[2] The Countess was also the first to draw blood, shooting Constable Michael Lahif when he tried to enter the Rebel position via the "Traitor's Gate".[3]

The Rebels seized the Green without any significant opposition. Expectant of encountering a British force, they had a woman, Margaret Skinnider, cycle ahead of their column as a scout.[4] To their surprise, she did not encounter any British troops besides one bored policeman. The Rebels marched with a determination up Grafton Street and seized the park before the British or the citizenry had any idea that a Rebellion was afoot.

The Green was not a very defensible position, but it was a vital intersection inside of Dublin. Ten different streets all interested there. A major blunder was the Mallin neglected to occupy the Shelbourne Hotel, a relatively high building that had fields of fire that covered nearly the entire park.[5] The ability to hold this terrain would significantly hinder British movement throughout the city and its recapture would be a critical priority for the British forces. Since the Green itself was mostly an open park, it provided very little in terms of cover and concealment.

[1] Michael Foy and Brian Barton, *The Easter Rising (*London: Sutton Publishing, 2004), p. 56.

[2] Max Caufield. *The Easter Rebellion* (New York, Holt, Rinehart and Winston, 1963), p. 87.

[3]Ibid, p. 88.

[4] Michael Foy and Brian Barton, *The Easter Rising (*London: Sutton Publishing, 2004), p. 56.

5 Ibid, p. 58.

So Mallin made the decision to occupy the nearby houses. Hence, this position closely resembled other Fenian positions: occupied buildings with knocked down internal walls supported by a series of outposts to create a defense in depth.

The Rebel positions did not fare well against the first British attack. Their hastily dug trenches and fortified positions were little match for the trained machine gun fire from the British troops who had occupied two buildings overlooking the Green – the Shelbourne Hotel and United Services Club - late on Monday night. The British took full advantage of the Rebel's relatively exposed position and fire power advantage, and instead of risking a frontal assault like the Lancers on Sackville Street who attached the GPO, they set up their weapons and attacked by fire instead.[6]

Commandant Mallin quickly realized that their position was untenable. By 6am on Tuesday morning he ordered his troops to retreat to the nearby position at the College of Surgeons. In the high-built urban environment that surrounded the Green trenches did not provide any cover from the British small arms and this failure to properly analyze their terrain and to anticipate British positions cost the Rebels the ability even put up a decent fight on a piece of key terrain.

---

[6]Max Caufield, *The Easter Rebellion* (New York: Holt, Rinehart, and Winston, 1963), pp. 122, 152, 154

Chapter 31: The General Post Office

The main body of the Fenian forces occupied the General Post Office (GPO), raised the flag of the new Republic and declared the new state. Padraig Pearse read out the Proclamation of the new Irish nation with James Connolly at his side under the portico. The response was underwhelming. The poet Stephen MacKenna recalled that there was no resemblance to the wild fervor that one expects from the people during an uprising. The crowd besides Nelson's Pillar met the words with a chilly shrug and went about their business.[1]

The Volunteers were on edge. Constant false alarms rang throughout the day. The Fenians were surprised by the malaise of the British response and the anticipation affected many of them. In fact, the first people to show up in response to the Rebellion were Separation Women (women whose husbands were serving in the British Army in France) who cajoled the Rebels and a group of Priests who appealed to their humanity to attempt to avert any bloodshed.[2] The inexperience of the Volunteers was also apparent. There was a constant stream of accidental shots going off throughout the building from Fenian rifles and shotguns.[3]

The Lancers under the command of Colonel Hammond arrived at the head of Sackville Street, beneath the monument honoring Parnell, and got their bearings on the situation before making any moves.[4] Their martial demeanor and rigid discipline were a stark contract to the ragtag Rebels who had fired more rounds by accident that morning than they had in anger.[5] The Lancers launched their assault just as a Rebel company from Rathfarnham dashed across Sackville Street. A cavalry charge against a defensive position with hardened fortifications in an urban is lunacy, but due to the inexperience of the Rebels, this assault only suffered three killed among the Lancers.[6]

The paved, relatively narrow street of Sackville Street was not ideal for the footing of charging horses. It's unknown whether this

[1]Max Caufield. *The Easter Rebellion* (New York, Holt, Rinehart and Winston, 1963), p. 95.
[2]Ibid, p. 96.
[3]Ibid, p.96
[4]Ibid p. 111.
[5]Ibid, p. 112.
[6]Ibid, p. 112.

charge was a meant as a demonstration to intimidate the Rebels into surrender or as an actual assault. There is no martial task that cavalry is more ill-suited for than assaulting a fortified position in an urban environment. While Colonel Hammond may have thought that the mere demonstration of the might of the Lancers may dislodge the Sinn Feiners, there is no reasonable outcome that would have resulted in success for his forces.

As the Lancers began their charge, the Irish prepared for battle. On the top floor, the O'Rahilly spread the word to hold their fire. Connolly gave the same order to the forces on the ground floor. By the time the Lancers approached Nelson's Pillar a member of the Fenians lost their nerve and fired the first shot. The Fenian plan was to let them come close enough to make up for the poor marksmanship of green revolutionaries. His comrades followed suit and a hail of bullets followed. Four Lancers fell from their saddles, three of them dead, and their troop turned and retreated. The only Fenain casualties came from friendly crossfire and an ill-trained Volunteer who accidentally shot himself in the stomach.[7]

Throughout the night, Fergus O'Kelly and other men who were stationed at the nearby wireless school attempted to control the narrative. The Fenians seized this critical installation in the initial attack on the GPO. At regular intervals, they sent out messages proclaiming that the Irish Republic had been declared and that all British assaults had been repulsed.[8] These messages were picked up and published by newspapers throughout Ireland and Britain. It is surprising that coupled with rumors of German landings and actions in outlying counties that such monumental news did not inspire more men did not muster and rise in areas outside of Dublin.

The most frustrating part of the day for the Rebels, besides the near constant accidental discharges of their rifles, was the lack of British action. Sackville street had far more looters on it than British soldiers.[9] This left the Rebels in a quandary. They knew that they needed the support of the people for eventual success and while they exhibited caution with the property they seized – minus the necessary destruction of in-

[7] Thomas Coffey, *Agony at Easter: The 1916 Irish Uprising* (London: George G. Harrap & Co, LTD, 1969), pp. 37-38.

[8] Max Caufield. *The Easter Rebellion* (New York, Holt, Rinehart and Winston, 1963), p. 158.

[9] Ibid, p. 166.

terior walls and erection of barricades to build their defensive positions – they were unsure of what to do with the looters.

General Lowe, the commander of British forces in Ireland, seemingly did not respond. While some of his subordinates launched attacks on their own initiative and other regular forces and auxiliaries secured critical positions such as Trinity College and the Port. But for the most part the British presence and response was unseen by both the civilians and the Rebels.

General Lowe had nearly a 5:1 advantage in manpower over the Fenians. He may have refrained from an immediate, overwhelming response in Dublin because of fears of a large uprising in the country or the need to hold a reserve to counter the threat of a German landing. This mirrors General French's response with the forces in England and shows a great amount of strategic patience. Lowe decided not to risk his forces in a series of frontal attacks, like the one that cost the Lancers so dearly in front of the GPO. Instead, he adapted to fighting in a British-owned urban environment and ordered a cordon around Dublin to isolate the city from reinforcements and to deny the Rebels the ability to break out and move into the countryside where they could more effectively execute a mobile guerilla war. He also ordered Colonel Portal of the Curragh Mobile Column to establish a line of fortified positions between key landmarks that the British occupied to ensure he was able to supply and support his forces. [10]

For their part, the Fenians were befuddled by Lowe's actions and did little to impede his movements.[11] As Lowe's noose slowly tightened, the Rebel positions became more and more isolated from one another. With communications severed and no enemy in sight, some of the commanders of the Rebel redoubts, such as Captain Cornelius "Con" Colbert in Watkin's Brewery, took it of their own initiative to consolidate to the main positions.[12] While many of the others held their positions, this unauthorized consolidation not only simplified the battlefield for the British, but showed the indiscipline and confusion in the Rebel ranks and eliminated a number of objectives that otherwise would have been seized by force.

---

[10]Ibid, p. 169.
[11]Ibid, p. 169.
[12]Ibid, p. 170.

Chapter 32: The of Battle Cork Hill

The Battle of Cork Hill was a small-scale fight that took place on the second day starting around 2pm. While most of General Lowe's forces were still consolidating blocking positions and communications posts throughout the city, a detachment of the 5th Royal Dublin Fusiliers under the command of Second Lieutenant F. O'Neill began their task of clearing the newspapers offices of the *Mail & Express* and the outfitters *Henry & James.*[1] This was the main Rebel position in the vicinity of City Hall. The attack began with sudden and withering fire from Dublin Castle. Many civilians were surprised by the attack and caught in the onslaught.

The British assaulted the Rebel position in five separate waves separated by about ten to twenty minutes each. With bayonets fixed and not suppressive fire, the first wave was quickly forced back by Rebel fire. Although the distance was no more than twenty yards from Dublin Castle to the Rebel position, the rifle fire was enough to stop the brash assault. The British adjusted, and the second wave had covering fire from the top of Dublin Castle. They were successfully able to gain a covered position outside of the Rebel defenses and prepared to breech. A more substantial British assault force attacked in the third wave. This wave also took advantage of the effective suppressing fire and made better use of the cover provided by the urban environment as they moved to join their comrades.[2] The fourth and fifth waves were progressively bigger and came with officers and stretcher bearers to tend to those wounded from the earlier assaults.

Following the breech, the fight became a room-to-room affair. As the Rebels ran short on ammunition, they resulted to fighting with the butts of their rifles.[3] Even in close and restrictive quarters, the mass of the British forces was simply overwhelming. At the price of twenty-two dead soldiers, the Fusiliers had fully seized the position and defeated and captured all Rebels just before three in the afternoon.[4] The capture of this position also completed the southern arm of General Lowe's cordon.

---

[1]Max Caufield. *The Easter Rebellion* (New York, Holt, Rinehart and Winston, 1963), p. 170.

[2]Ibid, p. 172.

[3]Ibid.

[4]Ibid.

Chapter 33: The Northern Suburbs

The Rebels had made no attempt to strongpoint in the northern suburbs of the city, being content to erect barricades along the North Circular Road and sabotage railways.[1] Part of the logic for this was Plunkett's desire to keep an escape route open towards Ulster if needed. The British in the north of the city had already secured the critical train depots at Amiens Street and North Wall terminal. The Rebels were met by a heavily armed British detachment traveling in an armored trail. The barricade erected on the North Circular Road received direct fire from an 18-pound gun that the British had quickly brought up from Athlone.[2] The Rebels were forced to fall back.

At three o'clock the men at the GPO heard a boom coming from the north. James Connolly, ever the Marxist, was staunch in his belief that the capitalist British would never use artillery in Ireland. "No capitalist government will use artillery and destroy the property of its own capitalist class."[3] The sound of an 18-pound artillery piece quickly destroyed the barricades in the Phibsborough-North Circular Road area in the northern suburbs of Dublin. This eliminated the primary planned escape route for the Fenains. The shrapnel from this gun quickly forced the rebels in the in Phibsborough-North Circular Road and Cabra Road railway bridge to retreat towards the Post Office. Many of them were taken prisoner, but a few made it to the Post Office.[4]

At the second position along the Cabra Road there were nearly thirty Fenians under the command of Joseph Canny. Braced for a bayonet attack – they could see the glimmering light flickering off the fixed bayonets of the British forces – they were instead met by rifle fire. They responded with their own fire and, for a moment, thought they had successfully repulsed the attack only to hear the boom of the 18-pounder. Within minutes their position was destroyed. The Rebels retreated, some killed, some captured and few making their way back to the G.P.O. With this defeat, Lowe's northern arm of the cordon was complete, and the Rebels in Dublin were isolated from the rest of Ireland and trapped in

---

[1] Max Caufield. *The Easter Rebellion* (New York, Holt, Rinehart and Winston, 1963), p. 173.

[2] Ibid, p. 174.

[3] Thomas Coffey, *Agony at Easter: The 1916 Irish Uprising* (London: George G. Harrap & Co, LTD, 1969), p. 102.

[4] Ibid, p. 107.

Lowe's slowly constricting cordon.[5]

The end of the Tuesday found the Rebels in little more than a state of delusion. Unbeknownst to them, General Lowe had completely encircled their position, cutting them off from outside help and from any avenue of escape. British reinforcements had also begun swiftly arriving in the city bringing with them not only a significant increase in manpower, but firepower that the Fenians could never match. The Rebel positions were consolidating either due nerves and indiscipline or due to tactical decisions to consolidate to more defensible locations. While these amateurs could hang their hat on a few fierce skirmishes, the Fenian lines had not held when the British tested them in force.

More important to the strategic position, the citizenry of Dublin had not mustered to their cause. There are no reports of men and women taking to support the barricade or rising to join their brothers in the fight. In fact, there are few if any remembrances of men who stayed home on Easter Sunday joining their comrades on Monday or Tuesday once the confusion over the countermanding order had cleared. The Rebels kept up their spirits with the ignorance of the British plan and rumors. In the trenches and barricaded houses that made up the de facto new Republic rumors of German landings, a countryside in flames and even Big Jim Larkin landing from America with an army of 50,000 made their rounds. This scuttlebutt came from the highest levels as well. Pearse said that the nation had risen in his Tuesday address and that the Rebels had been thus far victorious in near constant fighting.[6]

Wednesday morning saw the Rebel fortunes turn for the worse. A British gunboat name the *Helga* arrived on the River Liffey.[7] While the big guns and machine guns from the ship missed more often than they found their target, the arrival of the ship sunk Rebel morale. Despite the Connolly's belief that "when the British government uses artillery in the city of Dublin, it shows they must be in a hurry to finish the job – but there are probably some forces coming to help us" the Rebels were now fully isolated and on their own.[8]

Lowe was content. Having the Rebels encircled and no uprising in the countryside or mass movement in the city, he knew time was on

[5]Max Caufield. *The Easter Rebellion* (New York, Holt, Rinehart and Winston, 1963), p. 175.

[6]Ibid, p. 186.

[7]Ibid, p. 194.

[8]Ibid, p. 196.

his side. Further, with the departure of the entirety of the 59th Division, he would soon have an astounding numerical advantage. His plan was to continue to envelop and isolate the Rebel positions from each other, using his troops to make an increasing number of cordons and *the Helga* to weaken the strongest Rebel outposts.[9] Liberty Hall, although unoccupied, became the *Helga's* primary target since its location was critical to establishing one of the inner cordons.

9Ibid, p. 197.

Left - Michael Joseph O'Rahilly
Right - Eamon Ceannt

Top - Boland Bakery
Bottom - Marlborough Barracks

Left - Ivor Price
Right - Sean Heuston

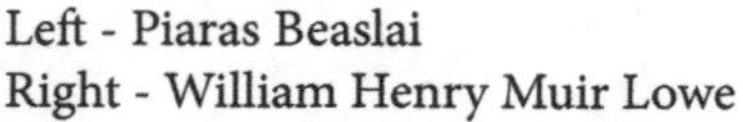

Left - Piaras Beaslai
Right - William Henry Muir Lowe

Jacob's Biscuit Factory

St Stephen Green Park - 1899

Left - Royal Hospital Kilmainhan
Right - Trinity College

HMS Helga

Section 2: The Counterattack

Chapter 34: Tuesday - The British Respond

The British did not mount an organized response until Tuesday morning. The shock and confusion of such a large scale and organized assault, the immediate need to secure Dublin Castle and its key personnel and the dispersion of British forces around Dublin made an immediate organized response impossible. The British can be forgiven for this. Volunteer marches and demonstrations were commonplace and such a large failure of the intelligence apparatus came as surprise to nearly everyone.

The Fenians did not have long to prepare their positions for the British counterattack. Early on Tuesday morning Brigadier General Lowe assumed command of all British forces in Dublin and arrived at the Kingsbridge station at the head of the 25th (Irish) Reserve Infantry Brigade.[1] His first action was a movement from the station south via Dublin Castle to Trinity College. Whether intended as a movement to contact or not, this movement was wholly unopposed. While the Rebels had planned to interdict the likely avenues of approach against their positions, they did not think to attempt to isolate key British positions. This was endemic of their 19th Century Revolutionary blurring of tactic and strategy to seize symbolic key terrain, throw up the barricades and fight a glorious defensive fight that inspires the people to rise. It also showed that their amateurish optimism would be in for a rude awakening once met with a modern military force.

General Lowe's patience and restraint was the pivotal decision of the battle in Dublin. Instead of throwing his forces rashly and headlong against the Fenian defenses like the Lancers had at the GPO, he secured the city and made the Fenian defeat all but a matter of time. Not only did this ensure a victory, but it also minimized collateral damage and conserved the lives of British soldiers needed on the Western Front. Long term, this maneuver also ensured that the Fenian forces would not be able to escape into the countryside and thus prevented a prolonged guerilla conflict. Had Maxwell followed this restrained path, the Rebellion could have stayed an isolated incident instead of evolving into a civil war.

---

[1]Joseph McKenna, *Voices from the Easter Rising: Firsthand Accounts of Ireland's 1916 Rebellion* (Jefferson: McFarland & Company, Inc., Publishers., 2017), p. 136.

By two o'clock in the afternoon on Tuesday, the first phase of Lowe's plan was in place.[2] The most important British infrastructure was secured, internal lines of communication were established and the two main Rebel positions – St. Stephen's Green and the General Post Office – were isolated from one another. While little of the fighting had taken place, the battle was already won. The decisive point for the British forces was isolation. The Rebels could not maneuver, the populace of Dublin and the rest of Ireland had elected to stay neutral and there were no lines of retreat. Had they taken no further action, they could have simply sat and starved out the Rebels at this point.

At midnight on Monday a small, thirty man contingent of previously uncommitted Fenian forces from the Hibernian Rifles was ordered first to the GPO, then at six in the morning it was sent to seize and secure City Hall. However, by early Tuesday morning, City Hall was back in British hands.[3] With a more advanced understanding of guerilla tactics, the Fenians could have left this force behind as small, mobile pockets harassing the British forces and forcing them into heavy-handed action that would sway public opinion and/or prevent them from massing against the Fenian strong points.

The events at the General Post Office were deflating. Small streams of reinforcements trickled into the post. Most were diverted to other redoubts like Kelly's Fort or sent to reinforce the Rebel position at City Hall, which had already retreated. A telegraph operator posing as a British headquarters intercepted a message that indicated that the rest of the country had not risen. This was kept secret from the rest of the men by Pearse and Connolly who kept up an optimistic disposition despite this fatal news.[4]

The anticipated assault never materialized. Instead, there was merely some minor sniping and skirmishing. Several Fenian outposts sensed the tightening noose and retreated to the main positions as the British continued their encirclement of Dublin. By this point, the Fenians at the main headquarters had a well-developed understanding of the British movements and position from reports from their outposts, telegraph intercepts and the work of the *Cumann na mBan*. It is important to note that this information was wholly unavailable to the other positions like St. Stephen's Green and the Four Courts since communications

[2] Ibid.

[3] Ibid, pp. 136-137.

[4] Ibid, p. 141.

were nearly non-existent between their positions. Despite their ignorance to the failure of the plan for all of Ireland to materialize and the optimistic 'news' from their leaders, the rank and file at the GPO were generally frustrated and disappointed at the lack of a British assault.

At the Four Courts, the Fenains were not left wanting for action. This was one of the first organized British counterattacks. After having reinforced Dublin Castle, the British launched a fierce bayonet assault supported by machine guns. Volunteer Dick Balfe remembered: "On Tuesday one of the famous British bayonet charges came down from the Royal Barracks with all regimental flags, fixed bayonets and swords. We used the same tactics we had on Monday, concentrating on the rear first and then the head of the column."[5] This halted the attack at the bridge and the fighting settled into stalemate and sniping. There was some similar skirmishing and sniping at the other outposts, but for now the British were content with probing attacks and conducting reconnaissance by fire.

At Boland's Mill the fighting was also sporadic. The men under de Valera kept busy by fortifying their positions and expanding their outposts. The most action they saw was a small skirmish near the Beggars Bush Barracks with some men of the Royal Irish Rifles.[6] By Tuesday morning, most of the outpost positions had consolidated back with the forces at Boland's Bakery due to both a realization of the indefensibility of the positions and a lack of supplies and communication. This was another amateurish mistake. Whenever outposts, big or small, became untenable the Fenian fighters would retreat to a larger Fenian position. The British had significant advantages in mass, firepower and logistics. Concentrating only made larger, easier targets for the British to concentrate on and added additional constraints to the Fenian supplies. Had these forces dispersed and spread outwards instead of inwards they could have greatly prolonged the conflict and become the core of the guerrilla forces that would become famous in the IRA.

Jacob's factory saw one of the most aggressive British attacks. A diversionary attack was launched by about a squad sized element of British soldiers on MacDonagh's two new outposts at Delahunt's pub and Byrne's store. This allowed a larger British force to move unimpeded down Charlotte Street, surround the two buildings and assault them.

---

[5] Ibid, pp. 144-145.
[6] Ibid, p. 148.

This forced both outposts to retreat to the Factory.[7] There was also a probing attack launched by the Fenians at Jacob's Factory against the British forces which accomplished little besides the death of one of the Fenians.[8] This attack was a needless expenditure of Fenian life, whereas one or two snipers could have practically halted or significantly hindered the British advance.

The South Dublin Union again saw, brief and ultimately inconsequential, skirmishing. The British launched small probing raids and sniper actions throughout the day, but never a full assault. Several of the Fenian outposts were abandoned in anticipation of a large assault that night. However, there was to be no assault.[9] General Lowe's headquarters pulled the Royal Irish Regiment back to the Kingsbridge Railway Station to await further orders. The official Regimental history clearly recalls that this was an unpopular order: "The battalion, under orders from headquarters, remained in occupation of the Union for the night (Monday) and on the following morning, for some extraordinary reason, it was directed to evacuate the Union and concentrate at Kingsbridge Station. This was done under protest."[10]

The fiercest fighting of the day was at St. Stephen's Green. A British force of about one hundred men and four machine guns were positioned on the upper windows of the Shelbourne Hotels.[11] The trenches dug by the Irish Citizens Army provided little protection from the plunging fire raining in on them from the upper levels. The British were careless in their target selection, openly shooting a tent designated with the international symbol for the Red Cross.[12]

Commandant Mallin ordered a withdrawal from the Green to the more protected College of Surgeons' building.[13] A detachment was ordered to provide covering fire from Little's Public House since the ICA members would have to move directly through the kill zone in order to evacuate. Once in the College, the ICA began to fortify this position to defend against a British assault. The British quickly realized where the

[7] Ibid, pp. 151-152.

[8] Ibid, p. 151.

[9] Ibid, p.151

[10] Stannus Geoghegan, *The Campaigns and History of the Royal Irish Regiment*, Vol. 2, *from 1900 to 1922.*

[11] Joseph McKenna, *Voices from the Easter Rising: Firsthand Accounts of Ireland's 1916 Rebellion* (Jefferson: McFarland & Company, Inc., Publishers., 2017), p. 156.

[12] Ibid, p. 157.

[13] Ibid, p. 158.

Rebels had withdrawn to and shifted their fires accordingly. By the end of the day Mallin and his men were struggling to occupy supporting building and to reinforce their positions. The British had them pinned and Mallin realized that his force was also cut off from a retreat to the main position at the General Post Office.

The Fenian's immediately surrendered any possibility of maneuver from the onset of hostilities. With improvised defenses, a lack of supplies, a lack of heavy weapons and a severe difference in manpower they condemned themselves to defeat from the start. Whether the leaders and planners knew or accepted this as a fact before the beginning of the conflict or held out far-flung hopes for German assistance or an island-wide rising can never be known, but the template for mobile, guerrilla war would have been known from the Boer War and could have been effectively emulated.

Chapter 35: Wednesday – The British Cordon

By Wednesday morning, the British forces had fully contained the Rebel forces and were beginning their offensive operations. Containment was the decisive point. There was no Fenian relief army marching towards Dublin, no supplies to sustain the Rebels through a siege, and no possibility of a breakthrough. The Rebels isolated from retreat and without any additional showing of popular support would either be defeated in short order by fire or starved into submission.

Fighting at the GPO began to intensify. The British intensified their sniping and usage of machine guns, but wisely chose not to launch any assaults. At the Four Courts the British launched some probing assaults, but their most effective tactic was the employment of an 18-pounder field gun to the corner of Exchange Street and Wood Quay which forced the defenders to withdraw from the southwest corner.[1]

There was already a British brigade in Dublin and another two were to land shortly from Britain. Further at eight in the morning, the gunboat *Helga* and the *Sealark*, its escort, began sailing upriver.[2] It commenced its bombardment of Liberty Hall, even though it was unoccupied. The Fenians again missed an opportunity. In the narrow channel of the river, a small number of sharpshooters could have limited the effectiveness of the gunboat and goaded it into increasing collateral damage. This could have helped divert or limit the effects of its guns and prove the ruthlessness of the British forces.

The Fenian position at the *Mendicity* was under the command of Sean Heuston, the youngest Commandant in the Rebel forces. The position was originally intended only as a temporary position to harass the British forces moving from the Richmond and Royal Barracks towards Daly's position at the Four Courts.[3] By Wednesday, Heuston and his forces were still holding the *Mendicity* and were by this time completely surrounded. The Rebels were running short on both food and ammuni-

---

[1]Joseph McKenna, *Voices from the Easter Rising: Firsthand Accounts of Ireland's 1916 Rebellion* (Jefferson: McFarland & Company, Inc., Publishers., 2017), pp. 167-168.

[2] Ibid, p. 161.

[3] Max Caufield. *The Easter Rebellion* (New York, Holt, Rinehart and Winston, 1963), p. 201.

tion, so Heuston sent two men off to the GPO for supplies.[4] At noon, the British launched a fierce assault supported by sniper fire. After crawling along the quay wall, the British threw grenades into the *Mendicity* and entered the building. The whole assault was brief, just fifteen minutes, and the remaining Rebels were all captured or killed.[5]

While Heuston's stand is romanticized, it was a foolish mistake. He chose to stay in a difficult to defend position without adequate supplies. He also abandoned the intent of his orders. The *Mendicity* was a logical harassing position that could have effectively disrupted British movements but was not a viable blocking position. Taking advantage of space, this small force could have harassed the British over a much larger geographical area and greatly limited the amount of mass the cautious British could afford to move on the Four Courts.

At around noon, Daly launched an assault against the Linenhall Barracks. A party under the command of Captain Denis O'Callaghan maneuvered to the front gates and demanded the surrender of a small British garrison. When they refused, O'Callaghan's men used homemade canister bombs in an unsuccessful attempt to breach the gate. While the charges failed to open the gate, the noise they created was enough to make the British forces think twice and they surrendered.[6] They were marched, along with thirty-two unarmed men and a policeman to the Father Matthew Hall. The Fenians, lacking in manpower, smartly chose not to occupy this position. This was one of the most successful and bloodless raids by either side during the whole of the conflict.[7] While the Fenians most likely could not have launched more raids like this, it was an effective offensive operation that they could have better exploited as a propaganda coup.

At the two in the afternoon, direct fire commenced on the General Post Office from multiple positions. The British had managed to manhandle several heavy machine guns and two light, 9-pound artillery pieces into positions without being detected by the nearby Rebels. An insurgent force should always have the intelligence advantage, but by concentrating into larger and larger positions the Fenians surrendered

---

[4] Joseph McKenna, *Voices from the Easter Rising: Firsthand Accounts of Ireland's 1916 Rebellion* (Jefferson: McFarland & Company, Inc., Publishers., 2017), p. 168.

[5] Ibid, p. 169.

[6] Paul O'Brien, *Crossfire: The Battle of the Four Courts, 1916* (Dublin: New Island, 2012), p. 42.

[7]Ibid, p. 42.

their ability to conduct reconnaissance and have enough mobility to avoid concentrated firepower. They had the two 9-pounders located at Trinity College and machine guns were located on the top of the Fire Station, the roof of the Custom House, the Tivoli Theater and on Purcell's corner.[8] The British opened fire simultaneously to the shock of both Rebel and bystander.

The Fenians in the GPO were mostly pinned down and helpless. The British were disciplined enough to make effective use of the cover provided by the city, so there were few opportunities for the Rebels to return fire. The range of both the artillery and the Lewis and Vickers machine guns were beyond the reach of Rebel rifles. There were a few opportunities to pick off a British soldier in khaki briefly darting in the open. On the rooftop, most of the Rebels took confession from Father John Flanagan. The senior Cumann na mBan women made a mad dash across Sackville Street to gather additional medical supplies.[9] For the most part, the Rebels were fixed by the British direct fire as their forces completed their envelopment of the GPO.

To make matters worse, the British improvised an armored car capable of carrying eighteen soldiers using two of the boilers from the Guinness Brewery and the Inchicore Railway Works.[10] Whether by mechanical failure or a lucky shot through the drivers slit by Volunteer Joseph Sweeny, the armored car was immobilized and spent the rest of the afternoon stalled in front of the Gresham Hotel.[11] The armored car did little damage, but it was another psychological assault on the hungry and tired Rebels. Not to mention and tremendous target to force them to waste their scarce ammunition. Despite all of this, the Fenian leaders, primarily Clarke and Connolly, remained cheerful. No one knows if this was joy and their belief that every brick destroyed further their cause, or they had begun to believe their own lies and had become delusional.

The British did develop a tactic where they loaded a team of soldiers armed with crowbars and other breaching tools into the back of the car, drove as close to the target as possible, use the armored car to provide cover while they breached and entered the building to secure a foothold. Once the foothold was secured, the car would pick up the

---

[8] Max Caufield. *The Easter Rebellion* (New York, Holt, Rinehart and Winston, 1963), p. 216.

[9] Ibid, pp. 220-223.

[10] Ibid, p. 223.

[11] Ibid.

next team.[12] While this had little effect on the actual battle in Dublin, it proved to be an effective technique and one that would see further development and adoption in future wars.

The adoption of these improvised tactics by the British shows what could have been. Lowe and the British government were wary of wasting soldiers that were needed to fight on the Western Front. A greater application of harassing fire and the use of snipers would have seriously hindered British mobility. The difference between the headlong charge of the Lancers on the first day and the improvisation of armored cars shows how effective even minimal harassment could have been against this force.

At Boland's Bakery, the Rebels under Eamon De Valera were preparing for a major attack. A small contingent of seventeen Fenians under the command of Captain Mick Malone held their positions on Mount Street and Northumberland Road. So far, their only action had been an ambush that left four members of the "Gorgeous Wrecks" – the jeering nickname for the mainly elderly British volunteer reserves – dead.[13] Despite the alternative avenues of approach, General Lowe ordered that the bridge should be taken at all costs.[14] While the rank and file of the rookie 59th Division may have been surprised when they landed in Ireland, the citizenry of Dublin's suburbs greeted them warmly, even offering them tea as they assembled near the Royal Agricultural Grounds.[15]

The newly arrived Sherwood Foresters launched a headlong assault at the Rebel position to heavy losses, who were fresh off the boat from England and, for some, had received their first training on the pier

---

[12] Michael Foy and Brian Barton, *The Easter Rising (*London: Sutton Publishing, 2004), p. 170.

[13]John Dorney. "Today in Irish History, April 26, 1916, The battle at Mount Street Bridge", April 2011[The Irish Story] Available from < http://www.theirishstory.com/2011/04/26/today-in-irish-history-april-26-1916-the-battle-at-mount-street-bridge/#.W48qYuhKjIV>; accessed 4 September 2018.

[14] John Dorney. "Today in Irish History, April 26, 1916, The battle at Mount Street Bridge", April 2011[The Irish Story] Available from < http://www.theirishstory.com/2011/04/26/today-in-irish-history-april-26-1916-the-battle-at-mount-street-bridge/#.W48qYuhKjIV>; accessed 4 September 2018.

[15]Paul O'Brien, *Crossfire: The Battle of the Four Courts, 1916* (Dublin: New Island, 2012), p. 41

at Kingstown.[16] Malone and his men at the Clanwilliam House put up a stiff resistance. Firing so quickly that many of their rifles began to overheat, dozens of British soldiers were killed or wounded in the attack.[17] The green British forces failed to conduct a reconnaissance of the Rebel positions. They identified the schoolhouse as their primary objective while failing to understand where the Rebel forces were concentrated or even identify the Clanwilliam House as a position until after the attack had begun.[18] A cease fire that allowed the British to reposition their forces and effective direct machine gun fire severely weakened the Clanwilliam House.[19]

On Wednesday afternoon, Brigadier General Maconchy made General Lowe aware of the heavy losses and informed his superior that it would take the remainder of the 2/7th Battalion as well as the 2/8th Battalion to take the bridge and surrounding buildings.[20] Citing the high commitment of forces and already high casualties, he asked if the situation required taking the bridge at all costs. Lowe ordered that it did.[21] Lowe surely had to be feeling the pressure to quickly resolve the Rebellion and knew the tolerance for his tactic of a slow and methodically tightening noose was losing patience.

On Wednesday the small band of Sinn Feiners under de Velera and Malone's commands inflicted heavy losses, but by Thursday of these positions would fall. Had de Velera reinforced and attacked, his large force could have inflicted a tremendous loss of the rookie troops. This would have been a tremendous coup and would have certainly altered General Lowe's plans and possibly even changed the perception of the Rebellion while there was still time.

De Valera knew that his position was untenable and planned and prepared for several offensive operations but failed to execute on any of them. Most of these plans were the desperate attempts of a military ama-

---

[16]John Dorney. "Today in Irish History, April 26, 1916, The battle at Mount Street Bridge", April 2011[The Irish Story] Available from < http://www.theirishstory.com/2011/04/26/today-in-irish-history-april-26-1916-the-battle-at-mount-street-bridge/#.W48qYuhKjIV>; accessed 4 September 2018.

[17] Paul O'Brien, *Blood on the Streets: 1916 and the Battle for Mount Street Bridge* (Dublin: New Island, 2012), p. 50.

[18] Ibid, p. 56.

[19] Ibid, p. 58.

[20] Ibid, p. 60.

[21]W. Cope Oates, *The Sherwood Foresters in the Great War, 1914-191 The 2/8th Battalion* (London: Naval and Military Press, 2015).

teur who fully realized the precariousness of his position. After realizing that the position at St. Stephen's Green was in dire straits, he planned a relief operation that was canceled once it was learnt that the Irish Citizen Army had abandoned the Green.[22] This plan got so far that the men selected for the mission were mustered and had pre-mission checks performed personally by de Valera in which he instructed them to leave their knapsacks for the sake of mobility.[23] Other canceled actions by de Valera's Battalion included a seizure of the key buildings surrounding his position like the Oriel House and the railway station at Kingstown.[24]

Fighting was also ramping up at the Four Courts. Early in the morning, an isolated Fenian position outside of the Mendicity Institute as the about 200-300 British soldiers prepared for an assault. The Fenian outpost had only about twenty-six Volunteers while and were not only helpless to interdict, but also helpless to move to a safer location.[25] Most of the action was a sniping duel between the men under Daly's command and the Fusiliers and from across the Liffey. The Fenians also had to deal with machine gun fire from the roof the roof of the Jervis Street Hospital.[26] Daly made the decision to burn down the Linenhall Barracks since he lacked the forces to hold it and needed to deny it as a position that the British could use.[27] At the end of the day, de Valera could not reconcile his plans to the low turnout of Volunteers. At a minimum de Valera planned to have 500 men and believed that it would require 800-1,000 to withstand the British counterattacks. With only 173 Volunteers fighting for him during Easter Week, fighting his own plan became more challenging than fighting the British counterattacks.[28]

Wednesday ended with General Lowe declaring by communique: "There is now a complete cordon of troops round the centre of town

---

[22] Michael Foy and Brian Barton, *The Easter Rising (*London: Sutton Publishing, 2004), p. 77.
[23] Ibid, p. 77.
[24] Ibid, p. 74.
[25] Paul O'Brien, Crossfire: The Battle of the Four Courts, 1916 (Dublin: New Island, 2012), pp. 37-38.
[26] Max Caufield. *The Easter Rebellion* (New York, Holt, Rinehart and Winston, 1963), p. 226.
[27] Ibid, p. 227.
[28] Michael Foy and Brian Barton, *The Easter Rising (*London: Sutton Publishing, 2004), p. 73.

on the north side of the river."[29] This greatly understated the actions that he and his troops had taken. The Rebels had lost several key positions, all remaining positions were isolated, threats German actions had not materialized, the countryside was quiet and everywhere the British were in direct contact with Rebel forces and delivering direct fire onto their positions. Further the Rebels were lacking food, ammunition and reinforcements. The city had not risen to the proclamation of the new republic and there was no additional aid coming to their position. By the end of Wednesday, Lowe's forces have reached the decisive point and it was just a matter of time before the battle would be over.

In the General Post Office, the reality was beginning to set in for the Fenians. Several positions had been overrun and other abandoned and their survivors retreated to the General Post Office. It was now obvious to the common rebels that support – both foreign and from their fellow country – was not coming. Defeat was inevitable and escape was impossible.

The Irish leaders, having scarcely slept since Monday, were once again woken up to the news that the British were using the rooftops on Henry Street to maneuver on the GPO.[30] Morale was quickly waning inside the GPO. Connolly, desperate to do something to change the narrative, started singing "The Soldier's Song", which by this time had become the unofficial anthem of the Irish Republic.[31] While eventually a few voices joined him, it was an awkward attempt to revive morale. Pearse stood watching the scene stone-faced and somber and reassured himself and Desmond Ryan, a former pupil of his from St. Enda's College, that: "When we are wiped out, people will condemn us and blame us for everything. But in a few years, they will see the meaning of what we tried to do."[32]

While there was some optimism among the leadership - especially Connolly – and in the ranks, most had begun to make the realization that defeat was imminent. While the Fenian leaders did their best to keep their spirits high and pass on positive reports, there is only so long that optimistic reports can maintain morale in the face of overwhelm-

---

[29] Max Caufield. *The Easter Rebellion* (New York, Holt, Rinehart and Winston, 1963), p. 231.

[30] Thomas Coffey, *Agony at Easter: The 1916 Irish Uprising* (London: George G. Harrap & Co, LTD, 1969), p. 152.

[31] Ibid, p. 153.

[32] Ibid, p. 154.

ing firepower. Many of the Rebels felt content that they had already achieved more than they had hoped for. The Countess even exclaiming late Wednesday evening: "Think of it! We've already done more than Wolfe Tone."[33] This even though troops under her joint command at St. Stephen's Green were literally fainting due to lack of food. Some young Rebels, who were still teenagers, having eaten nothing but jam or biscuits since they mustered on Monday.[34]

Despite General Lowe's success and the fact that the situation in Ireland was under control, Lord Kitchener informed Lord French that the government desired to have a more senior general office running things in Ireland.[35] The decision to bring a more senior office into command and unify the civilian and military roles was wise. The choice of the man to lead it was not. While Maxwell was more than qualified, had an impeccable pedigree and had recently performed well in his most recent post in Egypt he would receive the primary blame for turning General Lowe's effective campaign against the Sinn Fein Rebels into an utter disaster.

[33]Max Caufield. *The Easter Rebellion* (New York, Holt, Rinehart and Winston, 1963), p. 257.
[34] Ibid, pp. 256-257.
[35]Ibid, p. 259.

Chapter 36: Thursday – The British Counterattack

With each passing day, the Fenian position became worse and worse. By Thursday morning, all of the northern avenues of approach into (and out of) the city were sealed with British troops advancing from the north against the Four Courts and to strengthen the isolation of the GPO.[1] The arrival of the 2/6th South Staffords, hard-nosed men from the worst slums in England, further tipped the balance in the British favor. At 4am, British forces from both the 2/5th and 26th Sherwood Foresters took fire from Daly's 1st Battalion and suffered many casualties while moving towards Dublin Castle. The assault on the unoccupied and undefended Liberty Hall began again and ended with the Ulster troops launching a gallant yet useless bayonet assault.[2]

De Valera's position at Boland's Bakery was under heavy bombardment and on the verge of collapse. In one of the more brilliant ruses of the battle, he had his men under the command of Captain Michael Cullen raise the Green Flag up on an unused tower. This caused the British to assume the Sinn Feiners has moved positions and shift their targeting. It almost caused a British friendly fire incident when the shells nearly hit the *Helga* as well.[3] This greatly relieved the pressure and was a much-needed morale boost in the Irish ranks. A dispersion of skirmishers and snipers throughout his area of operations could greatly enhanced the effects of these success and provided a great deal of additional relief to the Rebels.

The British had no need to rush into an attack. Despite the Fenian wishes for a major clash, General Lowe was content to shell and slowly tighten his noose. He may not have known how dire the Rebel supply situation was, but his decision saved countless lives from a needless slaughter in the siege. Keeping containment as his priority was the right decision and the Fenian strategy effectively eliminated the most dangerous course of action from ever becoming a reality.

---

[1] Joseph McKenna, *Voices from the Easter Rising: Firsthand Accounts of Ireland's 1916 Rebellion* (Jefferson: McFarland & Company, Inc., Publishers., 2017), p. 195.
[2] Ibid, p. 195.
[3]Max Caufield. *The Easter Rebellion* (New York, Holt, Rinehart and Winston, 1963), p. 277.

Fighting was not going much better at the South Dublin Union where the 2/7th and 2/8th Sherwood Foresters engaged the Fenian positions in the late afternoon.[4] The Nurses' Home was occupied by exactly twenty-seven Rebels and their officers with an additional sixteen in the building fronting James Street. Accidental discharges by Fenians at the Jameson's Distillery spooked the Royal Engineers' horses and triggered a fierce British assault.[5] The British force under the command of Captain Oates began overwhelming covering fire. This allowed a relatively small contingent of British forces to seize the bakehouse.

While Fenian recollections of the battle strongly state that there was no panic in the Rebel ranks, Commandant Kent decided the position was untenable and began to order a withdrawal.[6] There were strong disagreements between Cosgrave, Joyce and Kent as to how much ground the British had seized and where the Rebels should make their stand. By nighttime, the position was abandoned and the men under Kent's command were making their way back to the Royal Hospital via the Rialto Bridge.

Meanwhile at the GPO, the British were still slow to attack and quick to shell. The Rebels tried to occupy themselves as best they could. Connolly dispersed his men into further blocking positions and ordered improvements in the barricades.[7] Others spread rumors of a column from Wexford marching on Dublin. Another popular rumor was that since the Rebels had held out for three days Ireland was now a fully recognized nation and due the right of a seat at the negotiating table when the Great War ended.[8] Mostly, the Rebels fought fires as the British shells had ignited and leveled most of Sackville Street. More than anything at this point, the resource-starved and isolated Rebels wanted an honest shot at attacking British khaki. They would still have to wait.

The British finally launched their attack in the early afternoon. Fighting quickly grew so intense that the Rebels had to replace over-

---

[4] Joseph McKenna, Voices from the Easter Rising: Firsthand Accounts of Ireland's 1916 Rebellion (Jefferson: McFarland & Company, Inc., Publishers., 2017), p. 195.

[5] Max Caufield. *The Easter Rebellion* (New York, Holt, Rinehart and Winston, 1963), p. 280.

[6] Ibid, p. 282.

[7] Joseph McKenna, *Voices from the Easter Rising: Firsthand Accounts of Ireland's 1916 Rebellion* (Jefferson: McFarland & Company, Inc., Publishers., 2017), p. 196.

[8]Max Caufield. *The Easter Rebellion* (New York, Holt, Rinehart and Winston, 1963), pp. 294-298.

heated rifles.[9] While the intensity of the Rebel fire was high, its accuracy left much to be desired. While Several advances were beaten back, it was still becoming apparent that the Fenians could only reasonably hold out for so long in the face of such overwhelming force. The Rebels were quickly wasting their limited supply of ammunition. Even with their limited intelligence the British would have been able to assume that the Fenians would not have large stockpiles of ammunition. Goading Rebels into wasting the ammunition supply may not have been a conscious tactic, but it was certainly effective.

Connolly personally exposed himself to direct fire, moving through the Rebel held positions and doing the best he could to redistribute men to alternate fighting positions and reinforce other positions. He was shot in the left leg, the bullet shattering the bone, and dragged back to the headquarters to be treated and given morphine.[10] This removed the most effective tactical leader the Rebels had at the GPO from the fight and was another needless and useless sacrifice of Fenian combat effectiveness in vainglory.

Friday

Friday morning saw the arrival of General Maxwell and a change in the tone of the British response in Dublin. General Maxwell and his staff arrived at the River Liffey at two o'clock in the morning to a city in flames. Still vocally bitter over of his removal from command in Egypt after having checked the Turkish advance and feeling as if he was unjustly receiving a share of the blame for the Gallipoli campaign, Maxwell had spent the past six months idly stewing in his own resentment while war subsumed all of Britain.[11]

Upon assuming his post in Dublin, he issued the following proclamation: "The most vigorous measures will be taken by me to stop the loss of life and damage to property which certain misguided persons are causing by their armed resistance to the law. If necessary, I shall not hesitate to destroy all buildings within any area occupied by the rebels and I warn all persons within the area specified below, and now surrounded

---

[9] Joseph McKenna, *Voices from the Easter Rising: Firsthand Accounts of Ireland's 1916 Rebellion* (Jefferson: McFarland & Company, Inc., Publishers., 2017), p. 197.
[10] Ibid.
[11]Max Caufield. *The Easter Rebellion* (New York, Holt, Rinehart and Winston, 1963), pp. 302-303.

by H.M. troops, forthwith to leave such area under the following conditions: women and children may leave the area by any of the examining posts set up for the purpose and will be allowed to go away free. Men may leave by the same examining posts and will be allowed to go away free provided the examining officer is satisfied they have taken no part whatever in the present disturbances. All other men who present themselves at the examining post must surrender themselves unconditionally together with any arms and ammunition in their possession."[12]

The assumption of command by General Maxwell did more harm than good to the British efforts. While it is understandable the British would want a more senior commander on site, it was a mistake to force a change of tactical command from someone who was already successfully countering the Rebellion. General Lowe already had the tactical situation well under control before Maxwell landed. An island-wide rising had not materialized, Rebel forces in Dublin were contained, a British headquarters was established and functioning and forces, including reinforcements, were arriving and being efficiently maneuvered into position. The plan to retake Dublin was simple and effective. First the British would continue to contain the rebel positions. Next, the British were to complete the isolation of the separate Irish commands from each other in order to limit communication and to be able to more easily defeat them in sequence. This too would be accomplished prior to Maxwell's arrival. Third, the British would leverage their direct fire superiority and indirect fire monopoly. The combination of machine gun, sniper and artillery fire would either force surrender without an assault or soften the Rebel positions in the preparation for an assault. This was in progress as Maxwell assumed command. Finally, the British would have to use their overwhelming manpower advantage to close with and destroy the Rebel positions in close combat. Both generals knew that most of their troops were untested so this action would result in a significant number of casualties on both sides.

Lowe had assigned the forces at his disposal with reasonable objectives. The 177th Brigade would be split with the 2/5th and 2/6th South Staffordshire regiments attacking Daly's position at the Four Courts. The remainder of the 177th Brigade under Carleton's command was to contain de Valera's position at Boland's Bakery in Ballsbridge. The newly arrived 2/4th Lincolnshire Regiment was to move along the line of the Grand Union Canal and with that, the south side of the city– in-

[12] Ibid, p. 303.

cluding de Valera's 3rd Battalion – was sealed off.[13] This action allowed the 2/5th South Staffordshire Regiments and the 2/6th South Staffordshire Regiment, which had previously been occupying the Grand Union Canal, to move to reinforce the Four Courts area where the fighting was the most fierce.[14] At 9am on the April the 29th, the Four Courts were isolated. Elsewhere throughout the city, other British forces continued to tighten the noose around the Rebel positions.

General Maxwell's arrival was not well received by the civilian administrators in Ireland. He wrote to his wife "They do not altogether appreciate being under my orders."[15] As the sun rose, Maxwell saw a Dublin that looked more like the battlefields of western France than the city he remembered when serving as the Chief of Staff for the Duke of Connaught in 1902.

Meanwhile, in the GPO, the Rebels were oblivious to the changes that were occurring in the British lines. Sensing the closeness of their demise, Pearse had ordered the women to begin packing their things so they could evacuate.[16] This order was met with a tremendous amount of resistance by the women, who intended to stay and fight until the end.[17]

The end came quickly. As the building caught fire and more and more Fenians fell wounded, the decision was made to evacuate all non-combatants and wounded at 7pm. By 8pm, the fire in the GPO became so bad that Pearse made the decision that it was necessary to evacuate the building.[18]

The British had the GPO well covered, and the chances of escape were scant. Only ten minutes after Pearse's decision, forty men under the command of the O'Rahilly lined up at the exit to Henry Street as an advance party and (despite the fact that many were lacking the necessary equipment) ordered to fix bayonets.[19] Many of these men were killed and most were wounded. A bayonet charge down 200 yards of

---

[13] Joseph McKenna, *Voices from the Easter Rising: Firsthand Accounts of Ireland's 1916 Rebellion* (Jefferson: McFarland & Company, Inc., Publishers., 2017), p. 217.
[14] Ibid, p.217
[15] Max Caufield. *The Easter Rebellion* (New York, Holt, Rinehart and Winston, 1963), p. 303.
[16]Ibid, p. 305.
[17] Thomas Coffey, *Agony at Easter: The 1916 Irish Uprising* (London: George G. Harrap & Co, LTD, 1969), p. 211.
[18] Joseph McKenna, *Voices from the Easter Rising: Firsthand Accounts of Ireland's 1916 Rebellion* (Jefferson: McFarland & Company, Inc., Publishers., 2017), p. 221.
[19] Ibid, p. 222.

open, urban street against even green soldiers armed with modern rifles was a fool's errand.[20]

[20] Ibid, p. 222.

Chapter 37: The Battle Outside Dublin

The original for a nationwide uprising was a romantic vision that never came close to materializing during Easter Week. However, had the Fenian leadership dispersed throughout the island and provided a unified message, this actually could have become a reality. There were many strong nationalist organizations outside of Dublin that were both armed and ready for the Rebellion. Since 1915 both the IRB and the Volunteers had successful recruiting and training programs throughout the country.[1] While Dublin would be the focal point, Plunkett envisioned rising in the western portion of the country that would divert British forces and, with the aid of success in Dublin and the arrival of German arms, inspire the rest of the country to rise.[2] The secondary hope was that the Germans who delivered the guns to the Rebels would see the opportunity to open another front against Britain and help persuade their government that Ireland was worth supporting.

In theory, success would breed success. As word of the Fenian victories in both the country and the city would reach Irish ears, men would march to the barricades in time for substantial support from the German military. However, the disagreements between the violent wing of the Fenians and the more passive voices like Hobson, MacNeill and The O'Rahilly created an air of extreme secrecy that eliminated the possibility of true coordination and prevented the country from effectively rising in unison.[3] This was also a flawed theory of glorious rebellion that rarely materializes in civil wars, even when there is popular support. The naivete and blind optimism of a people rising as one against their age-old oppressors should live more in the romantic plays of the Fenian revolutionaries than in the real world of combat and governance.

Due to the Countermanding Order and the runners that MacNeill sent to effectively deliver the message, there was no significant rebellion outside of Dublin. In Cork, the Volunteers did not mobilize. In Limerick, Commandant Colivet held a vote on Easter Tuesday and the decision was made by a ten to six vote not to fight. In Enniscorthy, the Volunteers did rise and were able to occupy the town but lacked the

---

[1] Annie Ryan, *Witness Inside the Easter Rising* (Dublin: Libertas Press, 2005) pp 56-63.

[2] Michael Foy and Brian Barton, *The Easter Rising* (London: Sutton Publishing, 2004) p. 27.

[3] Ibid, p. 30.

manpower to even take the police barracks.[4] This was a complete failure of the Fenian strategic plan and it allowed the British to concentrate all of their operations on Dublin and easily show that the Rebellion was an isolated incident and it did not have much popularity outside of a handful of radicals.

In Limerick, the day was filled with confusion and disappointment. The Limerick Battalion was tasked with holding the line of the Shannon from the Claire side and had expected to receive a supply of arms under the direction of Roger Casement.[5] The Battalion and its commander Commandant Michael Colviet were wholly unsuccessful in their missions. John Daly was able to watch from his window as 300 Volunteers marched past his home in Barrington Street, but the disappointment in their performance would sour the relationship between the Battalion and the Daly family for generations.[6]

While never clearly communicated or explicitly defined, the mission of the battalion was twofold. The first task was to assist in the disrupting operations by attacking British positions in Limerick, cutting telephone wires and destroying rail connections. More important than securing the city was to pin down as many British troops as possible and prevent them from reinforcing the troops in Dublin. The second task was that once their objectives in Limerick were completed, they would move as many men and arms as possible to Dublin to reinforce the Fenians fighting in the city. In all aspects and missions, Commandant Colviet and his men failed to achieve their objectives.

The one exception to the overwhelming Fenian failure was the Battle of Ashbourne on the northern outskirts of Dublin. About fifty men of the Finglas Volunteers under Thomas Ashe launched diversionary attacks to relieve some pressure on Dublin.[7] This group, which took on the designation of the 5th Dublin Battalion, had 120 men on its roster. Twenty were diverted to help with the fighting in Dublin and the rest failed to muster. While the legend of the battle far outpaces the actual fighting and its importance to the fighting in Dublin, the mythology of the tactically superior, yet out-gunned band of Sinn Feiners defeating their British foes was an important inspiration for future generations

---

[4] Ibid, p. 212.

[5]Helen Litton, *16 Lives: Edward Daly* (Dublin, The O'Brien Press, 2013), p. 128.

[6]Ibid, p. 117.

[7]Michael Foy and Brian Barton, *The Easter Rising (*London: Sutton Publishing, 2004) p. 214.

of Irish Rebels. In reality, the Volunteers did not perform that well and failed in both their tactical objectives of holding territory outside of Dublin, in their operational objective of forcing the British to divert forces outside of the city and in their strategic objective of establishing a guerilla presence and base of operations outside of the city.[8]

At noon on Easter Monday, the men of the company were mobilized and while fewer men than expected mustered the forty-five men that showed up were sufficient to accomplish the mission.[9] This diversionary attack was part of a greater plan to disrupt British operations in Dublin by forcing them to disperse forces to the countryside. The Irish knew strategically that the British calculus would have to favor the Western Front, so at a certain point they would not be able to spare the men to fight in Ireland, especially if they would have to fight and maintain a garrison throughout the island. In isolation, the Battle of Ashbourne was wholly insignificant and nothing more than a footnote to the larger uprising, but had it been one of several such actions it could have made it impossible for the British to concentrate their forces so quickly and overwhelmingly in Dublin. This would have radically altered Generals Lowe and Maxwell's plans and would have prolonged the fighting, diverted more troops from the Western Front, directly engaged more of the Irish populace and given the Germans more time to intervene.

The Volunteers moved quickly and assaulted the Royal Irish Constabulary Barracks at Ashbourne, which surrendered without much of a fight.[10] The Constabulary responded without rushing headlong into an assault. They utilized fifteen requisitioned cars and drove a force of fifty-four to sixty-seven officers under the command of County Inspector Alexander Gray directly to the seized police station.[11] The Fenians moved quickly, outflanking the Constabulary's position on the road and taking advantage of a high berm for cover. From that position they were able to conduct a well-executed linear ambush and force the surviving members of Gray's force to surrender.[12] The Rebel position remained strong for the rest of the week and did not see any additional organized attacks. The heartbreaking news came to them at eleven in the morning

[8] Michael Foy and Brian Barton, *The Easter Rising (*London: Sutton Publishing, 2004) pp. 214-217.

[9]Joseph McKenna, Voices from the Easter Rising: Firsthand Accounts of Ireland's 1916 Rebellion (Jefferson: McFarland & Company, Inc., Publishers., 2017), p. 257.

[10] Ibid, p. 264.

[11] Ibid, p. 265.

[12] Ibid, pp. 265-269.

on Sunday that the Dublin garrison had surrendered, and Ashe gave his own surrender around three in the afternoon.[13]

[13] Ibid, pp. 269-270.

Part 3: The End of Hostilities and Surrender

Chapter 38: Friday – End of the Fighting

At 9:30am Pearse published an official statement finally admitting that the British had severed communications between the Rebel positions and praising the gallantry of the Rebel soldiers – especially the wounded James Connolly. This was a simultaneous admission that the end was near and a rallying cry to keep fighting. While he lamented the Countermanding Order by name, Pearse spent most of the letter emphasizing the magnitude of what the Rebels had achieved: "If we accomplish no more than we have accomplished, I am satisfied. I am satisfied that we have saved Ireland's honour. I am satisfied that we should have accomplished more, that we should have accomplished the task of enthroning, as well as proclaiming, the Irish Republic as a Sovereign State, had our arrangements for a simultaneous rising of the whole country, with a combined plan as sound as the Dublin plan has been proved to be, been allowed to go through on Easter Sunday. Of the fatal countermanding order which prevent those plans from being carried out, I shall not speak further."[1]

Connolly issued a similar proclamation that contained little more than lies and exaggerations to bolster the Rebel morale. While both considered their "Fenian Duty" of martyrdom for Ireland as an important end state when they began their rebellion, Connolly continued to perpetuate the myth that victory was a possibility. He proclaimed: "Let us remind you of what we have done. For the first time in 700 years the flag of free Ireland floats triumphantly in Dublin City. The British arm, whose exploits we are for ever (sp) having dinned into our ears, which boasts of having stormed the Dardanelles and the German lines on the Marne, behind their artillery and machine-guns are afraid to advance to the attack or storm any positions held by our forces. The slaughter they have suffered in the last few days has totally unnerved them, and they dare not attempt again an infantry attack on our positions."[2] He continued to list the exploits of the subordinate commanders, to state: "we have confidence in our Allies in Germany and kinsmen in America are staring every nerve to hasten matters on our behalf" and to state that the Rebels are "in the hour of our victory".[3] All of these statements

[1]Max Caufield. *The Easter Rebellion* (New York, Holt, Rinehart and Winston, 1963), pp. 305-306.

[2] Ibid, p. 308.

[3] Ibid, p. 308

were false and while it is not known how much of this he fabricated in his own isolation after having been wounded, it is clear that the Rebel leadership decided that the statements were necessary for the ears of the starving fighters being bombarded and sniped at by the British.

In a desperate move on Sackville Street, The O'Rahilly and about forty men launched a daring assault to secure an escape route for the Rebels still inside the GPO. While the Rebels had been able to keep the flames at bay for most of the fighting, the fire had begun intensifying. The O'Rahilly and the Sinn Fein quartermaster Fitzgerald were in Coliseum Bar. Around seven o'clock, they launched their desperate assault. Against soldiers from both the Dublin Fusiliers and the Sherwood Foresters, the party failed in achieving their objective at a heavy cost. In the fighting, The O'Rahilly was killed, and the British were able to secure important documents, including Connolly's final order, which promptly made their way to General Maxwell's hands.[4]

Things were not going as well for the British forces facing against Ned Daly's battalion at the Four Courts. One of the major tactical mistakes made by General Lowe was to choose to use North King Street as the northern boundary of the inner cordon in that area.[5] While they intended to encircle the Rebel areas, poor reconnaissance and the confusion of the urban terrain led to the British to place their cordon right through the Rebel's stronghold at the Four Courts.[6] This area was so well barricaded and concentrated with Rebel firepower that the British infantry could not advance against it without the support of armored cars improvised from large barrels seized from the Guinness Brewery.[7] "Reilly's Fort", an empty public house, became the focal point of the British assault. The British under the command of Colonel Taylor resorted to adopting the Fenian tactic of braking through interior walls so that they could avoid the Mauser fire that they would face in open areas. Despite hard fighting and multiple assaults, the Rebels continued to hold their positions at the Four Courts.

---

[4] Ibid, pp. 323-326.

[5] Ibid, p. 335.

[6] Paul O'Brien, Crossfire: The Battle of the Four Courts, 1916 (Dublin: New Island, 2012), p. 106.

[7] Max Caufield, *The Easter Rebellion* (New York: Holt, Rinehart, and Winston, 1963), p. 336.

Chapter 39: Saturday – Surrender

Dawn on Saturday saw the Rebels close to breaking. The Rebels at the main position at the GPO were planning on how to breakout from their positions on Sackville Street with the intention of linking up with Daly's Battalion at the Four Courts. The Rebels made it as far as Hanlon's Fish Shop at no. 16 before the decision was made to stop. Connolly's foot had grown so gangrenous that he could no longer move and instead of abandoning their comrade, the Rebels halted their withdrawal turned the fish shop into their final headquarters.[1]

General Maxwell had completed his envelopment by 11am.[2] While the British had successfully contained the main Fenian positions much earlier in the week, secondary positions like Boland's Mill were finally cordoned off on Saturday morning. The British were also able to bring up heavy artillery, like the 18-pounder that they moved up Great Britain Street to help with the direct fires on the Rebel's urban fortifications.[3] The influx of several thousand British troops eliminated the possibility of an escape to the north, prevented Rebel positions from being able to consolidate with one another and kept the fighting as isolated from the rest of the city as possible. Restoring normalcy in Dublin was not a stated goal or objective and strict martial law was maintained.

The Rebels contemplated several plans for fighting withdrawals, diversionary attacks, and other means of escaping their current predicament. Slowly and somberly, the realization was made that any attempt to breakout would involve a tremendous loss of both civilian and Fenian lives.[4] With no other recourse, Pearse made the decision to find a white flag and surrender. At 12:45 under a white flag made out of a handkerchief and a Red Cross armband, a Miss O'Farrell presented the surrender of the Irish Republican Army to Colonel Portal.[5] General Lowe would only accept an unconditional surrender and after some back and forth with Miss O'Farrell acting as the messenger, Pearse surrendered

---

[1]Max Caufield, *The Easter Rebellion* (New York: Holt, Rinehart, and Winston, 1963), p. 344.

[2] Joseph McKenna, *Voices from the Easter Rising: Firsthand Accounts of Ireland's 1916 Rebellion* (Jefferson: McFarland & Company, Inc., Publishers., 2017), p. 231.

[3] Ibid, p.231

[4] Ibid, p. 346.

[5]Max Caufield, *The Easter Rebellion* (New York: Holt, Rinehart, and Winston, 1963), p. 348.

his sword to General Lowe at 2:30.[6]

The surrender letter that Pearse signed in front of General Maxwell at the Military Headquarters at Parkgate stated: "In order to prevent the further slaughter of Dublin citizens, and in the hope of saving the lives of our followers now surrounded and hopelessly outnumbered, the members of the Provisional Government at Headquarters have agreed to an unconditional surrender, and the Commandants of the various districts in the City and Country will order their commands to lay down arms."[7]

---

[6] Ibid, p. 351.

[7] Michael Foy and Brian Barton, *The Easter Rising* (London: Sutton Publishing, 2004) p. 155.

Chapter 40: Captivity and Martial Law

"I know what is going to happen to me, but I will do my best for you and the men"[1] -Eamon de Valera

"This is not the end of the fight for Irish Freedom – it is the beginning"[2] -The last words of Ned Daly to Liam Hogan of the 1st Battalion of the Irish Volunteers

Many of the Rebels met the news of the surrender order with resistance and disbelief. They fully believed in the Fenian message and intended to fight and die for the cause. While much of the resistance to the surrender order was bravado or an unwillingness to admit defeat, some of fighters believed that since they were likely to be executed anyways and that it was better to go down fighting. Tom Clarke was able to quell the near mutinous reaction with the promise that this was only a temporary setback. Clarke went among the men and said: "I'm fifty-nine years old, haven't I spent my whole life in the struggle for Irish freedom? For fifteen years I rotted in British prisons. But there'll be no more prisons for me this time. They'll be quick to eliminate the need. I'm well aware of that. So if I'm satisfied that surrender is the only course open to us, why shouldn't you be just as satisfied? Don't worry about them killing you. They'll only kill those who signed the Republican proclamation. And you needn't fight to the death to fell you've accomplished something here this week. You've already done more than anyone could have hoped. Because of men like you, Ireland's future is secure. When the people of Ireland hear the full story of Easter Week, they'll rise up en masse, and this poor bedeviled country will soon be free."[3]

Initially, the Rebels did not suffer any systematic physical mistreatment or retribution by their British captors.[4] There were some isolat-

[1] Sean Byrne, *Bureau of Military History, 1913-1921,* p. 422.

[2] Helen Litton, *16 Lives: Edward Daly* (Dublin, The O'Brien Press, 2013), p. 161.

[3] Thomas Coffey, *Agony at Easter: The 1916 Irish Uprising* (London: George G. Harrap & Co, LTD, 1969), p. 253.

[4] Max Caufield, *The Easter Rebellion* (New York: Holt, Rinehart, and Winston, 1963), p. 354.

ed incidents, but for the most part, the Dublin citizenry was more hostile to the newly surrendered Rebels than the British soldiers. Despite the consensus among the British soldiers a that the Rebels deserved swift and harsh punishment, they maintained their discipline and outbursts of retribution were few and far between. It took some time for the official surrender order to work its way through all the isolated Rebel the positions. Catholic priests like the Capuchin monks and Father Augustine played crucial roles as intermediaries for the Fenians and the British to support the veracity of the surrender order.[5]

The total costs to Dublin were enormous. Official numbers report that 1,351 people had been killed or severely wounded and that 169 buildings had been ruined beyond repair. The total cost of the damages was around two and a half million pounds sterling, an enormous sum for the time.[6] This was a far cry from the Marxist theology that Capitalists would never purposefully destroy their own means of production.

The tide of public opinion began to turn with the Bowen-Colthurst affair. A rampaging British Captain Bowen-Colthurst was alleged to have murdered at least six innocent civilians in cold blood during the fighting. Another fifteen allegations of murder were levied against the 2/6th South Staffordshire Regiment.[7] While there would have been some public tolerance for misdeeds and criminal behavior, General Maxwell's decision to cover up the atrocities and to disregard directives from London to prosecute the offenders was the beginning of the end for the British victory. Mr. Asquith applied direct pressure to General Maxwell and his staff to properly handle the cases, but it still took until June 6th before Bowen-Colthurst was court-martialed and the 2/6th were never properly tried for the bayoneting of fifteen innocent civilians on North King Street.[8]

Maxwell began to realize that he was not the officer to win the peace. To the credit of the British government and the formal civilian leaders of Ireland who all promptly resigned after the cessation of hostilities, they had all advocated for a more moderate approach and a more public prosecution of offenses by British soldiers.[9] In the end, Maxwell's tenure was short-lived and by October there was new leadership

---

[5] Ibid, pp. 335-358.
[6] Ibid, p. 359.
[7] Ibid, p. 370.
[8] Ibid, p. 371.
[9] Ibid, pp. 373-375.

in Ireland. But the damage caused by his policies was already done.

The words spoken at the surrender of the Third Battalion of the Irish Volunteers at the beginning of this chapter are ironic in the sense that Commandant de Valera was the only male leader of the Uprising to avoid the firing squad. These were not the executions of faceless enemy leaders, but well-known leaders of workers and educators. Although the last of the executions occurred between 3 and 12 May, a full list of those executed was not available to the public until May 24, 1916.[10]

Irish newspapers strongly urged for a reprieve for all minor actors in the Rebellion.[11] Letters sent by individuals and groups of citizens to August Birrell stressed that the opinion of most of Ireland was "most strongly against any further shooting as the result of court martial trails."[12] The executions turned outlaws into martyrs, and the people began to lionize them despite their earlier feelings.[13] The public outcry against the execution of the nineteen-year-old Sean Heuston, the proposed execution of a woman (Countess Markievicz), an American citizen (Eamon de Valera), and ninety-seven others led to the British government's intervention.[14] This uproar helped inspire a political movement against Home Rule and for Independence.

The desire to suppress the Uprising before it spread led to the heavy-handed British response that turned a failed uprising into the beginning of a war independence and a civil war. Most Irishmen were shocked and appalled with the actions of the Rebels and stood firmly behind the British response during Easter Week. The British attempted to capitalize on the pro-Empire sentiments of World War One and published a proclamation declaring that the revolution in Dublin was a result of German intervention and committed by a small, reckless force.[15] The inability of the British to prove this connection greatly hurt their popularity. The very next day a second proclamation declared martial law throughout the entire island, though Dublin was the only place to rebel.[16] Almost immediately, General Maxwell used his full authority to

---

[10] CSO, Regd. Papers, 8089/1916.

[11] "A Plea for Leniency," *Irish Independent*, 10 May 1916.

[12] CSO, Regd. Papers, 7860/1916.

[13] G.N. Plunkett, "Letter to the People of North Roscommon upon Election to Office" TCDMS 2074 (Public Letter, Dublin, 17 March 1917).

[14] Ruth Edwards, *Patrick Pease: The Triumph of Failure* (London: Victor Gollancz LTD, 1977), p. 323.

[15] Ivor Churchill, "A Proclamation No. 1," *The Irish Times*, 25 April 1916.

[16] Ivor Churchill, "A Proclamation No. 2," *The Irish Times*, 26 April 1916.

order secret court martial trails for the Fenian leaders and arrested over 3,000 alleged participants in the Uprising.[17]

The British declaration of martial law gave General Maxwell permission to act unilaterally and severely. This meant that despite objections to the executions in the House of Commons, Prime Minister Asquith gave Maxwell direct and total responsibility for the actions taken during the British response and their consequences.[18] Maxwell's experience in colonial warfare included fighting in the Boer War, Khartoum, and Egypt.[19] Acting with the typical British response, he intended the executions and arrests to serve as both a deterrent against further rebellions and means to quash all remaining resistance.[20] While the citizens of Ireland openly voiced their resentment to the executions and felt that the declaration of martial law and the "indiscriminate arresting of men throughout the country" was an insult.[21] The Fenians were a small, radical group disassociated with the main stream, yet according to the Deputy Leader of the Irish Parliamentary Party "the British Government treated Ireland, as if it were a sort of back-yard country in which the people could be trampled in the dust."[22] This harsh course of action aroused the nationalist spirit of a large majority of the island by illustrating that even after three attempts at Home Rule legislation the British would still abuse the Irish in the same way they abused their most primitive colony.

The execution of William Pearse is one of the most famous examples of the severity of the British response to the Rebellion. William was Padraig's brother whose most serious crime was found more in his surname than any action that he took during the Rebellion. While most accounts of him depict him as an unremarkable, the British assigned him a role of great importance during the Rebellion. He was cited as General Maxwell as "a brother of P.H. Pearse, the President of the Irish Repub-

---

[17] John McEwen, "The Liberal Party and the Irish Question during the First World War," *The Journal of British Studies* 12 (Nov. 1972): 114.

[18] Tyler Toby, "Exemplary Violence Used in British Colonial Policy: One Explanation for General John Maxwell's Violent Reaction to the Easter Rising of 1916" (Masters diss., University of Massachusetts Boston, June 1997), pp. 6-8.

[19] George Arthur, *General Sir John Maxwell* (London: John Murray, 1932), pp. 1-245.

[20] Tyler Toby, "Exemplary Violence Used in British Colonial Policy: One Explanation for General John Maxwell's Violent Reaction to the Easter Rising of 1916" (Masters diss., University of Massachusetts Boston, June 1997), p. 5.

[21] CSO, Regd. Papers, 7860/1916.

[22] *The Irish Times*, 16 May 1916, p.3.

lic. He was associated with the Sinn Fein movement from its inception. He held the rank of Commandant in the rebel army. He was present in the GPO during the fighting and was acting as an officer and surrendered with the rebels in Sackville Street."[23]

William Pearse recounted his role in the action differently: "I *had no authority or say in the arrangements for the starting of the rebellion. I was throughout - only a personal* attaché *to my brother P.H.* Pearse. I had no direct command."[24] Accounts of William Pearse's part in the action from the Fenian side were nearly universal in their accounting of his position. While his capabilities and involvement may have undergone some degree of exaggeration to create the narrative of the innocent martyr, his execution was nevertheless seen as wonton and vengeful. To almost all observers, it seemed as if the British executed him for his bloodline more than his actions, and in culture with a strong emphasis on family bonds, this vengeful action stood out and made many brothers, sisters, parents and cousins wonder if they would be punished for the actions or future actions of their kind.

One of the most disastrous decisions made by the British was the choice not to hold any individual soldiers accountable for their actions. This was specifically poignant when it came to the unnecessary deaths of non-combatants. There was a common belief at the lower levels that there was an order not to take prisoners. This led to reports, whether verified or not, of the wonton shooting of suspected Rebels. While the true number of non-combatants has never been disclosed, there was a common perception following the Rebellion that this practice was commonplace. An internal investigation after the Rebels found that since no order was given to take prisoners, it was interpreted amidst the chaotic situation as an order not to take prisoners and that the executions were merely soldiers trying to follow their understanding of their orders.[25] Regardless of the truth behind it, this became a major proof for the Fenians of British barbarism and it moved many Irishmen to join the effort to oust them from Ireland by force.

Irish stories of British atrocities never reached the level of depravity or hyperbole of the stories the British told of German atrocities

---

[23] General Sir John Maxwell. Transcript of Court Martial. May 1916. Available from <http://www.aoh61.com/history/easter_trials.htm>.

[24] William Pearse. Transcript of Court Martial. May 1916. Available from <http://www.aoh61.com/history/easter_trials.htm>.

[25] Helen Litton, *16 Lives: Edward Daly* (Dublin, The O'Brien Press, 2013), p. 150.

in Belgium at the beginning of the Frist World War. Ireland, however, had an interconnectedness, history and proximity that gave even the tallest tales more credence. Maxwell's refusals to prosecute and investigate any British misdeeds unintentionally gave a validity to any of these rumors. Further, the fact that so many of these incidents were true, made every reported act of murder and pillage feasible.

As an example, the story of Patrick Bealen became commonplace throughout Ireland. While the British would deny any inappropriate action, the common Irish citizen would hear of a poor innocent who was wrongfully imprisoned and sometimes even killed by overzealous and vengeful British soldiers. Bealen has been the foreman at a local pub. Only thirty years old, he was well known in his community and an everyman who would be familiar to anyone on the island. He was shot while in custody and without cause, from a distance by British soldiers and hastily buried in a shallow grave in the cellar. The commander of the British forces who conducted the incident, Lieutenant Colonel H Taylor of the 2nd/6th South Staffordshire Regiment reported that: "I am satisfied that during these operations the troops under my command showed great moderation and restraint under the exceptionally difficult and trying circumstances." This report directly conflicts with the county coroner's report of Bealen being shot in cold blood while he was an unarmed prisoner.[26] These actions played right into the hands of the anti-Home Rule Fenians. How could the Irish expect the British to give them any real form of sovereignty when British forces were willing to and able to murder innocent Irishmen in cold blood without so much as a slap on the wrist.

The Fenians were able to rebuild their decimated numbers and decapitated leadership with help from British officials. Harsh retributions and the secrecy surrounding the executions of the leaders drove many to support the rebels.[27] Inevitably, the British made mistakes and arrested men who had no part in any rebellious activity. Many began to view these arrests as unlawful and began to protest against the arrest of "probably innocent local [men] months after the Rising."[28] This was amplified in the jails as hundreds of innocent men were incarcerated for a crime they did not commit. The same Dublin jails that saw the exe-

---

[26]Helen Litton, *16 Lives: Edward Daly* (Dublin, The O'Brien Press, 2013), p. 147.

[27] Ruth Edwards, *Patrick Pease: The Triumph of Failure* (London: Victor Gollancz LTD, 1977), p. 324.

[28] CSO, Regd. Papers, 15168/1916.

cution of the leaders became the "universities for rebels" which led to a reinvigoration of the leadership.[29] The arrests became even more frequent throughout May, filling prisons with a new group a rebels.[30] The prisons created new rebels and the rash of arrests began to turn public opinion against Maxwell's policies.

Once a lack of evidence dispelled the reported German connection to the Uprising, the Fenian cause lost the blemish of wartime treason.[31] The message and sacrifices of the rebels coupled with the lack of evidence supporting a German link convinced the public that they, as the famous sign above Liberty Hall stated, "served neither King nor Kaiser, but Ireland", and were not German stooges. While Roger Casement was hung for his involvement, the Fenians quickly disavowed him as a major part of the conspiracy, claiming that he was unaware of the plans and of the strength and armament of the Volunteers prior to the Rebellion.[32]

As early as the end of May, the British began taking measures against the rebel propaganda movement.[33] Government correspondence reflected that public support, such as wearing the colors of the Irish Republican Brotherhood, was increasing among both youths and women.[34] This disaffection sowed the seeds of unrest, but it would take more than public outcry to create an Irish state.

---

[29] Dan Breen, *My Fight for Irish Freedom* (Dublin: Talbot Press, 1924), p.32.
[30] CSO, Regd. Papers, 8543/1916.
[31] Ivor Churchill, "A Proclamation No. 1," *The Irish Times*, 25 April 1916.
[32] Nora Connolly O'Brien, *The Irish Rebellion of 1916 or, the Unbroken Tradition.* (New York: Boni and Liveright, 1918), pp. 199-202.
[33] CSO, Regd. Papers, 8466/1916.
[34] CSO, Regd. Papers, 9531/1916.

Section 4: After the Rising

Chapter 41: The Catholic Church in the Aftermath of the Rising

"O Gentlest Heart of Jesus...have mercy on the souls of thy servants, our Irish heroes; bring them from the shadows of exile to the bright home of Heaven, where, we trust, Thou and Thy Blessed Mother have woven for them a crown of unending bliss."[1] -Prayer Card for those executed for 1916

The Catholic Church was a powerful force in the controlling the zeitgeist and actions of Ireland at the beginning of the twentieth century. Prior to the 1916 Uprising, the Catholic clergy of Ireland was among the staunchest opponents of the Fenians. The Church was fearful that new rebellions would result in a reestablishment of the Penal Law Codes and other restrictions. Many of the leaders of the Rebellion were atheist, socialist, or members of a movement with Protestant origins. Theobald Wolfe Tone, the father of the Fenian movement, was a Protestant.[2] The conversion of the Priests into Fenians was vital to the growth of nationalism following the Rebellion.

During the Rising, the brave actions of several Priests helped to hasten the surrender of the Fenians and saved Dublin from untold damage and additional casualties. Whether or not the Priests agreed with the Fenians ideals or methods at the time of the Rebellion is not stated, but there are several stories of selfless action on behalf of the Priests in an attempt to either prevent or end the fighting. Following the Rebellion, the attitudes of individual Priests followed the that of the general population of Ireland, gradually become more pro-Fenian in response to the court martials and other British actions. However, during the Rising the actions of Priests like the Capuchin Father Aloysius and Father Matthew Hall show that their priority was the preservation of lives and

[1] "Prayer Card for the Repose of the Souls of the Following Irishmen who were Executed by English Law, 1916" TCDMS 2074 (Prayer, Ireland, 1916).

[2] Lawrence McCaffrey, "Irish Nationalism and Irish Catholicism: A Study in Cultural Identity", *Church History* 42 (1972): 528.

the cessation of hostilities.[3] It is important to note that during the Rising there was never an official directive, despite the rumors in the Fenian fighting positions, of any official word of support or disapproval from the Catholic Church or its leadership in Dublin.

Prior to Easter Week, the Catholic Church as an institution had largely accepted the status quo of British rule in Ireland. In fact, the Church largely disapproved of Irish nationalism and was staunchly against the violence that the nationalist movement had caused in previous generations. This was not just a unique policy on Ireland, but one that extended to all the republican movements that had caused so much havoc in Europe and threatened the position of the Church in the previous century. "The anti-republican stance of the Church had deep roots in Catholic history and owed as much to the relationship of the Pope and the Vatican to Italian nationalism of the nineteenth century as to the activities of the Fenians. Moreover, during the nineteenth century, the Catholic Church in Ireland learned to live with English domination and English civilization in Britain."[4]

The same influences that inspired many members of the 1916 generations to nationalist ideals also affected their peers in the clergy. While some of these younger priests generally supported the rebels, the Bishops were unanimously against their actions.[5] Gradually, much of the clergy began to support the nationalist cause. This change could reflect the greater public outcry against the arrests and executions or because a shift in the background of the priests. As the dying words of incarnated and executed Fenians adopted a more religious tone, many of the younger members of the clergy who grew up with exposure to the Gaelic education movement were likely to support a nationalist revolution.[6] This change both reflected and helped to gain support for the changing popular opinion in Ireland.

The earlier conflicts between nationalists and the clergy made the Fenian attempt to gain the necessary public support even more difficult. In 1867 the Roman Catholic hierarchy had condemned the Fenians as being anti-Clerical because they disregarded a Church ban on

[3] Michael Foy and Brian Barton, *The Easter Rising (*London: Sutton Publishing, 2004) p. 200.

[4] Annie Ryan, *Witness Inside the Easter Rising* (Dublin: Libertas Press, 2005) p 198.

[5]Elsie Mahaffy, "Ireland in 1916: An Account of the Rising in Dublin" TCDMS 2074 (Diary, Dublin, 1916), p. 6.

[6] Irish Political Documents 1916-1949. "The death of Thomas Ashe." Ed. Arthur Mitchell and Padraig O Snodaigh. Dublin: Irish Academic Press, Ltd., 1985, p. 30.

advocating a violent revolution.[7] The resistance of the Roman Catholic Church stopped many in the mostly Catholic country from joining many of the Gaelic groups. The change in the opinion of the clergy was a grassroots movement. The younger generation of priests had grown up as immersed in the budding Irish cultural movements as their peers; in fact many of them took a covert, though active, part in Irish Republican Brotherhood activities.[8] In some cases there were close family connections between the Rebels and the Clergy. For example, Michael Mallin's, the second in command of the Irish Citizen Army, son was a priest and while he did not become a famous advocate for the rebellion, he certainly would have shared many of the same views with his parishioners.[9] The actions of other priests, such as facing British machine gun fire to lead prayer services for those who died in the rebellion, created the perception of clerical support for the Uprising.[10] This change in opinion within the priesthood was part of a larger change in Irish public opinion.

The growing support for the Fenian movement within the clergy did not fully emerge until after they had received some of the blame for the Rising. The first associations between the priesthood and the rebels came from private citizens. Many influential Irishmen, including many Catholics, such as Agnes Halton wrote to the British officials "at the expense of being called a traitor to my church" blaming "certain Irish Roman Catholic Priests" as being behind the revolt.[11] The public began to believe that the Church and the Rebels had been in cahoots and the post-1916 nationalist groups such as The Vigilance Committee - which warned young Irishmen against joining the British Army - began to exploit that perceived connection. One of their propaganda advertisements asked Irish youths: "why should you fight for the England? Is it in gratitude for the Priest-hunters and the rack of the Penal days!"[12] The

---

[7] Sean Duffy and Patrick Power, *Timetables of Irish History,* (London: Worth Press Limited 2001), p. 29.

[8] Peader O Cearnaigh, *Reminiscences of the Irish Republican Brotherhood and Easter Week 1916,* TCDMS 3560/2, p. 20.

[9] Lorcan Collins, "1916: The Easter Rising Walking Tour," Personal Interview. 13 July 2006.

[10] Kathleen Clarke, *Revolutionary Women: An Autobiography* (Dublin: The O'Brien Press, 1991), p. 128.

[11] CSO, Regd. Papers, 8442/1916.

[12] Vigilance Committee, "Poster Warning Against the Evils of the British Army" TCDMS 2074 (Political Poster, Dublin, 1916).

Gaelic cultural movements of the late nineteenth century and advertisements such as this may have instilled a spirit of nationalism the younger generation of clergy which manifested itself en masse after the British response to the Easter Uprising. General Maxwell believed that involvement of the Roman Catholic clergy would convert a large number of Irishmen into rebels, even hoping to get Papal assistance in distancing the Church from seditious behavior.[13] The perception of priests as being involved in the Uprising coupled with their support of the rebels and their widows after the executions firmly connected the two groups making the cause of Irish nationalism appear more acceptable from the Catholic perspective than it was prior.

[13]George Arthur, *General Sir John Maxwell* (London: John Murray, 1932), p. 261.

Chapter 42: Irish Women in the Aftermath of the Rising

"Until our arms have brought the opportune moment for the establishment of a permanent National Government, representative of the whole people of Ireland and elected by the suffrages of all her men and women..."[1] *-Poblacht Na H Eireann*

"It is a curious thing that many men seem to be unable to believe that any woman can embrace an ideal – accept it intellectually, feel it as a profound emotion, and then calmly decide to make a vocation of working for its realization – they give themselves endless pains to prove that every serious thing a women does (outside nursing babies or washing pots) is the result of being in love with some man, or disappointment in love with some man, or looking for excitement, limelight, or indulging their vanity. You do not seem to have escaped from the limitations of your sex, therefore you describe Madame [Markiewicz] as being 'caught up' by or rallying 'to the side' of Connolly, Larkin, or some man or other, whereas the simple fact is that she was working, as a man might have worked, for the freedom of Ireland. She allied herself with these later movements because they were advancing the ideals which she had accepted years before. We were writing about labour conditions – women's labour in particular – years before Larkin came to Ireland, and she never 'abandoned' or 'drew away from; that cause."[2] -Helena Maloney (second female President of the Irish Trade Unions and Cumann na mBan member) in a letter to Irish author Sean O'Faolain, 1934

[1]The Provisional Government of the Irish Republic, *Poblacht Na H Eireann*, (Dublin, 1916), p. 1.

[2]Annie Ryan, *Witness Inside the Easter Rising* (Dublin: Libertas Press, 2005) pp 107-108.

The female Rebels in the Easter Rebellion and its aftermath were essential participations in the propaganda war that turned a tactical and operational failure into a strategic victory. While often overshadowed by the actions of the men behind the rifles and the larger-than-life story of the Countess Markiewicz, there is no doubt without the women who belonged to and supported the Fenian movement that the Easter Rising would have been and shorter lived and more quickly forgotten affair. These women were absolutely essential to setting the conditions to foment a rebellion, providing the support to sustain the uprising and, most importantly, winning the hearts and mind operation following the surrender of at the GPO.

The supporting operations performed by the of the women of Ireland had a tremendous influence on change of opinion in the Irish Catholic Church, the international Irish community, and the average Irish citizen. Support for a Free State was not a foregone conclusion in April of 1916 and the collective writings and letters of the female Fenians created sympathy in the greater Irish zeitgeist and laid the groundwork for the acceptance of Fenian-inspired policy and creating the conditions to support a prolonged insurrection.

The long-term strategic objective of the Uprising – the creation of a free and independent Irish State – would have been completely unattainable without winning over people and organizations that were not radicalized. Prior to the Rebellion, most Irish men and women, even those who firmly believed in the independence, were against launching any revolution. The timing of a rebellion, the desire to support (and collect the pensions of) the sons and fathers on the Western Front and the perception of imminent Home Rule all made rebellion unpopular. After the hot war of Easter Week came a propaganda and information war, which in large part fell to the work, and more often the sacrifice, of Irish women that coupled with General Maxwell's response to change the public opinion and enable the next stage of the struggle – the Irish Civil War.

The commitment of Irishwomen before, during, and after the Easter Rebellion helped to win support for the Fenian movement. Echoing the contemporary violent suffrage movements of Emmeline Pankhurst in Britain, the promise of winning female suffrage in arms helped convince many of the benefits of the new ideology. Discussion about the influence that women had upon the revolution typically focuses on Countess Markiewicz and on the widows of the executed leaders, such as Kathleen Clarke, of the Rebellion. While these women sustained and expanded the Fenian movement after the deaths of the men, thousands of mothers and wives who did not achieve hero status also played their part in changing popular opinion. The rise of Sinn Fein and the Anglo-Irish War was truly a grassroots movement, and the influence of Irish women enabled great change to occur.

The Irish Volunteers knew the importance that women would play in the upcoming struggle. During Easter Week, all of the commanders with the exception of Eamon de Valera's Third Irish Republican Brotherhood Battalion had a contingent from the *Cuman na mBan* - the female auxiliary to the Irish Volunteers - to help sustain the men.[3] In some cases, women played a much more active role. Notably, Countess Constance Markiewicz co-commanded the Irish Citizen Army contingent at Saint Stephen's Green. The former wife of a Polish count, the close friend of James Connolly helped initiate hostilities on the Green by killing a police officer at point blank range.[4] The concept of a female commander in any military capacity was ludicrous in that time and society. Her role speaks not only to her command and leadership capabilities but to the progressiveness of the Fenian movement to align with her beliefs.

Her contribution to Republicanism extends beyond her actions in battle. She was the founder of the *Cuman na mBanand* and the co-founder of Na Fianna (Warriors of Ireland).[5] The *Cuman na mBanand* grew into the women's auxiliary of the Irish Volunteers. Like many other contemporary female auxiliary groups, this group was as primed for dramatic action as its male counterpart. Based on the actions of the Countess, it was probably more likely. While the name literally translates into "Women's Counsel" its members were clear to distinguish its Fenian prerogative by ensuring it was known as the Irish Women's Counsel when referenced in English. While not particularly numerous, seventy of their ranks were arrested following the events of Easter Week. During the hostilities, they performed many combat support and service support tasks. These included: couriers, intelligence gathering, medical aid (functioning under the banner of Red Cross workers in some cases)

[3] Conor Kostick and Lorcan Collins, *The Easter Rising: A Guide to Dublin in 1916* (Dublin: The O'Brien Press, 2000), p. 76.
[4] Ibid., p. 74.
[5] Tim Pat Coogan, *1916: The Easter Uprising* (London: Orion Books Limited, 2001), p. 50.

and moving supplies.

After the Rebellion, the British imprisoned the Countess for a number of years. While the British executed her peers within the Volunteers, her gender kept her alive and made her a popular rallying point for many Irishmen. She was the first women elected to the British Parliament at Westminster, but she never sat preferring to become the new Republic's first Minister of Labour in 1919. Her influence led to Sinn Fein's commitment to women's rights and suffrage which subsequently won them popular support.[6]

The Countess, whether rightly or wrongly, received much of the attention for the female role in the Rebellion. Partially due to her leadership role, partially due to her influence before the Rebellion and partially due to the blood directly on her hands, the legends of this aristocrat who fought and continued to fight for Irish independence overshadows that of many of her comrades, both male and female.

While their actions during Easter Week may be overshadowed by the Countesses' deadly pistol shot which initiated the fighting in St. Stephen's Green, in a city under siege it is impossible to underestimate the important role these women played. Without these women braving the bullets and barricades the British would have starved-out the Irish Republic in a short matter of days and with much less need for bombs or bullets. Without these women running communications between the multiple locations in an era before the common military or insurgent usage of the radio, the British could have much more effectively isolated the Irishmen and conducted directed information operations to convince each of the battle positions that the other had already surrendered or sued for a separate peace. While their actions in setting conditions for and capitalizing on the draconian British response had an immeasurable contribution to the strategic success of Easter Week in the cause of Irish independence, the brave actions of these women during the fighting did as much if not more to prolong the fighting as any individual rifleman.

The Countess' other founding claim, the *Na Fianna*, was also more militantly aligned than the average nationalist organization. Both organizations made significant contributions towards setting the conditions that made rebellion in Ireland possible. Having a strong youth movement is vital not only to providing a cadre to build a rebellion around, but to ensure that enough members of the next generation are

[6]Margaret Ward, *Unmanageable Revolutionaries: Women and Irish Nationalism* (London: Pluto Press LTD., 1983), p. 127.

indoctrinated with the ideals and mythos of Fenianism to ensure the movement's survival. The *Na Fianna* was co-founded by Bulmer Hobson and Countess Markiewicz in 1909. Unsparingly, the young men and boys involved with this group became the bedrock of the junior leaders of Easter Week. Starting in 1914 when they participated in the Howth Gun Running operation, this youth organization dramatically transitioned from a boy's hurling club and benign scouting organization founded along Lord Baden-Powell's scouting model into a revolutionary youth organization. With leaders such as Sean Heuston and Con Colbert amongst its ranks, it is clear to say that without this organization the ranks of the Easter Rebellion may have been much thinner and without some of its few competent members if the Rebellion were even able to occur at all.

The widows of the leaders executed in Kilmainham Goal did more for the propaganda war than any other group. After the *Rebellion*, women were responsible for the vast majority of the propaganda put out by the Republicans.[7] The whole world became heart-broken when newspapers worldwide reported that Grace Gifford Plunkett heard the gunshots that ended her husband's life just hours after they were married in prison.[8] As the executions continued, General Maxwell was attempting to decapitate the Fenian movement. The widows and relatives of the leaders of the Rebellion increasingly filled the void in leadership to ensure the movement did not die with their loved ones.[9]

None were more active than Kathleen Clarke, the elder stateswomen of Irish Nationalism. She founded the first Committee of the Irish Republican Dependent's Fund, restarted the central branch of the *Cuman Na mGael*, and founded the National Aid Committee for those who had fought during the Rising after their release from jail.[10] It was through these organizations that those who would fight for Ireland were able to survive. In fact, Kathleen Clarke supported Michael Collins, whose famous flying columns would wreak havoc upon the British in the Anglo-Irish War, immediately after his release from prison in 1917.[11]

---

[7] Ibid, p. 119.

[8] "Plunkett Married on the Eve of His Death," *The New York Times*, 7 May 1916, p. 1.

[9] Margaret Ward, *Unmanageable Revolutionaries: Women and Irish Nationalism* (London: Pluto Press LTD., 1983), p. 117.

[10] Kathleen Clarke, *Revolutionary Women: An Autobiography* (Dublin: The O'Brien Press, 1991), pp. 121-135.

[11] Margaret Ward, *Unmanageable Revolutionaries: Women and Irish Nationalism* (London: Pluto Press LTD., 1983), p. 122.

These women sacrificed as much as their more famous husbands did. They were essential to the transformation of the Easter Week Rebellion from a national disgrace into the foundation for a new nation.

Beyond their work as propagandists, female Fenians helped to convert a nation. The mothers pushed their families toward nationalist beliefs. Even the Fenian beliefs of Cathal Brugha, the second in command to Eamon Ceannt's Fourth Battalion, came from his family's political background.[12] The best 19th Century military leaders almost uniformly failed to understand the revolutions that were developing in 1916. General Maxwell, one of Britain's finest and most experienced officers, failed to grasp a concept a loosely organized group of women and auxiliary supporters of the Fenians were able to exploit masterfully. While Maxwell focused on the hard, tactical objectives the Fenians were able to seize the true center of gravity for a counterinsurgency: the support of the population.[13] The matriarchs of Irish households had an immeasurable contribution to the campaign to win popular support after the failure of Easter Week. Whether they understood the importance or effect of their work as part of a nested strategy or if they were just expressing their beliefs and experiences in a public domain, their actions had a greater effect on achieving an independent state than any single pull of a trigger could.

The Irish Free State considered itself the first nation to allow women to not only serve in support roles, but to serve shoulder to shoulder with the men on the front lines.[14] While this was not universal among all the commands and whether or not the Republic the Fenians declared could really be considered a nation, the role of the few women who actively took up arms and the female combat support elements was a start contrast from other modern nations. This is especially true when juxtaposed to what Emily Pankhurst and her fellow suffragettes were doing in Britain despite the war effort.

The female presence during and after was critical to Fenians efforts before, during and after the Rebellion and many of the males in the movement recognized this. While the dynamic does not meet the modern definition of equality, the relationship between the sexes was

---

[12] Alfred Burgess, *Bureau of Military History, 1913-1921,* p. 1634.

[13] Jonathan Klug, "Behind the Mosaic: Insurgent Centers of Gravity and Counterinsurgency" (Monograph for School of Advanced Military Studies, 2011), p. 4.

[14] Max Caufield. *The Easter Rebellion* (New York, Holt, Rinehart and Winston, 1963), p. 290.

decades ahead of its time. The number of critical leadership roles, from commander and Pearse's representative to General Lowe when negotiating the surrender, was later reflected in the prominent leadership roles and offices that women later held in the Irish Free State. Without the efforts of the women organizations during the Rebellion, the fighters would not have been able to communicate, receive medical treatment or sustenance during the fighting. More importantly, without their propaganda efforts, the Irish public would have accepted Maxwell's court martials and executions with a shrug and a sigh instead of a newfound resolve for self-determination.

Chapter 43: Power Shift in Irish Politics

"I do beg the government…not to show undue hardship or severity to the great masses of those who are implicated, on whose shoulders there lies a guilt far different from the instigators and promoters of the outbreak."[1] -Sir John Redmond to Sir Edward Carson

The most tangible change that occurred in Ireland after the 1916 Uprising was the power shift in Irish politics away from John Redmond and the Irish Parliamentary Party. It was this change that directly led to the Irish War for Independence and the Irish Civil War. After the executions and restrictions that followed in the aftermath of Easter Week, Sinn Fein usurped the Irish Parliamentary Party as the representative and legitimate voice of the Irish. This primarily occurred because John Redmond and his party could not deliver on their constituent's demands for the release of the prisoners of Easter Week.[2] Redmond and other influential Irishmen did all they could to ease the British treatment of the Rebels and their followers. Letters directly to the Chief of Staff pleaded that "the present unrest and disaffection in Ireland is due not only to the delay in the setting up of a Home Rule Government but also to the difference of treatment accorded to the Ulster Volunteers and the Irish National Volunteers."[3]

Even more devastating than the failure to secure freedom for the prisoners was the failure to secure freedom for Ireland in the form of the long-promised Home Rule Bill and the very real possibility that Britain, still desperately fighting in France, was going to extend conscription to Ireland. Redmond and his party had fruitlessly worked since the 1880s through diplomacy and bargaining in the Parliament to gain some measure of Home Rule for Ireland. Seven months after the end of a short-lived and vastly unpopular rebellion, popular outcry against martial law and executions had forced the new British Prime Minister David Lloyd George to set up the Irish Convention to begin to debate proposals for

[1] Irish Political Documents 1916-1949. "Redmond to Carson on the Rising, 3 May 1916." Ed. Arthur Mitchell and Padraig O Snodaigh. Dublin: Irish Academic Press, Ltd., 1985, p. 21.

[2] Tim Pat Coogan, *Ireland Since the Rising* (London: Pall Mall Press, 1966), p. 22.

[3] CSO, Regd. Papers, 7800/1916.

Irish Home Rule. The Irish people viewed this as a real step towards independence that came directly from the actions of the Rebellion and this success transferred into an explosive growth in Sinn Fein support.[4] Many in Ireland saw the contrast between Redmond's failure to use diplomacy to gain a similar convention in more than thirty years of trying and the immediate reaction gained by the *Rising* and began to see Sinn Fein as the best choice to enact change. By the 1918 elections, support for Redmond had dropped so much that even in public "he looked an absolutely broken man."[5]

The fear of the extension of conscription to Ireland was very real to the Irish people. The high casualty rates on the Western Front and the real and perceived racism towards the Irish made conscription akin to a death sentence. It was not until nearly the last minute that the government in Britain decided against passing the legislation. Ireland had lost many sons to the Great War due to the large volunteer turn out that Redmond's Party had pushed for and the salary and pension that came from enlisting. Conscription coming so close to fruition and the high cost in lives for those Irishmen who joined the British Army further undermined the support for Redmond and his party.

No group benefited from the 1916 Uprising more than Sinn Fein did. While the Rebels were an amalgamation of several factions, the decapitation of leadership of the other organizations and the common use of the name in the newspapers and by the British government made it the de facto identifier for the Irish nationalists. One of the hardest hit factions were the Socialists that Tom Clarke had led. With a Socialist influence waning and the Russian Revolution still in the future, no substantial castigation of Fenians as a radical communist organization developed.

Within the Fenian movement, Sinn Fein became the publicly active political party. They became synonymous and indistinguishable from the conglomeration of movements and organizations that rose on Easter Week in the press, the British government and in Irish minds. Sinn Fein came out of Easter Week more organized and united and with more of an existing leadership structure than the other various factions. The British decapitation of the leadership of the Rebellion did much to eliminate various centers of power and cults of personality. This allowed

[4] Tim Pat Coogan, *Ireland Since the Rising* (London: Pall Mall Press, 1966), p. 23.

[5] Thomas Pugh, *Bureau of Military History, 1913-1921,* p. 397.

for a new, more unified organization in terms of leadership, objectives and philosophy than the Easter Rebels had.

The popularity of Sinn Fein grew after the *Uprising* primarily because *The Irish Times* wrongly and unintentionally attributed the Rebellion to the group. If anything, the organization that Arthur Griffith founded in 1905 was a monarchist movement. Griffith has written a book called the *Resurrection of Hungry* that advocated a dual monarchy between Britain and Ireland. This all changed after 1916 when Sinn Fein became the blanket term for all Irish Nationalist groups.[6] Sometimes inaccurately called the "Sinn Fein Rising", this misnomer did have the positive effect of uniting all of Ireland's Nationalist groups under one, distinct banner.[7] The growing feeling of pride in the *Uprising*, the arrest of even suspected Sinn Feinners, and the ineffectiveness of John Redmond to intervene on the behalf of the Rebel prisoners grew the popularity of the party.[8] From the Rising came a new, powerful political party. Although the origins of its legitimacy are inaccurate, the work of its members after the Uprising and during the Civil War made it the political party that ensured the eventual independence for Ireland.

While an independent Irish nation did not emerge from the Rebellion, a political alternative to John Redmond's party emerged as a viable force in Irish politics.[9] Although in March of 1916 there were only about 2,000 Nationalist volunteers in Dublin as opposed to the 150,000 serving in the British Army and the 160,000 in Redmond's National Volunteers, their numbers may not be as telling as they appear.[10] There were several reasons that an Irish Nationalist might join with one of the pro-Union groups: the money that the British Army paid, the severance allowance it gave to spouses, anger over the German invasion of Catholic Belgium, the hope of a favorable return for Home Rule, and that no better political party than John Redmond's existed.[11]

---

[6] Tim Pat Coogan, *1916: The Easter Uprising* (London: Orion Books Limited, 2001), p. 48.

[7] Elsie Mahaffy, "Ireland in 1916: An Account of the Rising in Dublin" TCDMS 2074 (Diary, Dublin, 1916), p. 6.

[8] CSO, regd. Papers, 8543/1916.

[9] R. Dudley Edwards, "The Achievement of 1916," in *1916: The Easter Rising*, ed. O. Dudley Edwards and Ferguys Pyle (London: MacGibbon and Kee Ltd., 1968), p. 11.

[10] Leon O'Broin, *W.E. Wylie and the Irish Revolution 1916-1921* (Dublin: Gill and MacMillan Ltd., 1989), p. 1.

[11] Lorcan Collins, "1916: The Easter Rising Walking Tour," 13 July 2006.

On the Western Front, news of the Rebellion certainly had an impact on the Irishmen fighting in the British Army. While feelings were as mixed on the Front as they were back home in Ireland, the Rebellion did lead to several desertions to German forces.[12] However, the impact was minimal and far from what Roger Casement dreamed of while he was in Berlin.

In relative short order, most of the Catholic population shifted from Redmonite politics towards Republicanism, but that shift took a highly effective propaganda movement and direct action by the British against innocent Irish families to convince the populace that they would never have true self determination under a British crown. There was also an opposite reaction against Irish independence. The Ulster Unionist organizations were more organized and better equipped than the Irish nationalist organizations prior to the Rebellion. Easter Week was a call to arms for these Orangemen and caused many Protestants to move more towards a support of the British Empire. While the leaders of Easter Week Fenians were a mix of Catholic, Protestant and Socialist Atheists the aftermath of the Rebellion quickly saw the split along religious lines in the polarization between nationalism and loyalism.

The complete loss of faith in Redmond's ability to secure a Home Rule Bill and the proof that even the post-Victorian British Empire would still view the Irish as their subjects and subjugate them with martial law and draconian policies directly led to years of civil war and decades of troubles.

---

[12] Ronan McGreevy, "Secret files reveal how deeply the Easter Rising affected Irishmen serving in first World War" April 2018 [The Irish Times] Available from <https://www.irishtimes.com/news/ireland/irish-news/secret-files-reveal-how-deeply-the-easter-rising-affected-irishmen-serving-in-first-world-war-1.3486276>; Accessed 7 April 2018.

Left - Michael Mallin
Right - Peadar Clancy

Left - Alexander Gray
Right - Denis O'Callaghan

Makeshift armored car from the Guinness Brewery

Section 5: Analysis

Chapter 44: The Fenian Mission

Most modern, professional have very clear definitions for the critical planning features that are so vital to understanding not only how victory is defined, but what the critical subordinate tasks must happen in order to achieve this victory. Focusing on three of the most vital: Mission, End State and Decisive Point will help to clearly define the true objectives of the leaders of the Easer Rebellion.

This analysis will apply modern military definitions, theories and thought structure to the thoughts, plans and dreams of men who were executed over a century ago. While it is impossible to truly be able to capture or translate their designs, it is still useful to illustrate how a tactically and operationally failed campaign was still able to achieve the strategic objective of creating an independent Irish state. The Easter Rebellion did not directly create an independent Irish state much in the same way that any one battle does not directly win a war. From the Fenian perspective, the Easter Rebellion cannot be viewed in a vacuum as a separate and independent war. For the Irish nationalists, it was but another campaign – their generations turn to sacrifice – in a centuries spanning struggle against the English. An apt comparison would be the numerous conflicts between the kingdoms of France and England peaks and valleys across the spectrum of warfare that are now referred to as the Hundred Years War. Easter Week was the penultimate point to the establishment of the Irish Free State, but not to the end of the conflict. The Irish Civil War of the early 1920s and the *Troubles* of the 1970s were as much a continuation of the same conflict as the Easter Uprising was a continuation of Wolfe Tone's rebellion.

When creating a plan for an operation, there are several factors that must be taken into consideration. The US Army uses the acronym METT-TC. This stands for: Mission, Enemy, Terrain, Time, Troops and Civilian considerations. It is the final and most recent addition that would be the most important to the overall success of the Easter Uprising. Civilian considerations were not added to this planning structure until the US Army was several years into its longest wars – those in Iraq and Afghanistan. While the leaders of the Rebels placed more emphasis on glory and martyrdom then they did on creating a viable plan or building a force capable of executing it, this is still a useful framework to determine where they went wrong and where they went right.

The mission, being simply defined as the task, purpose and intent, was never clearly defined for the Fenian forces. Even though military planning and staff work was vague to the point of near non-existent by the standards of twenty-first century militaries the Fenians were severely lacking in defining their focus and goals. Each of the units were assigned an objective that roughly meshed into a larger plan. The organization and planning of the individual commands varied by the personalities leading them. There was not a clear picture as to what they were trying to achieve and how the success of the shaping operations would lead to overall strategic success. The missions for the supporting efforts was generally clear. They would seize and hold a politically and geographically important piece of terrain (like the Four Courts, Dublin Castle or St. Stephens Green) in order to disrupt the ability of the British forces to mass on the main objective/Fenian headquarters at the GPO.

Complicating this definition is the role that the other battalions outside of Dublin were to play in the Easter Rising. Planning for the Rebellion was very decentralized. The main Fenian planners concentrated their entire efforts on the planning for the battle inside of Dublin and left the other Battalions to their own devices. Even the signatories of the Easter Proclamation were unclear as to what the specific mission were for those battalions. Were they to fight in their own area of operations, like the 5th Battalion at the Battle of Ashbourne and force the British to disperse their forces throughout the countryside or were they to move towards Dublin to concentrate Fenian forces there? As evidenced by the variety of rumors during Easter Week, many propagated by Connolly himself, there was no clear plan on what they were supposed to do.

It is fairly simple to put a mission statement together for any of the supporting efforts. For example, the mission statement for the First Battalion under Ned Daly would have been: *The First Battalion of the Irish volunteers will seize the buildings the comprise the Four Courts extending up Church Street towards Phibsborough no later than 0900 on Easter Morning 04241916 in order to disrupt the movement of British forces north of the River Liffey.*

It is much more complicated to describe the mission of the forces of the GPO or the strategic mission of the entire Fenian force because their end state and decisive point is not clear and clouded in romanticism. The one thing that united this hodgepodge assembly of Irish nationalists is the belief the Britain should have no hand in the rule of Ireland. Therefore, the strategic end state is a free and independent Ireland.

However, it is unclear what the end state of this Easter Week operations would be. It is obvious that they would not have assumed success would have been as simple as seizing the GPO and declaring a nation. That the British would not just acquiesce, pack up after centuries of occupation, discharge the Irishmen on the Western Front and go back to their island.

There is no clarity on what the next phase of the operation would be, but it can be assumed that this was to be the opening salvo in a more geographically widespread war against the British. The Fenians believed that battalions throughout Ireland would need to rise and fight. A viable Fenian end state of the Easter Week Uprising could have been that more than X counties engaged in active rebellion against British forces.

While this construct would have nested well with both the ideology and common sense, it is highly likely that formal plans for the next phase of operations were disseminated or written down because they were never made. The strong emphasis on the glorification of martyrdom for the Fenian cause means that the end state could simply have been the Rebellion in and of itself. The Rebellion could have just been a grand gesture, a true suicide mission that was so realistic in its probability for failure that its only objective was to fight at all.

Defining the decisive point is another way to go about this. The decisive point is the tipping point of the battle. The point where once that task has been achieved, the mission has become successful. A simple, tactical example of this would be in an assault on an objective. If the objective is to seize a piece of terrain, a hilltop for example, the decisive point could be once the assaulting element has cleared past the last enemy defensive position. This could be written as: the deceive point is when the assaulting element has cleared the enemy bunker position located at "phase line black" on the military crest of the hill.

Each of the tactical actions have objectives that would change as the battle progresses, commonly known as phases. For example, in the Easter Rising, you could easily put three phases on the action. Phase 1 would be seizing key terrain like Jacob's Biscuit Factory or St. Stephen's Green. Phase 2 would be the defensive action against the British counterattack. Phase 3 would be expansion into a wider, nationwide Rebellion. The actions of Easter Week would, in and of themselves, be merely a phase in the larger, strategic, operation to secure independence from Britain.

It is doubtful that the Fenians thought beyond the second phase of operations for Easter Week, let alone the wider rebellion. There was no strategic vision or grand plan. There was no decisive point at which they could say, 'once we've achieved this, then we shall be successful.' A century's worth of continued violence and strife speaks to this.

At the tactical level, it is simple to determine what the decisive points would have been. Seizing objectives and defeating counterattacks have been codified down to a science by modern militaries. What is much harder to determine is what the decisive point for the third phase would be. How would the Rebels transition from defeating the initial British counterattack into defeating the British in Ireland? How would they coordinate with forces in outside counties and eventually mass them into a force large enough to fight an organized British Army? Were the plans coordinate further with German forces?

This lack of planning for the third phase of Easter Week and for the larger Rebellion betrays a combination of extreme martial incompetence coupled with an overwhelming delusional philosophical idealism of the Fenian forces. The romantic belief that once Pearse read the Easter Proclamation the people would rise and in unison repel the invaders as centuries of the ancestors could not. The alternative is that they did not bother to plan or think about this because they did not know how.

There is a fatalistic alternative that the Fenian leaders did not believe that they would survive the Rebellion, so there was no point in planning what they would not live to see. That their decisive point was merely Rebellion in and of itself. Whether they lived or died, succeeded or failed, the first pull of the trigger was enough to fulfill their duty and destiny to the Fenian cause.

Seventeenth, Eighteenth and even early Twentieth Century European and American armies would often define these statements in long, flowing prose. In style of the day, the Fenians could have stated their mission as: 'Irish Volunteer forces will seize key strategic and symbolic locations in Dublin in order to inspire the remainder to resist British Rule and initiate guerrilla warfare throughout the country.'

The Military Council may have anticipated that the Rebellion would fail during Easter Week. They probably did not foresee the countermanding order, but even the most romantic would have had to contemplate that the people would fail to raise to the barricades against the insurmountable might of the British Army. The Fenians would, however, most likely view this loss, plus the subsequent retributions, imprisonments, penalties and executions as a blood sacrifice that would lead to a dramatic change in public opinion. This change would be necessary to sway a nation on the cusp of Home Rule, whose populace is heavily involved in a foreign war in support on Britain and heavily dependent upon its pensions and welfare, to violently reject any form of British rule and rise in arms against the Crown.

The Fenian leaders did not have a clear mission or objective. Whether this was due to incompetence, a rosy vision of success or the foresight that this was rebellion was a sacrifice the Rebel efforts would have been more successful with this planning

Chapter 45: The British Mission

After the initial shock of the attack on Dublin Castle and Phoenix Park, the British responded to the Rebellion in a manner expected of a professional army. While the British did not expect an armed uprising on Easter Week, they did anticipate that such a rebellion was a possibility. There were both formal and informal plans in place on how Dublin Castle would orchestrate a response to insurgency ranging from a German landing to a labor strike. While in normal circumstances, the Marxist belief that a capitalist army would hesitate to destroy the means of production may have been held some logic and truth, the British Empire in 1916 was in far from normal circumstances.

Speed in defeating the Fenians was of the essence to prevent disruptions to the sustainment effort for the British Expeditionary Forces fighting abroad and to prevent diversion of combat troops. Stability, or at least suppression of hostilities and the reestablishment of a functioning port, was critical to allowing the highest concentration of British forces on the continent and to prevent any further disruptions to the flow of men and material.

The British plan had four phases. The first was to determine the scope of the Rebellion. This was quickly established using the modern telegraph and signals systems throughout Ireland and by reconnoitering possible Rebel positions in and outside of the city and probing their strengths. In a time where horse cavalry had been rendered ineffective by modern machine guns, the British horse cavalry was able to effectively accomplish its task of reconnaissance with support from Irish Constabularies and auxiliary forces like the Georgius Rex. The Lancers' Monday morning charge on the GPO being the best example of this. While they did not dislodge the main Rebel position, they were able to effectively determine the depth and extent of the Fenian locations around Dublin.

The second phase was containing the Rebels to Dublin. Preventing a breakout or the spread of hostilities to the countryside was critical to quickly putting the Rebellion down and minimizing the troops required. Occupying the entire island would have required tens of thousands of troops that were desperately needed in France. The British would accomplish this by encircling Dublin, ensuring that there were no communication stations in Rebel hands and cutting off all mass transportation into and out of Dublin. Simultaneous to this encirclement, they would ensure that all key terrain inside the city was held. The primary purpose of this was to deny the Fenians any propaganda victories. Sites like Trinity College and Dublin Castle were primary objectives.

The third phase was to isolate the Rebel positions from each other. After General Lowe established a cordon around the city, he moved his forces to separate each of the identified Rebel strongholds from each other. As British reinforcements came into the city and the threat of a Rebel column moving in from the countryside minimized, General Lowe was able to get more aggressive in advancing his columns along major thoroughfares to both isolate the Rebel positions from each other and to begin directly attacking locations like the GPO with a tremendous advantage in manpower. Conventional wisdom is that attackers need a three-to-one advantage in manpower to be successful. By the time Lowe began his advances, the British had an even stronger advantage than that.

The fourth and final phase was to attack. In this phase the British forces attacked the Rebel stronghold, not just with fire by with direct assault by infantry forces. All phases had some overlap and there was constant attack by direct fire throughout the entire operation. At this point, the British completed the isolation of the Fenian positions. Now the British had the initiative, and they could decide when and where to assault instead of merely relying on targets of opportunity and the aggressiveness of the on the ground commander. There was direct pressure from General Maxwell down quickly put an end to the Rebellion.

Even after the arrival of General Maxwell, General Lowe maintained his operational control of the fight. The British mission was simple: British forces were to isolate and destroy all Rebel held positions in Dublin and quickly restore normal order and functions to the city's vital infrastructure. The British had a completely enemy focused mission. Any thought of key political or civil terrain was at best an afterthought.

Chapter 46: Objectives

"Forward, the Light Brigade!"
Was there a man dismayed?
Not though the soldier knew
Someone had blundered.
Theirs not to make reply,
Theirs not to reason why,
Theirs but to do and die.
Into the valley of Death
Rode the six hundred.[1]

While historians can take advantage of the fact that they can take chapters to explain even minute points, militaries do not have luxury to be verbose when defining critical points and concepts. The leaders of the 1916 Rebellion were not military professionals. They did not think, speak or write in the curt and direct language of modern militaries. In the Victorian era, the language used in this issuance of orders by Western professionals of the highest military distinction and pedigree was far more vague than the modern standard, however it still did provide discernable and understandable directions and intent. Compared to the clearly defined, systematized structuring and language used in modern orders 19th and early 20th Century commands seem poetic at best, superfluous and open to interpretation as a rule, and confusing at worst. There are countless examples from the wars proceeding the Great War of a misinterpreted order leading to utter disaster.

If there were one leader of the Rebellion, all the men and women present that morning would have agreed that Padraig Pearse would have been the figurehead. There was no one leader of the Easter Rebellion. This violation of the military principal of unity of command not only resulted in the poor execution of the plan and the infamous countermanding order. This lack of unity and the reliance upon Pearse, a romantic and

[1] Alfred Lord Tennyson, "The Charge of the Light Brigade", December 2017 [Poetry Foundation] Available from < https://www.poetryfoundation.org/poems/45319/the-charge-of-the-light-brigade>; accessed 1 December 2017.

an academic, as the closest thing to a leader in the Fenian organization resulted not only in battlefield confusion and tactical failure, but also clouds the true objectives and end state of the Rebellion. The lack of a true commander was not the only violation of the principals of warfare committed by the Fenians. The lack of a clearly defined mission and objective, while not unique to 19th and early 20th Century operations, coupled with the inevitable overwhelming might of the British military to doom the self-proclaimed Irish Republic.

One of the most famous incidents in the history of the British Army came from a similar lack of a clearly defined order coupled with an enemy's insurmountable advantage in firepower. The famous Charge of Light Brigade just over sixty years prior and immortalized in Alfred Lord Tennyson's poem could not have been far from mind for any Englishman or Colonial coming of age in the Victorian era. While well within the practices and common standards for military orders of the time and Army, the simple order that Lord Raglan gave to Captain Nolan: "Lord Raglan wishes the cavalry to advance rapidly to the front – follow the enemy and try to prevent the enemy from carrying away the guns"[2] falls well short of critical information required of a modern military order. Lucan ordered Lord Cardigan and his Light Brigade into a suicide attack because there was no clear task, purpose or intent to the attack. Raglan, Nolan and Lucan all made fatal assumptions from their vantage points and prerogatives that in the end doomed one-hundred and seven men to their deaths.[3] While historians have reached the conclusion that if Lord Lucan had challenged the order or even asked for the slightest clarification, it would have averted the fateful charge.

The Fenians who planned and lead the Easter Rebellion would have been aware of this and countless other historical and contemporary examples of military disasters caused by a miscommunication. It is unreasonable to expect these men, who by profession were poets, aristocrats, schoolmasters and labor leaders, to have carefully studied and applied the lessons learned of this misinterpreted order. It is less unreasonable to expect these lifelong advocates of Irish independence would have studied the numerous European rebellions that occurred in

[2]Evans, Elanor. "The Charge of the Light Brigade: who blundered in the Valley of Death?" In History Extra. Winter 2016. Available from <http://www.historyextra.com/article/bbc-history-magazine/charge-light-brigade-who-blundered-valley-death>. Accessed 8 December 2017.

[3] Ibid.

the 19th Century. They must have known the likelihood of success of a movement that relied on the citizenry awakening from their slumber to rise in arms to join the barricades.

While idealistic, these were not the young men of Victor Hugo's Parisian coffee shops pontificating on the red and the black. While it is doubtless than many of the men who took up arms that morning held the same youthful idealism, the leaders of the movement were older, personally successful and well educated. They, especially Pearse, knew the lore and legend of previous failed Fenian uprisings. While they may have underestimated England's strategic position in the midst of the Great War and overestimated the nationalist zeal of an island with many of its young men voluntarily serving in and families dependent on salaries from their overlord's, it is hard to imagine that they would have so grossly overestimated their chance of winning nationhood by force.

Why then, launch such an obviously hopeless Revolution? While it is doubtless than many of the men and even some of the leaders had enough unsubstantiated illusions of success to justify mustering and striking on Easter morning, it is likely that there was an understanding of the low probability of success. Without clearly defining tasks and intent at the strategic, operational and tactical levels most historians have assumed that this was a poor plan, poorly communicated and poorly executed that only eventually succeeded because of the bungling and heavy-handed response of General Maxwell.

It is impossible to know if and to what extent this simplified version is true. While the Fenian leaders may not have planned the Rebellion as purely a sacrifice, it is more likely that they know that their tactical and operational success was not necessary to achieve the desired end state of Irish independence.

Chapter 47: A Fenian Analysis of Enemy (British) Forces

Taking this analysis from the Fenian perspective, there were two possible enemy forces. The first would be the official representatives of the British government in Ireland. This would include the Army and Naval forces as well as the police constabulary, investigative services and other official government representatives. The second forces were the unofficial or irregular forces. These pro-Union, largely Protestant forces did not have a noticeable presence in Dublin, but had the rebellion spread throughout the island as planned they would have become a more significant factor. Especially in the Northern counties as seen during the Irish Civil War and the Troubles.

The Fenians knew that the British forces and their government were rightfully focused on the Great War. The massive mobilization and unprecedented participation of every facet of British society and its empire was truly levee en masse on an unprecedented scale. The Fenians also would have understood that the British, while ever wary for Irish tumult, would not predict a home-grown Irish rebellion as the most likely course of action. Labor riots or strikes were by far the most likely course of action. As recently as August 1913, there had been labor strikes in Dublin with more than twenty thousand participants.[1] It is far more likely that the Constables who came searching Liberty Hall in the day months preceding the Rebellion were looking for indications of a communist inspired labor strike that would disrupt the flow of men and material to France. Those in the service of the crown who had an eye on a nationalist rebellion would also be more focused on a rebellion inspired, supplied and launched by the Kaiser's forces. Wild fears of a modern day Hoche Expedition launched from U-Boats must have haunted those tasked with keeping Ireland secure. Further, in the espionage and subterfuge filled world that would see these fears confirmed with the Zimmerman Telegram scandal – a telegram from German representatives to the Mexican government promising support for an invasion of the United States – the British would be incredibly wary of the opening of another front in their own empire.

---

[1]Hourly History. *Easter Rising: A History From Beginning to End.* Hourly History, 2016. p. 11.

While Ireland was on a war-footing and the martial presence was higher during the pre-war years, the island was not on lockdown. Some of this resulted from the support that John Redmond and his Home Rule Party gave to the war effort. This plus the large number of Irishmen fighting for the war effort and the even larger number of Irish mouths depending on those men's salaries for survival made it seem unlikely for a major revolution.

There were also questions of how willing the British would be to sacrifice men and capital to defeat the Rebels. Avowed Marxists within the Fenian ranks like Clarke believed that the British would never fire on their own city and risk destroying the means of production that made their Empire wealthy and supported the war machine. Others believed that the British would never risk a fight in Ireland when they faced an existential threat in the Great War. The realists thought that the British would use all means at their disposal to quash the Rebellion quickly. The reality on the British side was mixed. While none of the officers seem to indicate any desire to preserve property and minimize collateral damage, there was some disagreement as to what actions to take to minimize casualties. General Lowe's slow cordon and use of naval and land artillery and snipers shows a desire not to wontedly waste British lives for a quick victory. General Maxwell was more aggressive, but it is unknown how he would have approached the problem had the cordon not already been set. At the subordinate commands, there was also a difference of opinion. Colonel Machonchy, who commanded the Sherwood Foresters, was reluctant to attack without artillery support, while Colonel Oates was far more aggressive and believed, along with General Lowe, that they were asking no more of their men than Haig was asking of the troops on the Western Front.[2]

The Fenians had rough estimates and knowledge of the number and disposition of British forces on the island. The main army establishments were at Finner in Donegal, the Curragh in Kildare near Dublin and at smaller camps in Buttevant, Mallow and Fermoy. There were also small garrisons in Belfast, Dundalk, Mullingar and an artillery depot in Athlone. The total number of troops in Dublin were estimated at 5,000 and a total of 37,000 in Ireland. Additionally, there were 12,000 armed members of the Royal Irish Constabulary on the island.[3]

---

[2] Michael Foy and Brian Barton, *The Easter Rising* (London: Sutton Publishing, 2004), p. 79.

[3] Ibid, p. 14.

The one lucky break for the Fenians was that the British forces that they faced were hardly the hardened veterans of the Western Front. They were mostly green troops diverted from training who had minimal if any training in tasks as basic as marksmanship. Many had never even fired a live round while in uniform.[4] Further, while they knew that there was an emergency due to the rapid nature of the deployment, many of them assumed it was on the Western Front. Officers hurriedly purchased tour guides of Dublin because they lacked maps and many of the soldiers disembarked in Dublin assuming that they were in France.[5]

The Fenians had rough estimates of the quantity and quality of the British soldiers in Ireland. There is nothing to indicate that they viewed them as anything other than a superior and professional fighting force with tremendous capabilities. The Fenians also knew the British would send reinforcements and could only hope these would be undertrained and untested men with the similar inexperience and fighting capabilities as the Fenians. In this case, the Rebels got what they wanted. The North Midland Division was diverted from training near Hertfordshire to respond to the Uprising. This unit under the command of Major General A. E. Sandbach consisted of the 176th Brigade, the North and South Staffordshire Regiments; the 177th Brigade, the Lincolnshire and Leicestershire Regiments; and the 178th Brigade, the Sherwood Foresters ("The Robin Hood").[6] There are numerous stories where the soldiers of this division, completely unaware as to the events in Ireland assumed they were landing in France when they docked in Dublin. They came with minimal ammunition, no experience with war and no training in urban warfare. They were hardly the first choice for soldiers, and one of their officers, Captain E. Gerard of the Royal Field Artillery, described them as "untrained, undersized products of the English slums…The young Sherwoods I had with me had never fired a service rifle before. They were not even able to load them."[7]

In Plunkett and Casement's estimate to the Military Council, the: "British forces in Ireland are not an army nor even a garrison at present. There are a number of small, scattered garrisons and many large training camps. They are not equipped for the occupation of the country

---

[4] Ibid, pp. 165-166.

[5] Ibid, pp. 165-166.

[6] Joseph McKenna, *Voices from the Easter Rising: Firsthand Accounts of Ireland's 1916 Rebellion* (Jefferson: McFarland & Company, Inc., Publishers., 2017), p. 120.

[7] Ibid, p. 120.

much less to resist invasion. Those units that are intended for immediate service receive their equipment, munitions and stores in England when they leave Ireland on their way to the front."[8] Their estimation, and their proposal to the British, was that Ireland was ripe for the taking and could easily fall with minimal German intervention. The Germans were not interested.

There was also no unified command operating in Ireland. General Maxwell did not arrive in Ireland until Friday April 28th. While all representatives of the British government did report to a single person, the Lieutenant Governor of Ireland Ivor Churchill Guest the Viscount Wimborne, and he did have the ability to declare martial law at the beginning of the Rebellion, he was a civil, not military governor. The coordination between the civil government and military representatives was more focused on supporting the war effort than preventing or defeating a rebellion.

The Fenians were correct in their assessment that April of 1916 was a tremendous opportunity to strike. Limiting the initial action to Dublin eliminated a threat from irregulars. The government had threadbare forces focused on the defense of Ireland and few in leadership or planning roles could have imagined that Redmondite Ireland would rise without an external stimulus. Further, any action would most likely be dismissed as a less violent labor strike instead of a full armed uprising. The Fenians knew the fixed positions of all British forces in the city and were able to set up their secondary positions, like the Four Courts, to disrupt their effectiveness. They also knew the entirety of the focus of the British Empire was on the War and that they would be far less able to flex their overwhelming might on Dublin and that delay in time and economy of resources gave the kindling a chance to ignite a larger fire.

Despite weight of the factors against the British forces, they were still the Britain that ruled more of the globe than any Empire in history. Even at their least prepared and weakest disposition, they British forces had an almost incalculable advantage in men and material over the Fenian forces. It is doubtful that the Fenians thought that the British would surrender Ireland or that they would not have a hard fight against Unionist population and the Ulster League. While the element of surprise and Britain's focus on the Western Front gave the Rebels an advantage at the outset, Britain simply had such an overwhelming dis-

[8] Michael Foy and Brian Barton, *The Easter Rising* (London: Sutton Publishing, 2004) p. 15.

parity in resources and combat power that there is almost no way they could have lost the fight. The armed British and the pro-Union forces in Ireland the not only significantly outnumbered the trained Fenian forces but had a tremendous advantage in firepower and the knowledge that they could leverage the full resources of the already mobilized Empire if needed.

Chapter 48: Fenian Forces Analysis

The lack of follow-on plans and poor communication for the forces outside of Dublin indicate that the Fenians may never anticipated a successful operation. It is even more indicative that this was an entirely amateur operation, below the level of competence of most militia or irregular forces. The lack of planning, communication and other failures that doomed the Rebellion has received a lot of attention. Incompetence at the strategic and operational level doomed the Uprising.

What deserves more focus is that there was very little training or competence at the tactical level. The Fenian organization lacked any sort of real noncommissioned officer presence. The composition of the Fenian forces made the inclusion of experienced tactical level leaders an impossibility. However, with some rare exceptions, the same people were personally responsible for all actions on all levels. This meant that there was never any ability to train their force for combat and the poor, but brave, performance of the Fenians in most of the sectors is proof of this.

Even if the Fenians had developed a viable strategy and adequately prepared their forces and supplies, there was not a path to outright victory without external intervention. However, even if there was a German intervention it may have done more strategic harm than good. Nations do not like invasions and the presence of the Kaiser's troops would have galvanized the support not only of the Unionists, but of neutral and pro-Home Rule Irishmen. Additionally, an invasion would have prioritized Britain's need to defend Ireland and with Britain's control of the seas the German ability to land, let alone supply, an adequate force would have been dubious at best.

Due to the overwhelming amount power the British forces could mass against the Rebels, especially as the duration of the conflict went on, the only scenario in which the Fenians would have been able to win their independence by force in 1916 is if there had been a massive uprising throughout the entire country coupled with an overwhelming series of defeats on the Western Front give the Fenians a chance.

The troops available to the Fenians did not have the competency in their basic soldier skills or logistical support to be successful without a miraculous upswing of localized support. When looking at the troops available, the first blunder that the Fenians made was to concentrate all of their organization planning on the combat troops alone. The logistical aspects of the operation were clearly an afterthought. Part of this comes from the complacency of operating in their home city, part from an optimistic assumption that the people would rally to the barricades and part because most of the combat support and service support operations were delegated to the hands of the female supporters. While the skills and abilities of the Countess Markievicz were equally to any of her male peers, these functions were secondary, even in her mind, to the glory of actual rebellion.

One of the biggest failings for the Fenians was the lack of logistical planning. It is impossible to find success in a conflict if the basics of beans and bullets are not available. The Fenians planned a first phase that would be offensive, but the more critical second phase would be defensive. They knew that they would seize the relatively unguarded objectives easily and then face stiff assaults from a professional and well-armed military force. Knowing that they were walking into a siege, they did next to nothing to prepare for this. There was not much the Fenians could do to stockpile ammunition since the limited supply of ammunition that was largely smuggled into the country, food was a different matter entirely. Timing the operation to take place immediately following the Easter holiday meant that there would be little in terms of food reserves in the city for them to commandeer and even less for the citizens.[1] This drove most people in Dublin to initially support the British response and it put a time limit on how long the Rebels could hold onto their positions before being starved out.

The one glaring deficiency that the Fenians did acknowledge and actively work to correct was the disparity in firepower. Ireland had largely been disarmed following the failed Fenian Rising of 1867.[2] The Fenians knew that they would not be able to source any form of artillery or machine gun, but actively worked through the gun smuggling of Roger Casement and civilian shooting clubs to secure enough rifles for the Rising. They did not have the arms nor ammunition to support a war that lasted longer than a week. Many of the Rebels mustered without rifles, instead they were armed with ancient shotguns, ineffective homemade bombs and grenades and even pikes. While the lunacy of a man armed with a pike fighting against a machine gun during the years

[1] Max Caufield. *The Easter Rebellion* (New York, Holt, Rinehart and Winston, 1963), pp. 158-159.

[2] Joseph McKenna, Voices from the Easter Rising: Firsthand Accounts of Ireland's 1916 Rebellion (Jefferson: McFarland & Company, Inc., Publishers., 2017), p. 31.

of the Great War was not isolated to the Irish planners, it shows just how desperate and ill equipped the Fenians were.

The Fenians were severely limited in their expertise and resources for training. They were also severely hamstrung by the secrecy needed for the operation. This secrecy extended beyond just hiding their actions and intent from the watchful eye of Dublin Castle to the need to hide their true motivation from Eoin MacNeill and the more pacifist elements of the Volunteers. One of the ways they accomplished this was through classes and terrain familiarization. The Fenians had the ability to walk in small groups to their objectives to familiarize themselves with the area, scope out their future fields of fire and identify targets and reference points.[3] Further, there were engineering classes teaching the future Rebel officers how to make explosives (which later proved ineffective), to tunnel between buildings to create internal lines of communication and how to erect barricades.[4] The latter two would prove highly effective against the assaults of the inexperienced British forces.

Even with the primacy of combat, many of Fenian forces were completely green. Firsthand accounts, while optimistic, show that even the trained forces lacked any real training that would prepare them for combat. Instead focusing on marching and drill rather than preparations for marksmanship and urban combat.[5] A desire to preserve the scarce supply of bullets could be forgiven. The focus on the pageantry of playing drill became a vainglorious preparation for death more akin to the ancient Greeks than a serious military force. The troops available to the Fenian leaders did not have the logistical support to sustain prolonged defensive operations. Nor did these forces have adequate preparation for the tasks they were assigned. While some forces, like those under the command of Ned Daly, were well-drilled and proved competent enough to effectively seize an undefended objective and execute a disruption operation, they could never have properly executed a mission to hold that terrain against the British Army.

---

[3] Ibid, pp. 32-33.

[4] Ibid, p. 32.

[5] Nora Connolly O'Brien, *The Irish Rebellion of 1916 or, the Unbroken Tradition.* (New York: Boni and Liveright, 1918), pp. 5-7.

Chapter 49: Terrain

The Fenians showed foresight and competence in understanding the importance of Dublin as a physical and emotional center of gravity. However, their tactical-level were largely incompetent. While not flawless, the combination of choosing to seize high visibility areas that would catch headlines and more defensible secondary positions to support the main locations and create a defense in depth was very astute. The Fenians prioritized objectives of cultural and symbolic significance over their tactical importance. If the Fenians had focused their effort of defeating the British forces stationed in Dublin, they would have attacked their barracks. If their priority was to disrupt the British war effort, they would have concentrated on destroying the port and railhead. If they had decided to seize the most defensible position possible, it is doubtful that location would have been in Dublin. Instead, they would have operated across the breath and out of the less accessible portions of the island. This would have made a British response more cumbersome, been able to mitigate the British naval capabilities and extended the resources required to defeat the Rebellion.

From a purely military standpoint, Dublin was a terrible location to launch a rebellion. The Fenians were outnumbered, isolated from any reinforcements or material supplies, within range of British naval power, and in the epicenter of British logistics on the island. While it is doubtful that a choosing different target or a different plan would have altered the outcome of the Rebellion, it may have extended the length, or the resources required to defeat it. While the Rebels prepared as well as they could for the realities of urban warfare in their home city, they also knew the surrounding area very well. A mountainous countryside is much friendlier to guerrilla forces than the fixed confines of a city. The Rebels were not all native Dubliners, with many connections throughout the human terrain of the areas surrounding Dublin and the more far-flung counties of Ireland. The rank and file had also become familiar with the countryside due to the numerous route marches conducted there.[1]

Connolly was very innovative with the use of the urban terrain in Dublin. In a time before street to street fighting in a multi-story urban environment was common, Connolly saw the advantages that a defend-

[1] Joseph McKenna, Voices from the Easter Rising: Firsthand Accounts of Ireland's 1916 Rebellion (Jefferson: McFarland & Company, Inc., Publishers., 2017), pp. 32-33.

er could have. In addition to the multiple pieces of high ground and restricted areas of movements, Connolly was able to foresee that the Rebels would still be facing a vastly superior force with a tremendous artillery advantage. Therefore, static defensive positions would be obliterated by British forces. Instead, he favored using unmanned barricades to frustrate cavalry charges and restrict movement.[2] Coupled with loopholed buildings that allowed his forces to move between buildings by knocking holes in walls and never having to expose themselves gave the Rebels a tremendous mobility advantage while severely restricting British movement.

The Fenians, however, were not interested in defeating British forces on Easter Week or launching a Boer-style guerilla war. They were interested in being martyrs and having their sacrificed remembered alongside their idols for generations.

[2] Michael Foy and Brian Barton, *The Easter Rising (*London: Sutton Publishing, 2004) p. 26.

Chapter 50: Time Considerations

It would have been unconscionable for the Fenian forces to let the greatest threat to the British Empire since Napoleon pass without an attempt at a rebellion. Regardless of the unique circumstances that presented themselves in 1916, the Fenians felt honor-bound to fulfill their duty to and launch an honest attempt at achieving Irish independence at least once in their lifetimes. In a martial sense, the timing of an operation takes into consideration advantages that may be gained or lost by everything from light conditions to constraints on an enemy's resources. As with other aspects of their planning, the Fenians did not take all that sophisticated of an approach when considering the military implications of time.

It is safe to say that this generation of Fenians would have at least attempted some form for violent uprising against the British during their lifetimes. The scope and success of which would most likely have been dramatically different if not for the opportunity presented by the Great War and the cultural reawakening and organization that took place in the preceding decades. For most of the Fenian leaders, the time that concerned them the most was their own lifetimes. Men like Pearse, Clarke and Connolly who had dedicated their whole lives to the dream of Irish independence felt that they owed their ideology a personal sacrifice. That a quiet and peaceful death would render them no better than a false prophet who preached a fiery path to liberation without having the courage and honor to personally sacrifice.

Another lesser appreciated aspect of time was the health of the Fenian leaders. Plunkett was dying of glandular tuberculosis, MacDermott limped from Polio and Clarke was in perpetually ill health as a result of his fifteen years of confinement in English prisons.[1] Many of the planners of the Rising knew that they were not long for the grave and felt that they had yet give their personal pound of flesh for Ireland. While this was not a solitary driver behind the decision to rebel, it would no doubt have influenced the decision-making process for many of the planners. For the likes of Clarke and Plunkett whose personal end

[1] Max Caufield, *The Easter Rebellion* (New York: Holt, Rinehart, and Winston, 1963), p. 31.

was already very near, there was no difference between a British bullet and an unseen disease. The former's chance that it may lead to the completion of their life's work and at a minimum would only enhance their own personal legacy.

The First World War presented an opportunity that the Fenians could not pass up. With Britain at its weakest, they knew that there would never be a better time to strike. This obvious conclusion drove the rhetoric and preparations from theoretical to practical. The Rebels also knew that the longer their Free State lasted, the better chance it had to enact lasting change. In the immediate sense, this could come from inspiring a mobilization of a larger portion of the populace and cajoling those who obeyed to countermanding order to take up arms. It could have inspired a mutiny of Irish soldiers on the Western Front which would have further sapped British resources and/or served as motivation the British to grant independence as the lesser of two evils when confronted with the German threat. If the Free State survived long enough it could have even resulted in recognition and possible material support from the German and Austrian forces or it could have resulted in the large population of Irishmen living in America to force Wilson to exert pressure on the British allies. While these were all far-fetched ideas and goals, they were nevertheless possibilities. When war gaming the Rebellion, these could all be considered the most dangerous courses of action for the British Empire, and they all represented real fears that the British government had to take into consideration.

Even more important to the historically minded Fenians was that the longer the Rebellion lasted, the more prominence it would hold in the annals of Irish nationalism and the more likely it would be to inspire later generations. This generation of Fenians was acutely aware and drew their inspiration to launch a rebellion from the rebellions of previous generations, which was rooted in a European history of rebellion. Even if unsuccessful, the opportunity that the First World War presented offered them the opportunity to be the most successful of the lot; and, failing that, at least the opportunity to be the most tragic. The common assumption was that after the end of the war, the Redmondite faction would win a degree of Home Rule for Ireland. If nothing else, a glorious and tragic stand for true freedom could serve as a bulwark against the nationalist complacency that would come from the partial victory of Home Rule.

While there is some significance to choosing Easter Week – it was a major holiday in a strongly Christian, especially Catholic, Ireland. The choosing of the date had less to do with any deep religious significance then it did with a practical timing. It was the first opportunity when the Fenian forces would have sufficient arms, sufficient time to train in their use and to organize themselves. They could not wait too long. The longer they held off the greater the chances that the British would discover them and their motives.

The week of the Easter holiday also had the advantage that most of the British forces would also be in a state of low readiness. This would delay their reaction in the critical first hours and give the Fenians a tremendous initial advantage in establishing seizing and establishing their positions.

The more important consideration was not the week that they launched the Rebellion, but that the Rebellion occurred during the Great War. This event, more than any before it, taxed and strained the resources available to the British. The British Empire was at its weakest. The war against the Germans was far from decided, mounting casualties and an unprecedented scarcity of resources was threatening the very existence of the Empire. This generation of Irish nationalists would never in their lifetimes have a better opportunity to strike.

Chapter 51: Civil Considerations

The components discussed thus far are more military science than art. The analyses of troop strength, fields of fire, friendly forces available, etc are more or less mathematical and comparatively straightforward. This is not to belittle their importance or difficulty. It takes an incredibly competent professional or a uniquely gifted natural tactician to be able to look at a blank map and with limited or nearly absent information be able to determine the best course of action. It is an entirely different and rare person who is also able to enact these plans in an effective and competent way. The science of war, while not easy, is relatively mechanical in its analysis, planning and application.

On the other hand, the civil component is far more art than science. While it is reasonable to assume that modern military professionals and their civilian counterparts in the field of marketing will eventually advance this aspect of warfare to a near science as teachable as implementing overlapping fields of fire on a direct fire target or how to take advantage of the military crest of the ridge when emplacing a defensive position, the human center of gravity is far more complex than any other. In the planning of the Rebellion, the Fenians were not wholly incompetent. There were several places where they showed competence and others where they showed brilliance. Their efforts were earnest and above par when compared to their peers in both professional and irregular contemporary armies.

Where they excelled beyond their peers, and especially their British adversaries, was in their knowledge and handling of the civilian population. A sizable portion of which was vehemently opposed to their aims and the vast majority of which was opposed to a violent uprising giving the situation with both Home Rule and the Great War. By and large, and especially in comparison to the British forces, the Fenians showed restraint when interacting with the civilian population. The Fenians took care to avoid unnecessary bloodshed, were open about who did the shooting and were both quick and smart in their justification for shooting. A great example of this is in the killing of the fourteen-year-old son of the caretaker of the Magazine Fort at Phoenix Park.[1] The Fenians were quick to acknowledge that his death was both unfortunate and unavoidable. The boy was given the opportunity to surrender and chose to run to alert the British forces. That he was shot because of a

[1] Helen Litton, *16 Lives: Edward Daly* (Dublin, The O'Brien Press, 2013), p. 107.

willful action and with an understanding of the potential consequences allowed the incident to be justified in a way that seemed valiant in juxtaposition with the British execution of someone like Willy Pearse who was just a common soldier who surrendered in accordance with the customs of the time. The Fenians were aware of the importance of the negative repercussions of unnecessary killings and after the first day of the Rising, Padraig Pearse issued an order forbidding the killing of any unarmed man, even if they were in uniform.[2]

Arrests were another example of where the heavy hand of the British did more harm than good. The arrest of over 3,400 people immediately after the Rising may not seem all that egregious, especially when over 1,400 of them were released in the following two weeks.[3] More than even the executions, the arrests turned the tide of public opinion. A large part of this was the scope of the arrests ensured that someone's family member, neighbor or other relation was wrongfully imprisoned. In communities and family structures as tightknit as early twentieth century Ireland, a relatively small number could have a tremendous reach. These arrests made British transgressions real to the Irish citizenry. Nation's rarely change their politics and take up arms over the martyrdom of a few men. It may cause a temporary outrage, but that will subside. They will, however, have that change for their friends, family and neighbors.

This is one of the most dramatic differences between the 1916 Rebellion and previous Fenian uprisings. While none of them lacked for the dramatic story of the heroic martyr, the scope of the Rebellion was too small to make it personal. The British did the Fenians a favor with the nationwide arrests and reactions. They ensured that a movement that Fenian incompetence and internal conflicts contained to Dublin spread throughout the island.

---

[2] Max Caufield, *The Easter Rebellion* (New York: Holt, Rinehart, and Winston, 1963), p. 127.

[3] Helen Litton, *16 Lives: Edward Daly* (Dublin, The O'Brien Press, 2013), p. 168.

Irish Citizen Army, Liberty Hall, Dublin - 1914

Dublin Castle

Phoenix Park

Left - Ivor Churchill Guest
Right - Col. Ernest Machonchy

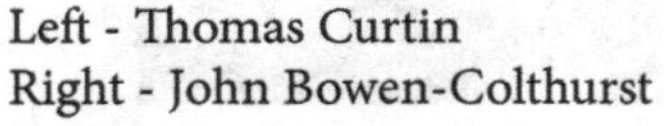

Left - Thomas Curtin
Right - John Bowen-Colthurst

Section 6: Conclusion

Chapter 52: Aftermath of the Rebellion

"It is horrible that the country has to stand silently by listening to the moans of decent young Irish boys being slowly done to death behind the walls of Mountjoy Prison by brutal tyrants."[1] -M. Fogarty, Bishop of Kiloloe

My sole object in 'surrendering unconditionally' was to save the slaughter of the civilian population; and to save the lives of our followers, who had been led into this thing by us. It is my hope that the British government who has shown its strength will also be magnanimous and spare the lives and give an amnesty to my followers as I am on the of the persons chiefly responsible, have acted as Commander in Chief and President of the Provisional Government. I am prepared to take the consequences of my act, but I should like my followers to have an amnesty. I went down on my knees as a child and told God that I would work all my life to gain the freedom of Ireland. I have divined it my duty as an Irishmen to fight for the freedom of my country. I admit I have organized men to fight against Britain. I admit having opened negotiations with Germany. We have kept our word with her and as far as I can see she did her part to help us. She sent a ship with arms. Germany has not sent us gold."[2]
-Padraig Pearse

Prior to the Rebellion, most common Irish people either accepted the status quo of British rule without or with minimal self-representation. After the Easter Rebellion, the perception shifted. Open support or action to advance Irish sovereignty was no longer relegated to fringe radicals. The Easter Uprising made open and active defiance of the British more acceptable. This was in large part due to the British government's reactions after the Rebel surrender under General Max-

[1] M. Fogary, "Letter on the Death of Thomas Ashe from the Bishop of Killoloe" TCDMS 2074 (Letter, Dublin, 30 September 1914).

[2] Padraig Pearse The National Archives of the UK (TNA): Public Record Office (PRO) PRO WO71/345.

well's direction. After the Uprising, the British did not accurately gauge the feelings of the Irish toward the Rebellion. As the arrests intensified during the month of May, many people became more and more disaffected with the British cause.[3]

The crucial misunderstanding on both sides was an overestimation of the innate support in Ireland for a violent Rebellion and to the extent of the conspiracy against the Crown. The British thought that most of the island was hostile to their rule and took actions that made this a self-fulfilling prophecy and the Rebels thought that the masses would rise to join them. The extremes of the British response are due in part to their focus on the war that was still underway in France combined with centuries of aloofness and unconcerned rule over Ireland. There was also a feeling that the major threat had been neutralized and an aggressive 'mopping up' operation to root out the remaining revolutionary elements was the logic course of action towards preventing another outburst.

The British did not realize that prior to the Rebellion the Irish were largely supportive of the Empire and viewed their rule as common fact. The ongoing war had actually increased the Empire's popularity. There was a feeling that the Irish contribution to the eventual victory in France and Parnell's emphatic support of the war effort would finally secure a Home Rule Bill. Many of the women were being supported by their husbands and sons fighting on the front or were receiving pensions from their deaths. Some Irish troops, but not all, felt betrayed by the Rebels and went out of their way to be aggressive and violent towards their prisoners.[4] The citizenry of Dublin had mixed opinions, but to the majority it was an unnecessary destruction of lives and property and a major disruption to their lives.

> "Look at what was trying to keep out the Government. You might as well try and keep out the ocean with a fork."[5] -Unnamed Dublin citizen to the surrendered Rebels

[3] CSO, Regd. Papers, 7860/1916.

[4] Joseph McKenna, *Voices from the Easter Rising: Firsthand Accounts of Ireland's 1916 Rebellion* (Jefferson: McFarland & Company, Inc., Publishers., 2017), pp. 236-237.

[5] Ibid, p. 297.

With the immediate rebellion suppressed, the British had to be cautious to ensure that the smoldering ashes from Dublin did not ignite fires in other parts of the island. Even before General Maxwell's staff learned of the countermanding order and the Fenian plans for the rest of Ireland, they had to assume, plan for and enforce the crowns position in the rest of the island. Many units who were either mid-training, en route to France or at home in England on a respite from the Western Front were recalled or diverted to Ireland. The mission of the 177th Brigade was typical of that performed by these forces. The 177th, was on leave the night before the Easter Uprising. Immediately recalled and quickly deployed to Ireland on the mail boat the SS Ulster, it the first deployed to Dublin instead of France. Their tasks in Dublin consisted of guarding key infrastructure like railways and bridges. Following that, on May 10th, they moved to County Kerry to help with the suppression of local pockets of resistance by conducting home searches and making arrests. Soon, they resumed their training, conducting route marches and finishing what they had begun in Britain before sailing to France.[6]

The Fenian protests, posters, speeches, songs, and newspaper articles became widespread and had an unquantifiable effect on Irish public opinion. These expressions of a revitalized nationalism were important because they created a relationship between the masses and the vanguards of the revolution.[7] After the Rebellion, the general tone of nationalist ballads turned from forlorn to optimistic.[8] Poems such as W.B Yeats' "Easter 1916" provided a foil to the brutality of the British by sharing Yeats' dream of a better existence in an Ireland free of British hegemony. Eventually, this disaffection began to manifest itself as political opposition and lobbying against the British policies and the perception it was creating abroad.[9]

The British, for their part, did little to counter the propaganda. They continued to rule by decree and made hardly any effort to understand, let alone sway, Irish public opinion. As Redmond lost power and influence and British eyes remained on France, the Fenians had nearly

[6] Andy Rush, "Hellfire Corner and the Easter uprising of 1916", February 2018 [Loughborough Echo] Available from <https://www.loughboroughecho.net/news/local-news/hellfire-corner-easter-uprising-1916-14218277>; Accessed 5 February 2018.

[7] Benedict Anderson, *Imagined Communities: Reflections on the Origin and Spread of Nationalism* (London: Verso, 1983), p. 80.

[8] Eimear Whitfield, "The Balladry of Revolution," in *Revolution? Ireland 1917-1923*, ed. David Fitzpatrick (Dublin: Trinity History Workshop, 1990), p. 63.

[9] CSO, Regd. Papers, 8081/1916.

free reign to control the Irish narrative.

Although the crowds that gathered to watch the beginning of the Rebellion on Easter Monday "seemed free from any strong partisan feeling," those who favored continuing British rule knew that it would not take a successful armed rebellion to undermine the Crown's position and authority.[10] Well-meaning Unionists sent the British authorities reports that greatly exaggerated the strength of the Rebel supporters and their secret sympathizers.[11] General Maxwell and his staff wrongly, but firmly believed that Ireland was full of 'Sinn Feiners' and that Sinn Fein was a singularly organized entity that controlled all of the known rebellious factions. This belief caused the severity and duration of martial law throughout the island.[12] Even the Dublin Chamber of Commerce deemed it necessary to hold an emergency meeting and send a message to the Chief of Staff for Ireland and the King's private secretary to swear their allegiance to the crown because by May 10th "so much of Dublin seems to have become Sinn Feiners."[13] While Sinn Fein was a general term used by the British to describe Irish Nationalists, the political party of the same name had successfully wed itself to the growing popularity of the Rebellion.

The restraint that the Rebels showed towards the populace of Dublin had a tremendous influence on public opinion. While physical violence against the citizenry is most often cited, the respectful handling of property and public spaces may be the more dramatic dichotomy. One of the most colorful examples is the recollection of Andrew Jameson, the owner of the Jameson distillery. After the end of the Rebellion, he praised Rebels stating that while the Fenians were in possession of his distillery they did very little damage even though they had enough whiskey to 'set all Dublin mad'.[14]

The Fenians took great pains to ensure that their fighters were respectful towards both people and property. This extended to their treatment of British soldiers and government officials. In comparison, the British felt the need to swiftly and severely punish the Rebels. Privately, to his wife General Maxwell wrote that: "some must suffer for their

[10] "The Sinn Fein Rising. Scenes and Incidents in Dublin Streets. A Citizen's Diary," *The Irish Times, 2 May 1916.*

[11] CSO, Regd. Papers, 7554/1916.

[12] George Arthur, *General Sir John Maxwell* (London: John Murray, 1932), p. 249.

[13] CSO, Regd. Papers, 7876/1916.

[14] Helen Litton, *16 Lives: Edward Daly* (Dublin, The O'Brien Press, 2013), p. 111.

crimes."[15] To Lord Asquith he justified his proposed response due to the severity of the damage to the city, the loss of life and the involvement of German support. He felt it was necessary, not out of revenge, but out of rule of law and to prevent further disturbances to "inflict the most severe sentences on the known organizers of this detestable Rising… It is hoped that these examples will be sufficient to act as a deterrent to intriguers and to bring home to them that the murder of His Majesty's subjects or other acts calculated to imperil the safety of the realm will not be tolerated."[16] This was not revenge, this was a decision to appear strong and decisive, to deter any further action and to reestablish the rule of law in Ireland.

The court martials were an involved affair. There were one-hundred and seventy men and one woman (the Countess Markiewicz) who were tried by court martialed. Only eleven were acquitted. Of those convicted, ninety received the death penalty.[17] This was far more than just isolating the most severe punishment to the leaders and it gave the surviving Sinn Feiners more than enough martyrs to rebuild the movement. As John Daly said as he was being led to his execution: "We die that the Irish nation may live. Our blood will rebaptise (sp) and reinvigorate the old land."[18]

Almost immediately, the Fenians and their support took steps to control the narrative. While the Fenians did have a printing press in Liberty Hall, the arrest of Tom Clarke and the prominent role to Volunteers played in the fighting eliminated that as a viable option for propaganda. Denied any printed means of communication, the Fenians initially had to rely on word of mouth and other oral means to begin to dictate the narrative of the Rebellion. While this would eventually spread to public speeches, the pulpit and eventually back to the printed page, initially even speaking out against the British response was a risky and highly monitored endeavor.

Fortunately for the Rebels, the British response did more than any slogan or oration could. The excessive arrests and executions gave many families and communities personal reasons to support the defeat-

[15] Maxwell, General Sir John. Letters to his wife, 12 May, Maxwell Papers, Box 6/9.
[16] Maxwell, General Sir John. Letters to Asquith, 9 May, Asquith Papers, BMS 41-3.
[17] Michael Foy and Brian Barton, *The Easter Rising (*London: Sutton Publishing, 2004) p. 232.
[18] Piaras F. MacLochlainn, *Last Words: Letters and Statements Of The Leaders Executed After The Rising At Easter 1916.*(Stationary Office, Dublin, 1990), p. 172.

ed Rebels when they otherwise may have stayed passively pro-independence, neutral or even pro-British. British action ensured that almost everyone was within a degree or two of separation from a reason to support the Rebellion. It also changed the Irish paradigm and made any tale or instance of British violence more believable and increased the overall distrust of the government in London and their Redmondite 'lackeys'. Before the Fenians even had the chance to rally and reorganize, the British had performed the Rebel's hardest task for them. Changing the public's perception throughout the island does not seem like it would have been that difficult, but that is because to modern eyes who witnessed almost a century of violence it is hard to image a British Empire that was at the moment peacefully exerting an uncontested and largely supported control over the island to include an unprecedented war effort. This abrupt transition was more the work of the heavy-handed British reaction than any effort of action by the Fenians.

For the British, the Easter Rebellion was always subsumed within the existential crisis of the First World War. The government and the populace at large cared less about the long-term ramifications of the British response then they did about ensuring that soldiers needed for the front were not stuck on guard duty in Ireland, the ports were open to move supplies and news of a fifth column was out of the headlines. General Maxwell did have a tremendous task on his hands. These were not tribesmen or colonist speaking a foreign tongue. While they may not have been English and the majority may have been Catholic, they were far more closely related than any of rebels he and his peerage had previously suppressed. With limited resources and ample pressure to get the job done and quickly, Maxwell could even be forgiven for his decisions.

There is ample evidence to show that for the most part British decision making was not motivated by spite. Rather, a desire to get back to face the real enemy and France and probably an assumption that the post-war leadership would grant the long-promised Home Rule Bill anyways. The British responses were not motivated by hate. Revenge, fear and indiscipline yes, but hate is not as likely.

In the end, the public in Ireland cared little for motivation or justification. The instances of improper and unnecessarily harsh responses took more mindshare than sympathy for the British or even pro government Irish perspective could. The prevalence of instances of British brutality created an environment where every story and slight were magnified and widely disseminated. The official British policies and proclamations of the British authority under General Maxwell re-inforced this image and furthered the rebel cause of sowing discontent against the British government. There is little to overtly show that the draconian action was intended to quickly get Ireland back to fully op-erating for the war effort, but that is probably because the need to do so went without saying. It is hard to fault this shortsightedness. In 1916 the Great War was at near its peak and even if the ports were still smolder-ing and the factories understaffed due to arrests, the men on the Front still needed the supplies to fight. The narrative had shifted, and it shifted away from Redmond and Home Role and to the Sinn Feiners.

Chapter 53: Success of Failure?

The 1916 Easter Uprising was a Pyrrhic victory for the Fenian cause. The Rebellion cost the movement its entire leadership structure, a large number of its most committed fighters, almost all of its weapons and ammunition, betrayed a conflicted leadership structure, destroyed the bravado of the organization in every location outside of Dublin and directly lead to martial law and a crackdown on dissenters and Independence activists. Despite all this loss and the failure to hold any territory or retain any objective, the events that it set in motion did eventually lead to an Irish Free State. Albeit partial since the complete unification of island under and Irish flag still remains an unfulfilled objective.

There were multiple lessons learned by the survivors that directly led to success in the subsequent Irish War of Independence. First, it proved that the continental style revolutions of the 19th Century could not survive modern warfare. The usage of effective sniper fire, innovations like the armored car and the effective usage of machine gun fire made static urban warfare a death trap for the under equipped rebels. Secondly, it disproved the Marxist theory popular among Clarke and the Irish Citizen Army that a Capitalistic power would not destroy its own means of production. Third, it proved that the Irish people were reluctant to engage in open and direct conflict with the British Army. Finally, it proved that a centralized, traditional command structure was a liability when fighting an insurgency. The revelations lead Michal Collins and later the Irish Republican Army to wage a guerilla war in the next iteration of the conflict.

Calling the Easter Uprising a success at any level relies too heavily on the outcomes of the Irish War of Independence to justify. While the Rebellion was absolutely critical and essential to setting the conditions for a successful Irish War of Independence and for the formation on the Irish Free State, by Friday of Easter Week it was clear that the Rebellion was a complete and unconditional failure for the Fenians.

Further, there was no immediate connection between the fighting during Easter Week and the Irish War of Independence. There was no force that broke out of Dublin to refit, regroup and reengage. While many of the leaders of the next phase of the centuries old conflict fought during Easter Week, they had to gain their freedom from British prisons before they could go to the next step. The three-year gap between the surrender of Pearse's forces and the founding of the breakaway Irish government (*Dail Eireann*) on January 21st, 1919, is more than enough of a demarcation between the two events to legitimately call separate wars in the same tradition.

Conflating tradition and the founding myth of the Irish Free State with an actual military and political end state has muddied the memory of the Easter Rebellion in Irish history. The story of a relatively cleanly fought, dramatic action with tragic sacrifices, heroic figures and a unification of different political factions for a common goal makes the perfect origin point for a new state. Despite the attractiveness of the story arch, the resulting shift in Irish public opinion, the harsh British reaction and the change in conditions that lead to a successful two and a half years of fighting throughout the countryside were never planned outcomes or results for the Military Council. It is fitting that a Rebellion lead primarily by nostalgic poets and nationalists with romantic views of an idyllic pre-British Ireland would be romanticized and immortalized for a Rebellion, that achieved nothing tangible for its cause.

Chapter 54: An Alternative Course of Action

The drama and devastation of a Rebellion in Dublin and the hoisting a green flag over the main symbol of the British Empire was meant to catalyze. It was meant to inspire and serve as a focal point to for the rest of the movement and to those who were undecided. It was a blood sacrifice and an event to spark a new resistance to the British in Ireland. It was not, however, the militarily prudent thing to do.

The most dangerous course of action that the Fenians could have chosen was to begin an insurgency. Forces could have dispersed among several major cities and launched bombing campaigns or concentrated in the more remote corners of the island and launched concentrated attacks where they could not just seize but hold British property. During this time, they could have slowly grown their force. Both strategies would be utilized to much greater success by the Irish Republican Army during the Irish Civil War and the Troubles.

History has proven that this course of action was not only more successful, but it would have been much more damaging to the British effort in the Great War. It would have had a much larger effect on the British supply chain, diverted far more men and material from the Western Front and the increased duration of the conflict would have done far more damage to the reputation of the British government. From a purely military standpoint, the Fenians blundered in their strategy and should have fought like guerillas and insurgents from the beginning.

It is essential for guerillas and insurgents to rally to the people to their cause. An element of drama and theater was needed to inspire a change in opinion in the Irish people. In this war, public opinion was the real center of gravity and the first strike needed to be something that would inspire it.

The argument that the Easter Rebellion was just the first battle in a larger war is a difficult one to justify. Ireland has a long history of ideologically congruent, but disconnected rebellions against British rule. The leaders of Easter Week themselves viewed their actions as their generations contribution to a struggle that went past Wolfe Tone. However, there was no formal plan that almost exactly six years after the surrender Michael Collins and his Irish Republican Army would fight and win the Irish Civil War.

The Fenians of 1916 had hoped and planned that other battalions throughout the country would also rise. These other forces were to follow the tactics of the Dublin units, seizing key government positions and fighting a wholly conventional defensive fight from behind urban barricades as was popular in the European rebellions of an earlier generation. The countermanding order is largely blamed for the failure to muster, but this affected the Dublin units as well as the outlying units.

Since all the Dublin battalions were extremely undermanned, the Fenian leaders had to quickly reorganize units, adjust objectives and alter the plan. The failure to seize Dublin Castle was a tremendous blunder. Flying a green flag over the most important building in Ireland for even an hour would have been ten times the propaganda coup that holding the Post Office was. While executing this reorganization, they should have sent one of the forces outside of Dublin to serve as a disrupting force and moved another from a less important position to Dublin Castle. This guerrilla unit would have disrupted British efforts, forced a greater commitment of forces and been able to increase the number of overall fighters. All of which were key stated objectives of the Fenians. It also would have provided a continuity of forces following the defeat of the positions in Dublin. A unit that after the surrender of the main force would continue to fly the green flag and fight the British.

The position at the Four Courts contributed the least to the overall fighting. While it was the scene of some bloodiest fighting, it held the least tactical and strategic importance and was the most isolated from the rest of the positions. Ned Daly was also the most capable commander and his men the best trained. While they would have resisted the last-minute diversion from the main action, they would have been the best choice to move to the countryside and begin a guerilla war. In this way the Fenians could have had their big, dramatic moment and been able to wage a war that would harm the British enough to force them to a negotiating table.

At any level, the 1916 Easter Uprising was a failure. It failed to meet any of its tactical, strategic or operational goals past the third day of fighting. The change of conditions in Ireland that it brought about were pure happenstance that relied upon a combination of the draconian British response, the effective propaganda campaign of the survivors and ideologically aligned Fenians who abstained from the fighting and, most importantly, the actions taken during the far more successful Irish War of Independence. The positive, for the Fenians, outcomes of the Uprising were beneficial to the Sinn Fein efforts in the subsequent war, but not wholly necessary. Had the Easter Week Fenians adopted those tactics and strategies, one conflict instead of two could have sufficed and it would have done far more damage to a Britain strained by world war. Easter Week was a failure in a decades and centuries old string of failure, but it was nevertheless critical to the subsequent conflicts that established Irish independence.

Chapter 55: Conclusion

"Now and in time to be,

Wherever green is worn,

Are changed, changed utterly:

A terrible beauty is born."[1]

-WB Yeats

The Easter Week Rebellion both failed and succeeded. The rebels fought and many gave their lives for four objectives: an independent, Gaelic, republican and united Ireland. At the end of Easter Week, they had briefly attained two of those things before being fully defeated. Today, Ireland is a free republic, but it is not united and it is hardly more Gaelic than it was a century ago.[2] The Irish Volunteers were unable to preserve their provisional government through the hail of British gunfire, the country did not rise to meet Dublin's call and Irishmen in the British Army did not defect as Pearse had proclaimed from his headquarters in the General Post Office.[3] By Friday, the British Army had met its objectives of defeating all Rebel positions, restoring order in Dublin and preventing further immediate hostilities. The Rebellion did incite a British response which proved to be swift and harsh, but well within the norms and standards of the playbook that Britain used for its overseas colonies.

It was this response created discord in Ireland and the ensuing grassroots political response changed the ethos of the island. The executions, arrests and martial law made many in Ireland realize that if the government in London treated the Irish as harshly as they would the Indian, Malay or other Zulu they would never grant self-determination of Home Rule. Home Rule no longer seemed to be an imminently achievable goal that Redmond could achieve after the Great War or the next

[1] William Butler Yeats, "Easter 1916," in *Collected Poems, (*New York: Macmillan, 1956), p. 177.

[2] Alan J Ward, The Easter Rising: Revolution and Irish Nationalism, Second Edition. (Wheelilng: Harlan Davidson 2003), p. 147.

[3] Irish Political Documents 1916-1949. "First Bulletin of the Provisional Government" Ed. Arthur Mitchell and Padraig O Snodaigh. Dublin: Irish Academic Press, Ltd., 1985, p. 18.

political milestone. It was a carrot that a superior race would perpetually keep dangling in order to continue the good and passive behavior of a subject people.

General Maxwell was unable to comprehend the disaffection that the execution of cold-blooded murders and traitors under the powers granted to him in the Defense of the Realm Regulations caused in Ireland.[4] The rise of Sinn Fein as the dominant political party and the popularization of the Fenians made the Irish nation ready to fight for self-determination with arms instead of words. The men who fought on Easter Week were once the youths of the Gaelic Athletic Association who watched the plays of Yeats. The youths who witnessed the events and repercussions of Easter Week would comprise the majority of the Irish Republican Army during the ensuing civil war.[5] The Rebels of Easter Week most likely could not have ever defeated the might of the British Army, but their glorious failure catalyzed a movement that for decades had existed in various forms and without much success. By failing and dying, the Rebels became martyrs for Ireland and upset the stagnant political climate of the colony.

General Lowe had nearly a five-to-one advantage over the Fenians. He may have refrained from an immediate, overwhelming response in Dublin because of fears of a large uprising in the country and the threat of a German landing. This mirrors General French's response with the forces in England and shows a great amount of strategic patience. He was criticized, especially by his contemporizes, for not being more aggressive. This reserved response seems even more timid in comparison to the actions that General Maxwell took when he assumed command. Isolating the unpopular Rebellion and allowing the Rebellion to slowly fizzle out in a protracted siege would have not only minimized the damage to Dublin, but the damage to the popular opinion of the Rebels.

The British commission into the Rebellion exonerated all of the principal administrators of Ireland, but concluded that Sir Matthew "did not sufficiently impress upon the Chief Secretary during the latter's prolonged absences from Dublin the necessity for more active measures to remedy the situation in Ireland."[6] They further concluded that the Re-

[4] George Arthur, *General Sir John Maxwell* (London: John Murray, 1932), p. 247.

[5] Peter Hart, "Youth Culture and the Cork I.R.A," in *Revolution? Ireland 1917-1923*, ed. David Fitzpatrick (Dublin: Trinity History Workshop, 1990), pp. 10-11.

[6] Joseph McKenna, Voices from the Easter Rising: Firsthand Accounts of Ireland's 1916 Rebellion (Jefferson: McFarland & Company, Inc., Publishers., 2017), p. 325.

bellion was that Ireland "had been administered on the principle that it was safer and more expedient to leave the law in abeyance if collusion with any faction of the Irish people could thereby be avoided."[7] Shockingly, there were no mentions of the delay in Home Rule, centuries of tyrannical administration, the growing threat of the Ulstermen or any of the other seemingly apparent sparks to the revolt. Centuries of detached rule and the cataclysm of the Great War made the British incapable of sympathizing or empathizing with Irish cause and that unwillingness to compromise with their subjected nation cost them union with the southern counties.

[7] Ibid, p. 325.

The Post Office

Bibliography

Primary

Brady, Christopher. *Bureau of Military History, 1913-1921.* 705.

Breen, Dan. *My Fight for Irish Freedom.* Dublin: Talbot Press, 1924.

Brennan, Michael. *The War in Clare 1911-1921: Personal Memories of the Irish War of Independence.* Dublin: Irish Academic Press, 1980.

Burgess, Alfred, *Bureau of Military History, 1913-1921.* 1634.

Byrne, Sean. *Bureau of Military History, 1913-1921.* 422.

Chief Secretary's Office, Registered Papers, 7319-15168/1916.

Churchill, Ivor. "A Proclamation No. 1." *The Irish Times*, 25 April 1916.

Churchill, Ivor. "A Proclamation No. 2." *The Irish Times*, 26 April 1916.

Clarke, Kathleen. *Revolutionary Women: An Autobiography.* Dublin: The O'Brien Press, 1991.

Connolly, James. *Labour and Easter Week 1916: A Selection from the Writings of James Connolly.* Dublin: Sign of Three Candles, 1949.

Connolly, James. "The Irish Flag." *Worker's Republic,* 8 April 1916.

Daly, Ned. Transcript of Court Martial. May 1916. Available from < http://www.aoh61.com/history/easter_trials.htm>.

Devoy, John. *Recollections of an Irish Rebel.* Shannon: Irish University Press, 1969.

Fogary, M. "Letter on the Death of Thomas Ashe from the Bishop of Killoloe." Trinity College Dublin Manuscripts 2074. Letter, Dublin, 30 September 1914.

Headquarters, Irish Command. "General Maxwell's Report to Field-Marshal, Commanding-in-Chief, Home Forces. Dublin, 25 May 1916.

"Inquiry into the Rebellion." *The Irish Times*, 20 May 1916.

Irish Political Documents 1916-1949. "First Bulletin of the Provisional Government." Edt. Arthur Mitchell and Padraig O Snodaigh. Dublin: Irish Academic Press, Ltd., 1985.

Irish Political Documents 1916-1949. "A Public Meeting in Galway Reacts to the Rising, 29 April 1916." Edt. Arthur Mitchell and Padraig O Snodaigh. Dublin: Irish Academic Press, Ltd., 1985.

Irish Political Documents 1916-1949. "Redmond to Carson on the Rising, 3 May 1916." Edt. Arthur Mitchell and Padraig O Snodaigh. Dublin: Irish Academic Press, Ltd., 1985.

Irish Political Documents 1916-1949. "The Death of Thomas Ashe." Edt. Arthur Mitchell and Padraig O Snodaigh. Dublin: Irish Academic Press, Ltd., 1985.

S.L King. Transcript of Court Martial. May 1916. Available from < http://www.aoh61.com/history/easter_trials.htm>.

Kitchener Papers PRO 30/57/55; see also Asquith to King George V, 27 April in PRO Cab37/146 and cabinet discussion in PRO CAB41/37.

Markievicz, Constance. "Dail Eireann debate – Debate on Treaty." *Tithe an Orieachtais House of the Oireachtas*, 3 January 1922. Available from < https://www.oireachtas.ie/en/debates/debate/dail/1922-01-03/2/>.

Maxwell, General Sir John. Letters to Asquith, 9 May, Asquith Papers, BMS 41-3.

Maxwell, General Sir John. Letters to his wife, 12 May, Maxwell Papers, Box 6/9.

Maxwell, General Sir John. Transcript of Court Martial. May 1916. Available from < http://www.aoh61.com/history/easter_trials.htm>.

Mahaffy, Elise. "Ireland in 1916: An Account of the Rising in Dublin." Trinity College Dublin Manuscripts 2074. Diary, Dublin, 1916.

Murphy, Sean, *Bureau of Military History, 1913-1921.* 204.

NOW. "Poser Against an English Garrison in Ireland." Trinity College Dublin Manuscripts 2074. Political Poster, Dublin, 1916.

Oates, W. Cope. *The Sherwood Foresters in the Great War, 1914-191* The 2/8th Battalion. London: Naval and Military Press, 2015.

O'Brien, Nora Connolly. *The Irish Rebellion of 1916 or, the Unbroken Tradition*. New York: Boni and Liveright, 1918).

O'Brien, W. "An Irish Soldier and the Rebellion." *The Irish Times*, 9 May 1916, p. 25.

O Cearnaigh, Peader. *Reminiscences of the Irish Republican Brotherhood and Easter Week 1916.* Trinity College Dublin Manuscripts 3560/1.

O Cearnaigh, Peader. *Foundlings of the Irish Republican Brotherhood.* Trinity College Dublin Manuscripts 3560/2.

Official Report by General Sir John Maxwell on the Easter Rising, April 1916. Source *Records of the Great War, Vol. IV*. Edt. Charles F. Horne. National Alumni, 1923.

Pearse, Patrick. "O'Donovan Ross's Funeral Address at Graveside." Speech. Glasnevin Cemetery, Dublin, 1 August 1915.

Pearse, Padraig. "The Coming Revolution." *An Claidhamh Soluis,* 8 November 1913, p. 6.

Pearse, Padraig. Transcript of Court Martial. May 1916. Available from < http://www.aoh61.com/history/easter_trials.htm>.

Pearse, Padriag. The National Archives of the UK (TNA): Public Record Office (PRO) PRO WO71/345.

Pearse, William. Transcript of Court Martial. May 1916. Available from < http://www.aoh61.com/history/easter_trials.htm>.

Plunkett, G.N."Letter to the People of North Roscommon Upon Election to Office." Trinity College Dublin Manuscripts 2074. Public Letter, Dublin, 17 March 1917.

"Plunkett Married on the Eve of His Death." *The New York Times*, 7 May 1916, p. 1.

"Prayer Card for the Repose of the Souls of the Following Irishmen who were Executed by English Law, 1916." TCDMS 2074. Prayer, Ireland, 1916.

Pugh, Thomas. *Bureau of Military History, 1913-1921*. 397.

Redmond, J.E. What Ireland Wants (Dublin, 1910), pp. 14-15 (excerpted from Mitchell, Arthur, and O Snodaigh, Padraig, (editors). Irish Political Documents 1869-1916. (Dublin: Irish Academic Press), 1989. p. 129.

"Rossa Buried in Dublin." *The New York Times*, 2 August 1915, p. 5.

"The Proclamation of the Republic" *The Irish Times*, 6 May 1916.

The Provisional Government of the Irish Republic. *Poblacht Na H Eireann*. Dublin, 1916.

"The Sinn Fein Rising. Scenes and Incidents in Dublin Streets. A Citizen's Diary." *The Irish Times*, 2 May 1916, p. 4.

Vigilance Committee. "Poster Warning Against the Evils of the British Army." Trinity College Dublin Manuscripts 2074. Political Poster, Dublin, 1916.

Yeats, William Butler ."Easter 1916." *Collected Poems*, 177-180. New York: Macmillan, 1956.

Secondary

Anderson, Benedict. *Imagined Communities: Reflections on the Origin and Spread of Nationalism.* London: Verso, 1983.

Arthur, George. *General Sir John Maxwell*. London: John Murray, 1932.

Bew, Paul. "Moderate Nationalism and the Irish Revolution, 1916-1923." *The Historical Journal* 42 (1999): 729-749.

Boyce, David. "British Opinion, Ireland, and the War, 1916-1918." *The Historical Journal* 17 (Sept., 1974): 575-593.

Caufield, Max. *The Easter Rebellion.* New York: Holt, Rinehart, and Winston, 1963.

Clarke, Vivienne. "Maxwell did not like ordering 1916 executions, says great grandson." March 2016. Available from https://www.irishtimes.com/culture/heritage/maxwell-did-not-like-ordering-1916- e x e c u - tions-says-great-grandson-1.2585599.

Codd, Pauline. "Recruiting and the Responses to the War in Wexford." *Ireland and the First World War*, ed. David Fitzpatrick, 1-24. Dublin: Trinity History Workshop, 1986.

Coffey, Thomas. *Agony at Easter: The 1916 Irish Uprising.* London: George G. Harrap & Co, LTD, 1969.

Collins, Eamon. *Killing Rage.* London: Granta Books, 1997.

Collins, Lorcan. "1916: The Easter Rising Walking Tour." Personal Interview. 13 July 2006.

Coogan, Tim Pat. *1916: The Easter Uprising*. London: Orion Books Limited, 2001.

Coogan, Tim Pat. *Ireland Since the Rising.* London: Pall Mall Press, 1966.

Coogan, Tim Pat. *The IRA.* New York: Palgrave, 2002.

Cronin, Sean. *Our Own Red Blood.* New York: Irish Freedom Press, 1966.

Curtis, Liz. *The Cause Of Ireland*. Beyond the Pale Publications, Belfast 1994, pg 190.This quote was taken from the original, in Padraig Pearse's book The Murder Machine

De Rosa, Peter. *Rebels: The Irish Rising of 1916.* New York: Fawcett Books, 1990.

Dorney, John. "Book Review – Crossfire, The Battle of the Four Courts 1916", February 2013 Available from < http://www.theirishstory.com/2013/02/18/book-review-crossfire-the-battle-of-the-four-courts-1916/#.WnB1K6inHIU>; accessed 30 January 2018.

Dorney, John. "'Slaves or Freemen?' Sean McDermott, the IRB and the psychology of the Easter Rising", April 2011 Available from < <http://www.theirishstory.com/2011/04/23/%e2%80%98slaves-or-freemen%e2%80%99-sean-mcdermott-the-irb-and-the-psychology-of-the-easter-rising/#.XX6EBChKiUk>; accessed 15 September 2019.

Dorney, John. "The North King Street Massacre, Dublin 1916", April 2012 Available from < http://www.theirishstory.com/2012/04/13/the-north-king-street-massacre-dublin-1916/#.WpW3g6inHIW>; accessed 27 February 2018.

Dorney, John. "Today in Irish History, April 26, 1916, The battle at Mount Street Bridge", April 2011 Available from <http://www.theirishstory.com/2011/04/26/today-in-irish-history-april-26-1916-the-battle-at-mount-street-bridge/#.W48qYuhKjIV>; accessed 4 September 2018.

Duffy, Sean and Patrick Power. *Timetables of Irish* History. London: Worth Press Limited, 2001.

Edwards, R. Dudley. "The Achievement of 1916." *1916: The Easter Rising.* Edt. O. Dudley Edwards and Fergus Pyle. London: MacGibbon and Kee Ltd., 1968.

Edwards, Ruth. *Patrick Pease: The Triumph of Failure.* London: Victor Gollancz LTD, 1977.

Evans, Elanor. "The Charge of the Light Brigade: who blundered in the Valley of *Death?" In History Extra. Winter 2016. Available from <http://www.historyextra.com/article/bbc-history-magazine/charge-light- brigade-who-blundered-valley-death>.*

Feeny, Brian. *Sinn Fein: A Hundred Turbulent Years.* Madison: The University of Wisconsin Press, 2002.

Gibney, Jojn. "Sites of 1916: The Four Courts and Church Street" In Century Ireland. 2016. Available From <https://www.rte.ie/centuryireland/index.php/articles/the- four-courts-and-church-street>

Geoghegan, Stannus. *The Campaigns and History of the Royal Irish Regiment, Vol. 2, from 1900 to 1922.*

Feeney, Brian. *16 Lives: Sean MacDiarmada.* Dublin: The O'Brien

Press, 2014.

Foy, Michael and Brian Barton, *The Easter Rising.* London: Sutton Publishing, 2004.

Hart, Peter. "Youth Culture and the Cork I.R.A." *Revolution? Ireland 1917-1923*, ed. David Fitzpatrick, 10-11. Dublin: Trinity History Workshop, 1990.

Hobsbawm, E.J. *Nations and Nationalism Since 1780: Programme, Myth Reality.* Cambridge: Cambridge University Press, 1990.

Hochschild, Adam. *King Leopold's Ghost*. New York: Mariner Books, 1998.

Hoff, Matthew. "The Foundations of the Fenian Uprising." Term Paper for History of Great Britain in the Nineteenth and Twentieth Centuries, United States Military Academy, 2006.

Hourly History. *Easter Rising: A History From Beginning to End*. Hourly History, 2016.

Kelly, Matthew. "Dublin Fenianism in the 1880s: 'The Irish Culture of the Future'?" *The Historical Journal* 43 (2000): 729-750.

Kostick, Conor, and Lorcan Collins. *The Easter Rising: A Guide to Dublin in 1916.* Dublin: The O'Brien Press, 2000.

Klug, Jonathan. "Behind the Mosaic: Insurgent Centers of Gravity and Counterinsurgency." Monograph for School of Advanced Military Studies, 2011.

Lee, Joseph. *The Modernization of Irish Society.* Dublin: Gill and MacMillan Ltd, 2008.

Litton, Helen. *16 Lives: Edward Daly*. Dublin: The O'Brien Press, 2013.

MacAtsaney, Gerard. *Sean MacDiarmiada, The Mind of A Revolution*, Nure: Drumlin, 2004,

MacLochlainn, Piaras F. *Last Words: Letters and Statements Of The Leaders Executed After The Rising At Easter 1916.*(Stationary Office, Dublin, 1990).

MacPherson, Hamish. "James Connolly – The Scot Who Died for Ireland and Irish Freedom". In The National. Available from: <http://www.thenational.scot/news/16240567.James_Connolly_____the_Scot_wh o_died_for_Ireland_and_freedom/>.

Martin, F.X. ed. *The Irish Volunteers 1913-1915: Recollections and Documents.* Dublin: James Duffy & Co. LTD., 1963.

McCaffrey, Lawrence. "Irish Nationalism and Irish Catholicism: A Study in Cultural Identity." *Church History* 42 (1972): 524-534.

McEvoy, Dermot. "Easter Rising Leader Executed in 1916: Edward Daly".

May 2017. Available from www.irishcentral.com/roots/history/easter-rising-leader-executed-in-1916-edward- daly.

McEwen, John. "The Liberal Party and the Irish Question during the First World War." *The Journal of British Studies* 12 (Nov. 1972): 109-131.

McGarry, Fearghal. *The Rising, Ireland, Easter 1916.* Oxford: Oxford University Press, 2010.

McGreevy, Ronan. "General who had Easter Rising leaders shot was 'able, level-headed and clear-sighted'." March 2015. Available from https://www.irishtimes.com/news/ireland/irish-news/general-who-had-easter- rising- leaders-shot-was-able-level-headed-and-clear-sighted-1.2127915.

McGreevy, Ronan. "Secret files reveal how deeply the Easter Rising affected Irishmen serving in first World War" April 2018. Available from https://www.irishtimes.com/news/ireland/irish-news/secret-files-reveal-how-deeply-the-easter-rising-affected-irishmen-serving-in-first-world-war-1.3486276

Macgowan, Alva. "Boland's Bakery and 1916". May 2016. Available from https://thearchaeologyof1916.wordpress.com/2016/05/05/bolands-bakery-and-1916/ea

McGuffin, John. "Internment – Women Internees 1916–1973". Irish Resistance Books. (1973) Available from <http://www.irishresistancebooks.com/internment/intern6.htm >.

McKenna, Joseph. *Voices from the Easter Rising: Firsthand Accounts of Ireland's 1916 Rebellion.* Jefferson: McFarland & Company, Inc., Publishers., 2017.

Moloney, Ed. *A Secret History of the* IRA. New York: W.W. Norton & Company LTD., 2002.

Monaghan, Charles. "The Revival of the Gaelic Language". *PLMA* 14 (1899): xxxi- xxxix.

Moore, Robert. "1916: the Easter Rising." In *Library Journal* [journal online] EBSCO Publishing. Winter 2002. Available from < http://bir1.epnet.com/BIRApp/BIR /results.aspx?sid=6B-059F12EE454FDFA5A698679EA9ECE7@sessionmgr2&control=brd&booleantext=%28%28XX%20%221916%3A%20The%20Easter%20R ising%22%29%29&fuzzytext=&key=BJBG.THE.EASTER.RISING.COOGAN.T IM.PAT.Adult.NonFiction&ui=BK0006148769&sort=Standout&starthit=18&pre vEndHit=28&displayText=1916%3A%20The%20Easter%20Rising&pagenumber=2&displaystarthit=11&prox=255>.

National Library of Ireland. "The 1916 Rising: Personalities and Perspectives", February 2018. Available from <http://www.nli.ie/1916/exhibition/en/content/executed/edwarddaly/index.pdf>.

O'Halpin, Eunan. "A History of Ireland in ten Englishmen (7): General Sir John Maxwell – The Man Who Lost Ireland?", Online June 2015 Available from < https://rgshistory.wordpress.com/2015/06/02/a-history-of-ireland-in-ten-englishmen-7-general-sir-john-maxwell-the-man-who-lost-ireland/>.

O'Malley, Connor . "The Secret Meeting: Setting the date for the Easter Rising.", March 2018. Available from <http://www.rte.ie/centuryireland/index.php/articles/the-secret-meeting>.

O'Brien, Marie and Connor Cruise. *Ireland: A Concise History.* New York: Thames and Hudson Inc., 1999.

O'Brien, Paul. "Heuston's Fort – The Battle for the Mendicity Institute, 1916", August 2012 Available from < http://www.theirishstory.com/2012/08/15/heustons-fort-the-battle-for- the-mendicity-institute-1916/#.Ww6tk0gvzIW >

O'Brien, Paul. *Blood on the Streets, 1916 and The Battle for the Mount Street Bridge,* Dublin: New Island, 2008.

O'Brien, Paul. *Crossfire: The Battle of the Four Courts, 1916,* Dublin: New Island, 2012.

O'Broin, Leon. *W.E. Wylie and the Irish Revolution 1916-1921*. Dublin: Gill and MacMillan Ltd., 1989.

Porritt, Annie "The Irish Home Rule Bill." *Political Science Quarterly* 28 (1913): 298-319.

"Rebels: The Irish Rising of 1916." In *Kirkus Reviews* [journal online] Proquest Online. February 1991. Available from <http://bir1.epnet.com/BIRApp/BIR/results.aspx?sid=F8C9F042-961D-4DE7-A1056FBD-8B47AB58@sessionmgr7&control=brd&booleantext=%28%28TX%20%22peter%20de%20rosa%22%29%29&fuzzytext=&key=REBELS.THE.IRISH.RISING.OF.BJBG.DE.ROSA.PETER.Adult.Fiction&ui=BK0001833741&sort=Standout&starthit=27&prevEndHit=36 &displayText=peter%20de%20rosa&pagenumber=3&displaystarthit=21&prox=255>.

Rush, Andy. "Hellfire Corner and the Easter uprising of 1916", February 2018 Available from <https://www.loughboroughecho.net/news/local-news/hellfire-corner-easter-uprising-1916-14218277>

Ryan, Annie. *Witness Inside the Easter Rising.* Dublin: Libertas Press, 2005.

Ryan, Desmond. *The Rising, The Complete Story of Easter Week.* Dublin: Golden Eagle Books Limited, 1957.

Sullivan, Tim. "Irish Home Rule and Resistance, 1912-1916." Term Paper, Loyal University. 2003. Available form <http://people.loyno.edu/~history/journal/Sullivan.htm> .

Tennyson, Alfred Lord. "Charge of the Light Brigade." December 2017 . Available from https://www.poetryfoundation.org/poems/45319/the-charge-of-the-light-brigade.

Tierney, Michael. *Eoin MacNeill: Scholar and Man of Action 1867-1945.* Oxford: Clarendon Press, 1980.

Toby, Tyler. "Exemplary Violence Used in British Colonial Policy: One Explanation for General John Maxwell's Violent Reaction to the Easter Rising of 1916." Masters diss., University of Massachusetts Boston, June 1997.

Townsend, Charles. *Easter 1916: The Irish Rebellion.* Chicago: Allen Lane 2005.

Ward, Alan J. *The Easter Rising: Revolution and Irish Nationalism, Second Edition.* Wheelilng: Harlan Davidson 2003.

Ward, Margaret. *Unmanageable Revolutionaries: Women and Irish Nationalism*. London: Pluto Press LTD., 1983.

Whitfield, Eimer. "The Balladry of Revolution." *Revolution? Ireland 1917-1923*, ed. David Fitzpatrick, 61-63. Dublin: Trinity History Workshop, 1990.

INDEX